The Donnellys Must Die

The Donnellys Must Die

ORLO MILLER

BICENTENNIAL
1807
WILEY
2007
BICENTENNIAL

John Wiley & Sons Canada, Ltd.

John Wiley & Sons Canada, Ltd.
6045 Freemont Blvd.
Mississauga, Ontario
L5R 4J3

First published in Canada in 1962 by
The Macmillan Company of Canada Limited

National Library of Canada Cataloguing in Publication Data

Miller, Orlo, 1911-
The Donnellys must die / Orlo Miller.

ISBN-13: 978-0-470-84055-9
ISBN-10: 0-470-84055-2

1. Donnelly family. 2. Murder—Ontario—Lucan. I. Title.

HV6810.L8M56 2006   364.152'3092271325   C2006-905211-5

Production Credits
Cover design: Ian Koo
Interior text design: Pat Loi
Front cover photo: NordicPhotos/FirstLight
Back cover photo: The London Free Press Collection of Photographic Negatives,
                   UWO Archives
Printer: Printcrafters

Printed in Canada
1 2 3 4 5 PC 10 09 08 07 06

Dedicated to my good friend
JAMES P. DUNN
who has waited so long for this book

Contents

Foreword

THE brutal murder of an old farmer named James Donnelly and four members of his family near the village of Lucan in south-western Ontario in 1880 has long fascinated the public and students of crime. The murders were the climax of a feud that is unique in Canadian crime and almost unparalleled in recent times in the western world.

The story has been told so often that it is now almost in the realm of legend. Legend has been recited as fact for so long that the truth lies buried fathoms deep.

I have attempted to reveal that truth.

The sole source of facts for all previously published accounts has been the newspaper reports of the trial of six of the suspected murderers in London, Ontario, in November 1880 and January 1881. Many articles and books have been based on this source, including W. Stewart Wallace's scholarly resume in *Canadian Murders and Mysteries.*

It has always seemed surprising to me that, in spite of the deep interest of the reading public in this case, no writer previously has consulted the thousands of legal documents, letters, and journals which relate to the feud, the murders, and the trials. I have used these sources as well as the newspaper accounts and a number of Irish source materials.

In addition to telling the story of the Canadian feud I have tried to describe its origins in Ireland. It began in Tipperary in 1766, came to Canada with the great Irish migrations of the 1830s and 1840s, and reached its climax on the night of February 3, 1880. On that night, a gang of men killed James, Johannah, Thomas, Bridget, and John Donnelly. Although eyewitnesses identified the killers in court, there were no convictions because the feud filled the jury with fear.

There are in this book a few outbursts of personal anger which I trust will be considered justified. There is no question that upon occasion the members of the Donnelly family committed misdemeanours. There can equally be no question that they did not merit the savage punishment meted out to them by their neighbours. I consider their unavenged deaths an unexpunged blot on the Canadian judicial system.

I believe that blame for the circumstances leading up to their deaths must rest with the Roman Catholic Church, the Orange Order, the Protestant churches, the two great Canadian political parties and their local news organs. If all, or any, of these institutions had taken decisive action before 1880, lives might have been saved.

There is dialogue in this book and occasional detailed descriptions of events to which I was not a witness. These are not products of imagination; I claim no poetic licence. Where they occur, they are based upon statements made in the witness-box, under oath. I am aware that much of the testimony given at the trials of the conspirators was perjured, and I have attempted to discern and eliminate such perjured statements, or at least to draw attention to their unreliability.

I am indebted to more persons than I can conveniently list, or even remember. My special thanks go to the late Dr. Edwin Seaborn, who, in the course of research on another subject, discovered many details of interest pertaining to this book; to Dr. James J. Talman, librarian of the University of Western Ontario, who provided facilities and encouragement; to L. N. Bronson of *The London Free Press*, who dug up many things out of the old files of that paper which I might otherwise have missed; to my good friend, Mr. John F. Malone, formerly of Manchester, England, who provided some vital Irish background, and to Dr. Fred Landon, my mentor in all matters historical. I acknowledge a very special debt to many friends whose number and personal modesty preclude my listing their names, and to my wife, who not only has lived uncomplainingly with this book for twenty-five years, but has been the source of all that may be considered good in its style and manner of presentation.

O. M.
London, Ontario
August 1962

PHOTOGRAPHS OF THE PLACE AND TIME

A popular postcard from the late 1800s depicting the Donnelly house near Lucan, Ontario. The Donnellys pictured here were all murdered.

A typical street scene, circa 1875–1878.

A composite photograph of the male citizens of Lucan, circa 1890.

An elegant home on Main Street, Lucan, circa 1870.

Sir Hugh MacMahon, one of the defense counsel. None of those arrested for murder was convicted.

The Donnelly gravestone, erected in August 1963 by descendants of the family. The marker does not mince words; it reads that John, James, Johannah, Thomas and Bridget were "murdered" on February 4, 1880.

Murder

CHAPTER 1

There's one did laugh in's sleep, and one cried,
"Murder!"

Shakespeare: MACBETH

ON the last day of his life old Jim Donnelly harnessed up the mare and drove into Lucan to do some shopping. One of his sons, Tom, went with him.

Neither man had much to say on the short trip into the village. The ground had been thoroughly covered already in the family's discussions. They had to appear in Squire Casey's court at Granton in the morning—that much was fact. The rest was speculation and the chewing over of old grievances. What else was there to say, except to damn the black soul of that bastard Jim Carroll, author of their latest misfortunes?

Carroll may have been watching when the pair drove into the village. As constable, it was his job to observe the comings and goings of the residents of the most lawless town in Canada. He could probably have told Jim Donnelly it was the last day of his life, but he had other matters to attend to.

Maybe Jim himself knew it in some secret corner of his heart. Or maybe it was just a goose walking over his grave that made him say what he did to a clerk in one of the stores.

"Going to pay cash, Jim—or do you want to charge it?" the clerk asked.

"Charge it to the Queen, boy," the old man said. "I may not be around to look after it."

Donnelly's manner, more than the words themselves, stayed in the clerk's memory. He told the story to a newspaper reporter the next day when Jim's name had become famous posthumously.

The old man made his few modest purchases in a leisurely way, seeking out no man, avoiding none. Some of those who met him, or purposely avoided him, must have had guilty foreknowledge of the manner of his passing. The Vigilance Committee was said to number more than one hundred men, most of them with families who were also privy to the secret.

Those who covenanted in murder (and their descendants to the present day) would have it differently, but the fact is Jim Donnelly had friends as well as enemies and perhaps as many of the former as of the latter. On that afternoon of February 3, 1880, he greeted many of his friends and clasped a hand or two for the last time.

Among his friends were the O'Connors, who lived just outside the village. It is to young Johnny O'Connor that we are indebted for the story of what happened between 5 o'clock and midnight on February 3.

Tom Donnelly and his father called for Johnny just before suppertime. Johnny's little sister went off to get him where he was working on a neighbouring farm. Although he was only eleven years old, Johnny was a good hand with cattle. Someone was needed to look after the beasts while the family was at Granton answering the latest charge preferred by the Vigilantes.

Johnny had no hesitation in accepting the responsibility, nor did his parents object to his going. Whatever the nature of their relationships with their adult neighbours, the Donnellys seem to have had an excellent reputation for kindness and thoughtfulness among the youngsters who worked for them from time to time.

When Johnny was ready, Tom wheeled the wagon out of the farmyard and headed down the Roman Line for home. The road was called by that name because of the large number of Roman Catholic Irish families who had first settled it thirty years before. Its more prosaic proper name was Concession Six, Biddulph Township.

From the village to the Donnelly farm was about a three-mile drive. The road was hard with frost and there was a sprinkling of snow in the furrowed fields and ditches. The sky was overcast and threatened more snow before morning.

No one has left any record of what the three of them talked about as they clattered along through the metallic stillness of the winter twilight. They were good friends, so perhaps Jim or Tom told the boy some of the family's plans. The old folks were thinking of packing up and leaving the township after the winter wheat was harvested. Indeed, Jim's wife, Johannah, was insisting on it. Hadn't she told Father Connolly less than a week ago that she was tired of living in terror?

As they approached the one-and-a-half-storey log building the Donnellys called home, lamps were coming on in the farmhouses. There was no warmth or cheer in their light that night, nor did they stay on long. All lamps in the homes of the guilty and the innocent alike were extinguished early in Biddulph Township on the night of February 3, 1880.

II

Johnny O'Connor had been at the Donnelly house before. He knew most of the family—Tom and John, Johannah their mother, and the Tipperary cousin, Bridget. John came out to help put up the mare, while the old man and the boy went into the house to get warm. Later, Tom asked Bridget to get them some apples to eat. The men sat and munched on these while the women got supper.

Afterwards Jim took Johnny to the barn to slop the pigs and to explain the next day's chores. Meanwhile, John Donnelly rode off to the home of his elder brother William, three miles away, in order to borrow a cutter to take the family to the court hearing. With the snow coming on, they would need the cutter.

Later still there was more apple-eating and, it appears, some talk about the impending trial. Much of it was either over Johnny's head, or of little interest to him.

About 9:30 old Jim stretched and announced he was going to bed. He turned to the boy, who was munching apples steadily by the stove, and spoke:

"You'll sleep along of me, boy."

Johnny finished his apple and waited to be shown where he was to sleep, while Donnelly got down on his knees by one of the kitchen chairs and said his prayers. Then he led the way into the bedroom at the front of the house.

In the fashion of the farm people of that day, Jim Donnelly slept in his long underwear. Johnny peeled off his shoes and the topmost of the two pairs of trousers he wore and then he, too, was ready for bed. He climbed into the big old four-poster over Jim, who merely grunted, and settled himself next to the wall.

On the border of sleep he heard voices in the kitchen. One of them belonged to a new arrival. Johnny recognized the voice to be that of Jim Feeheley, a friend of the younger Donnellys. He listened drowsily for a few moments to the buzz of talk and then drifted off. He did not hear Feeheley leave.

III

The Township of Biddulph in 1880 had a population of approximately 3,000. The movements and actions of most of the 3,000 on the night of February 3 are wrapped in obscurity. In the cases of all but a few the anonymity of their movements was accidental and proper; in the case of perhaps two hundred people it was intentional and criminal.

Here and there among the recollections of the innocent—
the guilty were almost instantly stricken with mass amnesia—
one finds a vivid cameo of some event, major or minor. One is
Johnny O'Connor's self-portrait of his youthful preoccupation
with the contents of the Donnelly apple bin. Another, with
more sinister overtones, is the story told by two cousins, Thomas
and Robert Keeffe. The parents of both youths were long-time
friends of the Donnelly family and hence presumably innocent
of foreknowledge, although in Biddulph Township that night
this would not have been a safe presumption.

About the time Jim Donnelly and Johnny retired, the two
young men were lounging by a farm gate not far away, idly
chatting. As they talked they heard a horseman approaching on
the Roman Line.

The sky had cleared in patches. The night was moonless but
there was enough starshine to silhouette the horseman and partially reveal what he carried in his hand, half-concealed within
his coat. Tom Keeffe took a few steps towards him, the better to
see who it was, but the horseman rode away without any words
being exchanged.

"Who was it?" Bob asked.

"Pat Ryder," replied his cousin.

"The old man?"

"No. Young Pat, his son. Did you see what he was carrying?"

Bob took a little time to think that one over. Neither young
man was particularly noted for intelligence and an outright
question without a known answer called for deep thought.
Finally he ventured an opinion:

"It looked as if it might be a stick."

"It was a gun," said Tom with the satisfaction some people
reserve for bad news. "He was hiding it inside his coat. The
part that stuck out was covered over with a piece of cloth or
paper—something white."

"What's he doing with a gun?" Bob asked.

Tom looked his contempt at this thoughtless question and replied:

"He's going around to gather the faction. You watch, they'll be shooting up the country at the trial tomorrow!"

Tom Keeffe was wrong. The Vigilantes were not going to wait until the morning.

IV

By midnight the Biddulph innocents were all asleep—or at least in their beds. Only the guilty were abroad.

Some time later—the only witness was an eleven-year-old boy who did not own a watch—Johnny O'Connor was wakened from a dreamless sleep. Old Jim Donnelly stood by the bed struggling into his trousers and muttering to himself. In the doorway stood a thick-set, dark-faced man. The lamp in his hand threw the jet-black spade beard into relief and the eyes into shadow.

Donnelly finished doing up his trousers and turned to the intruder:

"What have you got against me now?" he asked.

"I've got another charge against you," the dark man said in a half-snarl. Then he turned and went into the kitchen where the boy could hear him whistling as he walked back and forth. At this stage he seemed to be alone.

The boy cowered against the wall and listened. He heard two heavy thumps as Donnelly stamped into his big farm boots. There was a pause and then, from the kitchen, he heard the old man's startled exclamation:

"Tom! Are you handcuffed?"

Tom Donnelly's voice answered:

"Yes. He thinks he's smart."

The old man clumped his way back into the bedroom, mumbling something about finding his coat. Johnny realized he was using it as a pillow. He dragged it out from under his head and held it towards his host:

"It's here," he said.

The dark-faced man with the lamp was again standing in the doorway. Something about his shadowed eyes made Johnny shiver. He could have sworn the man was staring straight at him, but with the light held that way he could not really tell. Then he heard Mrs. Donnelly in the next room call out:

"Bridget! Get up and light the fire!"

Bridget answered the summons. Johnny heard her lifting off the stove lids. There was an indistinguishable murmur of voices and then Tom's, loud and clear:

"All right. Now read your warrant."

"There's lots of time for that," said the voice of the man with the black beard who had held the lamp.

He lied. There was no time at all for the Donnellys.

No sooner were the words out of the speaker's mouth than there was a shout, the kitchen filled with men, and the night's work of murder began.

It is a wonder the boy remembered anything of what happened next. At the first shout Bridget raced upstairs with Johnny close behind her. She must have thought he was one of the attackers, for when she reached the head of the stairs she slammed the door in his face. Johnny hesitated only a moment, then ran back down the stairs to the bedroom he had shared with Jim Donnelly, dived under the big four-poster and hid behind a laundry basket.

It is difficult to understand how the presence of the boy— first in the bedroom and then in the kitchen—could have been overlooked by the murderers. Of course they were at the time engaged with bigger game. Whatever the reasons, it was for them a near-fatal oversight.

From his sanctuary under the bed Johnny saw feet clad in heavy farm boots turn the floor of the kitchen into a muddy, bloody mess. In spite of his fear he peeked out once or twice and recognized a few faces. Others were disguised; one was daubed black with burnt cork. One wore a woman's dress, another a long duster. Somebody asked where the girl Bridget was and then several of them sought her out. Amid the thumping, yelling, screaming and moaning, Johnny O'Connor could not tell when and how she died.

Tom Donnelly took the longest. Bursting from his captors, he 'ran outside, but with his hands manacled he was no match for them. Some of them dragged him back into the kitchen and threw him on the floor. Johnny caught a glimpse of a fear-contorted face, quite unlike the Tom he knew, then he heard a voice say:

"Hit him with a spade and break his skull open."

By the time the blow fell, Johnny was behind the laundry basket, being sick.

Later, when the noise died down a bit, some of them came to the bedroom where Johnny was hidden, poured kerosene on the bed and set it on fire. There was one final thunder of feet and then silence.

It was getting hot under the four-poster. Johnny crawled out, took one horrified look at the blazing bedding and bolted for the door. He suffered a moment of sheer panic when the door stuck against some obstacle in the kitchen. He forced it open and in leaving, stepped on the obstruction.

It was the body of Mrs. Donnelly.

He slithered his way across the kitchen by the light from the burning bed. Somebody was breathing in an odd way. At that moment, one of the four victims was still alive. He should have given help, but Johnny was only an eleven-year-old boy and a very frightened one.

As he reached the outer door he saw an odd something by the stove which he said afterward "looked like a dog's head." Then he was out under the clean stars in a light snow, barefoot and running for the nearby home of Patrick Whelan.

More Murder

So, fair and softly, John he cried,
But John he cried in vain.

Cowper: JOHN GILPIN

JOHN Donnelly reached his brother's home shortly after dark. William was at the woodshed behind the house with a close friend, James Keeffe, splitting wood for the evening.

William came to meet his brother, his lame foot dragging slightly as he walked. Even in his work clothes he was a distinguished-looking man. His curly hair was worn long, and with his neat Vandyke beard he strongly resembled Buffalo Bill. The long face, its length accentuated by the beard, had a theatrical quality—John Wilkes Booth being played by John Carradine.

Keeffe went on splitting wood while William helped his brother stable the horse. Then William returned to the chopping while John went into the house to chat with his brother's wife, Nora, generally referred to by her husband in the Irish manner as "the woman" or in the Canadian manner as "the missus."

Nora Donnelly, daughter of John Kennedy, Senior, an early settler in Biddulph Township, emerges from the records as a taciturn, somewhat mousy woman. Her only outstanding physical characteristic was her slight deafness. She was not too warmly regarded by her in-laws, a feeling she reciprocated, except for a fondness for John Donnelly, whom she usually called "Johnny."

It was an emotion shared by many. Even the worst enemies of the Donnelly clan spoke rather well of John.

The two sat cozily chatting by the kitchen stove until about eight o'clock when they heard the two men outside greeting another visitor. A few minutes later three men trooped into the kitchen, stamping the cold from their feet. The newcomer was Martin Hogan, also a long-time friend of the Donnelly family. Each man bore an armload of wood which he deposited with great thumping in the wood-box by the stove.

Nora suggested tea, which Hogan alone declined; perhaps he would have preferred a stronger brew. As the others sat about drinking the scalding liquid, the talk turned to the Vigilance Committee. Nobody afterwards would say what they talked about but from all indications it was bitter talk. Unlike their elders, the younger Donnellys and their friends were not yet weary of battling their enemies.

Nora Donnelly took little part in the conversation and at nine o'clock she rose and announced her intention of going to bed. No one urged her to stay; and when she had gone the talk was probably freer, for some of it would undoubtedly have had to do with her family.

It was nearly eleven o'clock when Keeffe rose to go. It was a late hour for people who usually retired at nine, but the occasion was special. It was true the immediate topic was only a court hearing and the Donnellys were veterans of scores of such affairs, but there seemed that night to have been a shared feeling of something unusually unpleasant in the offing.

Hogan did not accompany Keeffe. However, shortly after the latter's departure he rose and put on his outer clothing. He was drawing on his mitts when John Donnelly proposed he spend the night there. Will Donnelly seconded his brother's suggestion and after winding the clock he took a lamp and led his two guests to the bedroom they were to occupy.

While John and Hogan undressed, Will sat on the foot of the bed and they continued the interrupted conversation. From later hints, the talk there ranged over a long period of time.

There seem to have been many references to the ashes of long-dead fires and the bones of long uneasy corpses.

It was half an hour past midnight before the three friends were talked out. Will left the others still murmuring drowsily and limped off to his bedroom to undress in the dark. Hearing Nora move, Will spoke to her:

"Are you still awake, Nora?"

"Yes."

The voice came from an unusual quarter. Will put out a hand in the dark and found his wife was sleeping on the outside of the bed instead of her usual position next the window. The whim of Nora Donnelly in changing her sleeping position was destined to have a far-reaching influence on the lives of several persons. On this occasion, it called only for a moment or two of good-natured marital chaff.

"Push in to the other side of the bed," Will commanded.

Nora giggled in the dark.

"No. I'm not going to warm your side of the bed for you."

Will by now was too sleepy to argue. Standing on the bed, he stepped over Nora. As he settled himself, flinching between the cold sheets, he aimed a hard-handed slap at his wife's rump.

As he lay in the dark waiting for sleep to come, he could hear a murmur of voices from the other bedroom. As far as he could remember later, his brother and Martin Hogan were still talking when he finally dropped off, around one o'clock in the morning.

II

It was about twenty minutes after two when Will Donnelly awoke to a presence in his bedroom. Struggling out of the first deep sleep of the night he heard a voice calling his name.

It was his brother.

"What's wrong, John?"

"Somebody's hammering at the door and hollering 'fire.'"

As John opened the door to the kitchen, Will could hear the noise too. Somebody was banging at the door and two voices were calling out:

"Will! Open up!"

"Open the door! Fire!"

As John hurried to the door, Will Donnelly leaned over and raised one corner of the window blind next to him an inch or two.

As he told it later at the inquest, he recognized three men instantly—James Carroll, the village constable, with his jet-black spade beard, John Kennedy, his wife's brother, and Martin McLoughlin, a prominent local farmer and one-time friend of the family. At some distance beyond them, near the fence, he thought he recognized three other men.

The act of recognition was instantaneous. A breath later his attention was jerked away from the window by a great blast of sound. Two explosions in rapid succession came from the direction of the outer door. The echo hurtled around the kitchen, rattling the pans on the wall. As it died away there was a whimpering moan and the crash of a body hitting the floor.

As the acrid smell of gunpowder filled the house, John's voice came from the floor near Will's door.

"Will! Will! I'm shot and may the Lord have mercy on my soul!"

As Will stirred in the bed a harsh whisper came from the other bedroom. It was Hogan.

"Lay quiet or we'll all be killed! It's *you* they want!"

The last words were almost drowned out by another burst of gunfire from near the road—seven shots in all, Will later claimed.

Will lifted the edge of the blind again. The group of men was by the fence now. A voice said:

"What next?"

And another voice, well known to both Will and Nora, said:

"Brother-in-law is easy at last!"

There was more conversation but the words were lost to Will Donnelly as Nora sat bolt upright in the bed and declared:

"I'm going to get up whether I'm shot or not!"

Will sat in rigid silence while Nora lit the lamp, closed the outer door and dragged John's bleeding body nearer to the stove. He was choking with the blood in his throat.

"O Lord!" she cried, "he's dying!"

Hogan slid into the bedroom. Will started to speak to him but was silenced again:

"Don't talk! If they find out it wasn't you they shot, they'll be back to get the pack of us!"

Hogan seized the dying man by the arm and pulled him into Will's bedroom. John could not speak. He moved one hand feebly. Nora sensed what he wanted.

"I've got a piece of blessed candle," she said.

In a moment she was back with the butt of candle. Hogan pressed it into John's hands and held it there.

The end came five minutes later.

Will Donnelly spoke for the first time since the shooting—in a whisper:

"Nora! Go and look at the clock."

She was back in a few moments.

"It wants a minute or two of half-past two."

They sat by the body until daybreak.

The Witness

Now, what I want is, Facts. Facts alone are
wanted in life.

Dickens: HARD TIMES

THE first outsider to learn of the murders was Patrick Whelan, whose house was directly opposite the home of old Jim Donnelly on the Roman Line.

The Whelans had been up late. There had been a number of visitors—Martin McLoughlin, William Feeheley and the ubiquitous Jim Feeheley. The last of the visitors left shortly after ten o'clock and the family, consisting of Mr. and Mrs. Whelan, their sons William and Joseph and a daughter, were all in bed by eleven.

At half-past one they were wakened by a frantic pounding on the back door. Mrs. Whelan, who slept with her husband in a ground-floor bedroom, called out to ask who it was.

"Johnny O'Connor," said a boy's voice.

Whelan got up immediately and lit a lamp, but before the flame illuminated the room the boy had pushed open the un-latched door and entered the kitchen. They found him standing there, barefooted, sobbing and shivering, his coat clutched under his arm.

"Who are you and what are you doing out at this time of night?" Whelan asked.

"Johnny O'Connor," repeated the boy. "I'm frozen."

"But what are you doing out?" Whelan persisted.

"I'm frozen," said the boy.

That was all he would say until Mrs. Whelan had brought him warm wraps and Pat had started a fire in the stove. Then he spoke again.

"The Donnellys are killed."

Whelan stared at the boy a moment and then crossed to a window overlooking the Donnelly homestead. He saw what appeared to him to be a light in a window.

"Better call out the men to quench the fire," the boy said to Mrs. Whelan.

Whelan wheeled on him.

"What fire?"

"They set the place on fire after they killed the Donnellys," the boy replied.

"You're fooling," Whelan charged. "There's no fire at the Donnellys. I just looked."

The boy was silent. After a moment's indecision Whelan returned to the window. Two windows were lit up now and the light seemed to be increasing. He got his boots and began pulling them on.

"Where are you going?" Mrs. Whelan asked.

"I'm going up the road to get John and then I'm going over to the Donnellys," he replied. "The boy's right. The place is on fire."

Johnny watched Whelan put on his outer clothing.

"Jim Carroll was there," he said conversationally.

The couple stared at him.

"Carroll, the constable?" Whelan asked.

"Yes," said the boy. "That's him."

"Carroll's got a case against us in court at Granton in the morning," Whelan mused. "Against the Donnellys, too."

"Well, if what the boy says is right," Mrs. Whelan said, "there won't be any case now."

"Tom Ryder was there too," Johnny said. "So was John Purtell."

There was a thick silence.

"You better be careful what you're saying, boy," Mrs. Whelan said slowly.

"That's right," said Pat, putting on his muffler. "You listen to the missus."

"Were the Donnellys quarrelling among themselves?" the woman asked the boy.

"No."

"Did they have any liquor?"

"No."

"Then what happened?"

"I told you."

"No, you didn't."

"Jim Carroll and the others came and they tied up Tom Donnelly and then they killed the old man and—"

"Shut up!" rasped Whelan.

"You don't know what you're saying!" the woman said fiercely. The boy subsided into frightened silence.

Seeing that she had scared the boy the woman went on more gently:

"You may not have it just right, boy. It's better not to say anything. You see, if you're not careful we might all be summoned up to the court about it. You don't want us all to come before the court, do you?"

The boy guessed he did not want that. The woman pressed the point.

"You may not have the whole truth of it. And if the court catches you out and finds you're not telling the truth—well, you know what happens to people who tell lies in court, don't you?"

The boy did not, but he was not going to reveal his ignorance, so he kept silent.

By now the daughter and Joe, the elder of the two sons at home, had joined the trio in the kitchen. Fifteen or twenty minutes had elapsed since Johnny's arrival—and still no one had gone to the burning house. It was to be another quarter-hour before anyone made the short journey to the funeral pyre of the Donnelly family.

II

The home of John Whelan, Patrick's son, was only one hundred and thirty yards from the Donnelly homestead. When the old man reached there it was to find his son already up and dressed. He explained that one of his children had awakened him with the news that the Donnelly house was on fire. He had not seen fit to look into the matter. According to the evidence John Whelan gave at the inquest it was a half-hour after his first knowledge of the blaze before he went to the scene.

It is doubtful that the lives of any of the victims could have been saved had their neighbours not shown such a pronounced reluctance to approach the burning structure, but much useful evidence might have been spared destruction.

As it was, the fire was well advanced when Patrick Whelan and Johnny O'Connor reached the site. When John Whelan arrived a few minutes later it was agreed among the three of them that nothing could be done to save the building or its occupants. An attempt to enter the front door, which faced south, was prevented when the door burst from its hinges and volumes of smoke poured out. Through a back window Pat thought he saw a body through the wreathing smoke, but could not be sure.

All three witnesses saw tracks in the light snow around the building and patches of blood on the ground in front of the house.

The progress of the fire, which had been slow up to this point, now accelerated and the building was soon a tumbling, seething mass of flames.

Chilled by the night air and perhaps by their thoughts as well, the three watchers shortly returned to their homes. Johnny went along with the older man and was put to bed with Joe Whelan.

At nine o'clock in the morning the whole family went to the scene of the fire. The building was levelled and in the ashes were seen the charred remains of four bodies.

There were several other people there as well. One was James Keeffe. His face was white and set. He spoke to no one. After a few minutes he rode off rapidly in the direction of Lucan.

III

The three living occupants of Will Donnelly's house finally stirred from their trance just before daybreak. Nora started a fire in the kitchen stove while Will lit a lantern.

He opened the kitchen door cautiously. A light snow was falling, but a six-foot projection of the kitchen roof over the door had preserved two sets of footprints—one set made by a pair of boots, the other by a new pair of overshoes.

Stepping carefully round the tracks Will walked the twenty-five feet to the home of his nearest neighbour, William Blackwell. When he rapped, the door was opened immediately by Blackwell himself, fully clothed.

"Isn't this a nice thing?" was Will's opening conversational gambit.

"What?" asked Blackwell carefully, with just the right shade of indifference. He admitted later in court that he had heard the shots but "didn't want to be mixed up in the muss."

"The shooting of my brother John," Will replied.

"Your brother John—shot?"

"Murdered."

"Who did it?"

"They did."

Blackwell asked no more questions; he did not want to know the answers.

At Will's urging he went over to the Donnelly house and examined the tracks. There were more footprints around the house, partly filled with snow; the tracks, Blackwell testified, of a party of twenty or more men.

Shortly afterwards, Will saddled John's pony and rode off to see his friend Jim Keeffe who lived three-quarters of a mile distant. There were more tracks on the road; the group of men which had made them had apparently gone half-way to Keeffe's in a body, hesitated in indecision and then dispersed.

Keeffe was in bed; he listened to Will's story in silence, then advised him to say nothing until the detectives were brought up from London. Will returned home while Keeffe saddled up to take the bad news to John's father and mother.

Later he rode to Lucan and wrote out a document in shaky hand-writing in the office of Thomas Hossack, the Lucan coroner:

I hereby certify that I found the remains of four bodies which I believe to be that of James, Julia, Bridget and Thomas Donnelly lying in the burnt ruins of James Donnelly's house and to further the ends of justice I request you, one of Her Majesty's coroners for said county of Middlesex to hold an inquest as it does not appear to me that deceased came to death from natural causes or mere accident.

Bloody Tipperary

CHAPTER

The community has been horror-stricken by a san-
guinary case of lynching; for such evidently is the
nature of the Biddulph tragedy, though there is mingled
with it something of the Tipperary feud. "There's
Tipperary, bluidy Tipperary!" we remember hearing one
Irishman exclaim with gusto, as he caught sight of the
well-known hills.

THE BYSTANDER (Toronto) March, 1880.

THE murder of five members of one family in the Canadian
backwoods during the early morning hours of February 4, 1880,
electrified the newspaper readers of the continent. Before the
ashes of the Donnelly farmhouse were cold, newspaper correspondents from the great papers of the United States and
Canada were clamouring for accommodation in Lucan village
or the nearby city of London, Ontario, midway between Toronto
and Detroit.

It is not difficult to assess the reasons for the public interest
in what was at once christened, in the romantic tradition of the
Victorian press, "The Biddulph Horror."

It was not the number of victims. There had been mass
murders before, and have been many since, which claimed more
than the five lives of the Donnelly massacre. Multiple murders
were not unheard of even in the general area of the crime, the

peninsula of south-western Ontario. Forty-eight years earlier a crowd of three thousand people at London had witnessed the public execution of one Henry Sovereign for doing away with his wife and five children in a moment of pique.

Mass murders are generally (if we admit a few classic exceptions) sloppy, messy affairs, performed on the spur of the moment with whatever tools are readiest to hand. They are often the work of minds temporarily or permanently unbalanced. They create a momentary excitement on the part of the curious and are speedily forgotten.

The murderers of the Donnelly family were by no means morons, misfits or maniacs. They were farmers and business men, stage-coach owners, carpenters and peace officers. Furthermore, they performed their grisly task in no moment of emotional unbalance, but deliberately, coldly, and savagely, with malice aforethought.

Within twenty-four hours of the commission of the crime, newspaper readers all over the continent knew the murders to be the outcome of a vendetta as bitter as anything that ever came out of Corsica. They knew, further, that the murders were the work of an organized body of men acting, however falsely, in the name of law, order and the Roman Catholic Church, and styling themselves, in a manner more closely associated with the early history of the Far West, a Vigilance Committee.

It soon became apparent also that the visitors who called on the Donnelly family that winter morning were members of no ordinary lynching party. This crime has no close parallel in the lurid history of interracial relations in the southern United States.

Lynching parties are usually motivated by mob hysteria, but no hysteria was exhibited by the Biddulph night raiders. They did their job efficiently and thoroughly, making only one major mistake. The man they were most anxious to eliminate escaped the clubs, the bullets and the buckshot.

William Donnelly lived to prosecute them.

II

William Donnelly was born in 1845, the son of James and Johannah (sometimes called Judith or Julia) Donnelly of County Tipperary, Ireland.

This county, one of those which together form the province of Munster in Southern Ireland, had long been a cradle of violence. For nearly two hundred years prior to the birth of William Donnelly the county had been the scene of civic disturbances on numberless occasions.

The initial cause of the social cancer referred to somewhat vaguely as "the Tipperary feud" was religious. In that bloody conquest and resettlement of Ireland which has caused the name of Oliver Cromwell to be forever execrated by the Irish, a colony of German and French Protestants was planted in the northern half of what was, and still is, a predominantly Roman Catholic county. Thus, as an eighteenth-century writer said: "Religious intolerance gave new stimulus to the disorders which poverty had occasioned."

Prior to the Cromwellian "plantation" or resettlement of Ireland, the Donnellys were persons of substance in their native Tipperary, where they had anciently been chiefs of Muscraighe-Thire. They were at no time a numerous group and are today represented by a relative handful of descendants. According to a recent work on Irish family names, there are now nearly 20,000 persons bearing the name Donnelly in Ireland, but most of these are descended from a very prolific North Ireland family whose name, spelled differently in Gaelic, has been anglicized in the same manner as that of the Munster family. The Tipperary Donnellys had ceased to be powerful leaders towards the close of the eleventh century.

From 1695 until the passage of the Emancipation Act of 1829, the Roman Catholic majority in Ireland was utterly crushed beneath oppressive laws which made them virtually the serfs of the Protestant minority. In no part of Ireland was the lot of the landless Roman Catholic peasant worse than in the fertile county of Tipperary.

If the English preyed on the Irish, the Irish preyed on one another. To the immediate horrors of war was soon added a more subtle and soul-destroying form of abasement. A class of middlemen arose which took tracts of land from absentee English landlords at a moderate rental and sublet it to peasants and small farmers at rack-rents that left barely enough to support life. The tenants were kept always in a state of the greatest poverty, quite at the mercy of their immediate landlord.

To these injustices was added still another in the eighteenth century. Near many of the villages were commons—stretches of grassy land or bogs which had been free to the people to use for grazing or for cutting turf and which had formed one of their chief ways of living. These had belonged to the people from very ancient times, but about 1760 the landlords began to enclose them as private property, used chiefly for grazing.

The removal of even this poor privilege finally brought rebellion—if the "Whiteboys" movement can be dignified by such a term. The movement and the name originated in Tipperary in 1761. The best available evidence indicates that the Whiteboys directed their activities against the oppression of individuals, not against the government, although attempts were made to prove that they swore a Jacobite oath and received monetary support from France.

Bound together by semi-religious oaths in secret societies, the Whiteboys travelled the country by night, their fraternity identified by white shirts worn over their coats. At first their targets were inanimate; they levelled all the new fences that enclosed the commons and dug up pasture land. Soon, however, they went beyond their original design, setting themselves up as redressers of all sorts of grievances. They committed outrages on all those who became personally obnoxious to them, perpetrating finally deeds of torture and villainy equalling the worst excesses of Cromwell's armies.

The ordinary processes of law proved totally inadequate to deal with Whiteboy terrorism and a military force under the Marquis of Drogheda was sent into Tipperary to smoke out and intimidate the night raiders while a legal commission gathered evidence in an attempt to bring their leaders to trial. The Marquis fixed his headquarters at Clogheen, a notable centre of Whiteboy disturbances. The parish priest there, Father Nicholas Sheehy, came under suspicion almost immediately.

Nicholas Sheehy was a native of Fethard, Tipperary. He received his training for the priesthood in France and on his return to Ireland assumed the curacy of the parish of Clogheen. He made no secret of his hostility to English rule in Ireland, nor of his advocacy of the original purpose of the Whiteboys.

Sheehy was several times arrested, indicted and tried for implication in the Whiteboys' activities and several times acquitted. Evidence was adduced at the trials to show that the priest had extensive knowledge of the organization and indeed, that he had on many occasions lent it tangible assistance.

This evidence—much of it of dubious value—provides most of what is known about the inner workings of the society. Solemn and binding oaths of secrecy were taken, extending to the names of the members, as well as the nature of their organization. The Whiteboys were known also as "Sive Oultho's Children" and "Shaun Meskill and her Children," the derivation of both terms being unknown.

The charge on which the Anglo-Irish authorities finally convicted the parish priest was complicity in the murder of an informer, an erstwhile Whiteboy named John Bridge. The body of the alleged victim was never found and stories persisted in Tipperary for many years after that Bridge had actually fled Ireland and had been seen in Newfoundland. However, Sheehy himself, in a letter written immediately prior to his death, was most explicit: "The fact is that John Bridge was destroyed by two alone, who strangled him on Wednesday night, October 24, 1764. I was then from home, and only returned home the 28th and heard that he had disappeared."

The implication is strong that the information came to the priest through the confessional and hence in such a manner that he could not make use of the information for his own preservation. Whatever the facts, Sheehy was adjudged guilty and was hanged, drawn and quartered at Clonmel, the assize town for the South Riding of Tipperary, on March 15, 1766. His head was fixed to a spike over the gates of Clonmel jail, where it remained for twenty years.

Of the effect of Sheehy's execution on the Roman Catholics of Tipperary, a nineteenth-century writer had this to say:

> The circumstances of the trial, and the fact that Sheehy alone of the Whiteboy victims was in holy orders, left a deep and lasting resentment in the popular mind. The grave of Sheehy was honoured like that of a saint. A Sheehy jury became a proverbial expression in Ireland for scandalous partiality. Stories were collected and believed of how all the chief persons connected with the tragedy came to some unhappy end, and the executioner of Sheehy was, some years later, murdered in a fierce popular outbreak.

The effects spread far beyond the geographical limits of Munster, or even of Ireland. In Canada, throughout the thirty-five years of arson, murder and rapine that culminated in the murder of five members of the Donnelly family, the record is dotted with references to "Sheehy's Day." Furthermore, in the later years of the Canadian feud, disorders tended to reach annual climaxes in mid-March on the anniversary of Father Sheehy's execution, tapering away thereafter to a low point in the summer months when the crops needed tending.

The importance attached to "Sheehy's Day," the establishment in Biddulph of an oath-bound secret society, even the implication of a parish priest in the activities of the society, all point so strong a parallel to the Whiteboys agitation as entirely to preclude mere coincidence. Between the death of Father Sheehy in 1766 and the beginnings of the Biddulph feud in the mid-1840s there is a gap of only three-quarters of a century—little enough time for the Irish mind to forget a grudge.

The gap furthermore is not without its connecting links. The Whiteboys were not smashed. They merely went underground and their acts of terrorism became even more vicious. By 1785 they had adopted a new name—the Right Boys. The following year there was a particularly savage outbreak which led to the passage by the Irish Parliament of a repressive act which provided punishment for membership in such illegal associations up to and including the death penalty.

While the severity of the legislation brought a few years of relative peace to Tipperary, there was no corresponding mitigation of grievances nor abandonment of the Whiteboys' cause. Similar societies sprang up throughout Ireland, causing great unrest which culminated in the abortive and bloodily suppressed rebellion of 1798.

The proliferation of secret societies in Ireland during this period makes it difficult to establish a true pedigree for their lineal descendant, the Vigilance Committee of Biddulph Township, in Canada. The Munster Whiteboys had their Ulster counterpart in the Defenders, and early in the nineteenth century both became submerged in the Ribbon Society which, with considerably altered objectives and methods, remains as a movement to the present day.

Whiteboys, Right Boys, Defenders and Ribbonmen shared a common purpose and swore similar oaths. Their objectives were only occasionally political, in marked contrast to that other great Irish secret society, the United Irishmen. They were, quite simply, anti-Protestant and anti-landlord.

While the form of oath differed from society to society, a Ribbonman oath attested to by the Irish novelist, William Carleton, contains features common to all. The third, fifth, sixth and ninth clauses of this curious oath, quoted below, are identical with the practices of the Vigilance Committee of Biddulph Township:

> 3rd. That I will duly and regularly attend on the shortest possible notice, at any hour, whether by night or by day, to

perform *without fail or enquiry*, such commands as my superior or superiors may lay upon me, under whatever penalty he or they may inflict for neglecting the same.

5th. I also declare and promise, that I will not admit or propose a Protestant or heretic of any description as a member of our Fraternal Society, knowing him to be such.

6th. That whether in fair or market, in town or country, I will always give the preference in dealing to those who are attached to our national cause, and that I will not deal with a Protestant or heretic—but above all with an Orangeman—so long as I can deal with one of my own faith on equal terms.

9th. That I will not, under the penalty inflicted by my superiors, give evidence in any Court of Law or Justice against a brother, when prosecuted by an Orangeman or heretic; and that I will aid him in his defence by any means in my power.

William Carleton is also the authority for the meaning of the Ribbonmen's badge: "The two ribbons are to be two signs that will guide you—the green one is for Ireland and friendship, and the red one for revenge and blood; the one is for your friends—the other for your enemies."

John Heron Lepper in his "Famous Secret Societies" says that after 1803 Whiteboys, Defenders and Ribbonmen were interchangeable and convertible terms "employed to describe one organized body" which he identifies as the Ribbon Society. This may well be true applied to Ireland generally, but in Southern Ireland, and particularly in Tipperary, the oldest of the three terms continued current at least until the export of the Tipperary feud to Canada in the mid-1840s.

In this brief exploration of the historical background of the Tipperary feud, the emphasis so far has been placed on one group of belligerents. It is now time to examine, equally briefly, the objects of the Whiteboys' hatred.

As has been indicated earlier, the wrath of the Whiteboys was at first directed against the property of the landlord class, most of them absentee landowners. As time passed and they

became bolder, they began to victimize their Protestant neighbours, most of whom were descendants of the German Lutheran
and French Huguenot settlers brought in by Cromwell.

Their most vicious acts and most virulent hatred were
reserved, however, for those of their own Roman Catholic faith
who collaborated with the Protestant enemy or defected from
their allegiance to the Whiteboys. For defectors there were terrible penalties ranging from the mutilation of livestock and arson
through immersion in pits filled with cold water and thorns up
to and including death by strangulation or other even more
unpleasant means.

There was still another group of Tipperary Roman Catholics
who not only refused to join or to sanction the activities of the
White boys but placed themselves actively in opposition. Many
misdemeanours were charged against them—they associated
with Protestants, did business with Orangemen, used the processes of English law for the redress of grievances and were
even known to give evidence against Whiteboys.

To this group belonged some of the oldest and most
highly respected native Roman Catholic families of Tipperary.
Prominent among them are family names that will appear again
and again in this narrative, including Nangle, Keeffe—and
Donnelly. Again and again in this story the bearers of these
and other equally ancient Tipperary patronyms will be found
asociating with Tipperary Protestants, doing business with
Orangemen and voting the Protestant ticket in politics.

In Biddulph Township these families were known as
"Blackfeet." It seems likely, from the obvious contrast with the
name of the Tipperary terrorist society, that the term was imported from Ireland along with the feud and its participants.

This is the true genesis of the "Biddulph Horror," which
was the legitimate heir of the "Munster Terror." This is the real
background of the events that turned a Canadian township into
a seething cauldron of hatred and claimed a score of lives. It is
a background that has been obscured by a conspiracy of silence

for more than a century. Only now and then does the veil lift—an unguarded reference by a garrulous oldster to "Sheehy's Day" or "John Meskill," or a baffled comment by a reporter on a sign reading "No Water for Blackfeet." With the Tipperary background as a guide, however, these scattered pieces of evidence suffice to reveal the shape of an ancient grudge demanding its victims from generation unto generation.

Martin O'Sullivan, writing in 1824 under the pseudonym "A Munster Farmer," has left a vivid word picture of the tragic passage of the feud from one generation to another. He speaks sorrowfully of his loss of influence over the younger people and records the sad words of the father of one young man:

> I tell you, there's something that's not right among them boys; they are grown so dark, and getting together in holes and corners; and when I speak to them about the ould times, and the bloody year ninety-eight, and the hard summer that came after, to frighten 'em, 'tis that that only sets them wild entirely.

To which O'Sullivan adds his prophetic comment: "The poor old man did not know that, in memory, hatred and revenge are only one remove from horror."

Green Wounds

A man that studieth revenge keeps his own wounds green.

Bacon

THE Tipperary feud was savage and deep-seated. It was also intensely localized, depending for its fury and persistence on the constant maintenance in the same proportions of its three explosive ingredients—Whiteboys, Blackfeet and Cromwell Protestants—within a confined area. The removal or dilution of one of the three elements disarmed the compound.

Between the close of the Napoleonic wars and the outbreak of the American Civil War thousands of Tipperary families migrated to North America. Most of them were assimilated peacefully into new neighbourhoods and soon forgot the old hatreds. In one small area only were the exact conditions of the Tipperary mixture duplicated. By 1845 two adjoining townships in the western portion of what was then called Upper Canada had precisely the right number of Whiteboys, Blackfeet and Cromwell Protestants to pick up where they had left off in Tipperary.

It came about in this manner.

In 1821 and again ten years later, food shortages in Tipperary—precursors of the great potato famines—led to savage but short-lived outbreaks of Whiteboy terrorism. At the close of the latter incident a Tipperary Protestant, James Hodgins, was awarded £50 by the grateful authorities for signal services as a constable in the "troubles." With this money, a sizable amount of capital for those days, Hodgins, then a man of forty-nine, decided to emigrate. It may well be that his decision was dictated to some extent by concern for his personal safety.

In his choice of a location in Canada he was influenced by the experience of a group of Tipperary Protestants, some of whom he may have known. In 1818 sixty-five Tipperary families, led by their squire, Richard Talbot, scion of an ancient Anglo-Irish connection, had emigrated to Canada, settling in the Township of London, immediately south of Biddulph Township.

Hodgins, a man of great energy, obtained employment with the Canada Land Company shortly after his arrival, assisting in the survey of some of the Company's one million acres of farmlands in Huron, Bruce and Perth Counties. As partial payment for his services he got patent for Lot 39, Concession 3, Biddulph Township. Shortly thereafter he became agent for the Company and was largely instrumental for the settlement of the Township.

Hodgins was not the first settler in the township. In 1830 a group of refugee Negro slaves from the United States cleared land there and established a settlement named Wilberforce after the great English abolitionist. By one of those exquisite ironies with which the history of the Biddulph feud is larded, the first community in Biddulph was built under the auspices of the Society of Friends. Descendants of some of the original slave settlers still live in the township. The presence of the Negro community in the township had no bearing on the Irish feud.

Constable Hodgins was soon joined by other Tipperary families, including a number of close relatives and family connections, most of them Protestants. Some of the names give clear indication of German and French origin, including such obviously anglicized surnames as Shoebottom and Courcey.

Theirs was at first a peaceful community. Although the Tipperary families in Biddulph and London townships were not all from the same community, they had many bonds in common.

They shared a mutual relief at escaping from the rigours and terrors of life in Ireland; they rejoiced together in the joys of owning their own land—and they attended the same church.

In the middle 1830s the magnet of cheap land coupled with continued distress in Ireland attracted many of the Tipperary Catholics to Canada. Some did not complete the long trek inland from Quebec to the western peninsula, settling instead in more easterly communities like Kingston, where their presence later provided the tinder for outbreaks of religious strife.

Enough of them, however, travelled half-way across the continent to the new homes of their former enemies, to re-create in short order the old grudges and grievances and the old feud, in a new setting.

By the middle 1840s the explosive mixture was well prepared, the fuse was lit, and the joyful sound of Irish club meeting Irish pate was being heard almost daily throughout the two townships.

There is reason to believe that some of the bolder spirits among the Tipperary Protestants were not altogether sorrowful at the renewal of old Donnybrooks. Life in the wilderness was boring, and a brawl at a tavern or a cross-roads was a welcome relief from monotony.

The story is told of the meeting of two Tipperary natives at a tavern in the Queen's Bush, as the Canada Company tract was called. Each recognizing the map of Ireland on the other's face but not being sure of religious affiliations, one tossed off his drink, stared at the other and declared in a loud, firm voice:

"To hell with the Pope!"

The second man responded in an equally formal manner. Draining his glass and setting it firmly on the bar, he made his declaration:

"To hell with King Billy!"

The line thus being clearly drawn the two divested themselves of their jackets and fought an hour's battle to a draw. As they lay panting side by side on the floor, each extended a hand to the other, and a lifelong friendship was sealed.

Not all such encounters had pleasant endings. In Biddulph they tended to result in injury and, on occasion, death.

The record of the early years of the "trouble" is fragmentary and confused but an impression of continuing violence is impossible to avoid. Some of the occurrences can be traced to the inevitable wildness of pioneer times. The Queen's Bush was frontier country. Life was hard, conditions were difficult and of a nature to breed crimes of violence, as early court records attest. To these generally prevalent causes can be set down many of the tavern brawls with their often fatal consequences.

By December, 1845, however, violence had taken a definite form and the Tipperary feud was well under way. A newspaper in the nearby town of London reported the first murderous incident in its issue of January 3, 1846:

BRUTAL OUTRAGE

We are informed that some difference lately arose, or perhaps previously existed between two *Parties* assembled at a Bee, in Biddulph. It seems that the next day, being Sunday, they again fell in with each other, whether by design or accident we cannot tell, at a place to which we are told people improperly resort on Sundays. After partaking freely of stimulating liquor they were again excited to malicious indignation; and our informant says that, when one party was going home in a sleigh, the other, who were previously prepared with weapons, met them in the Woods and beat them most unmercifully, killing one, and wounding two others so severely that it was doubtful whether they would recover. We understand the accused have gone away and hitherto escaped apprehension.

Communications in the Canadian backwoods were poor in 1846. It is impossible now to put together a connected story of the battle in the woods. *The London Times* made no further mention of the affair and no files now survive of other local newspapers of the period.

The item as it stands strongly hints at a previous basis for the dispute which erupted in so violent a manner. From other scraps of evidence it appears that the tavern at which the decision to fight was taken was one operated by the Keeffe family near the present hamlet of Elginfield, south of Lucan. This tavern looms largely and ominously in the story of the Biddulph vendetta. Thirteen years later, as we shall see, the incident of the 1845 manslaughter was curiously and almost exactly repeated, at the same tavern.

In fact, the pattern was to become almost monotonously familiar to the people of Biddulph during the next thirty-five bloody years. A dispute at a bee, twenty-four hours of brooding on the real or fancied grievance, a thorough lubrication at a convenient tavern—and bloodshed.

One specific point is established by the story of the 1845 affair. All previous writers have assumed the Donnelly family to be the principal instigators and cause of the Biddulph feud. They have been aided in arriving at this conclusion by the understandable desire of the murderers of the Donnelly family and their descendants to obscure the real issues. The battle in the woods indicates ill-feeling of a more than transitory nature. By no stretch of the imagination can this first blood be laid at the door of the Donnellys.

It occurred almost two years before the Donnelly family arrived in Biddulph Township and probably before they had even arrived in Canada.

Death's Shadow at the Door

All things they have in common being so poor,
And their one fear, Death's shadow at the door.

Edmund Blunden

IN 1844 James Hodgins (formerly Tipperary Constable James Hodgins), Justice of the Peace, landowner and agent for the Canada Land Company, returned to Tipperary. His major object was to secure more settlers for the Company's lands. The state of his native county being what it was, his visit was signally successful. This time the immigrants were mostly Tipperary Catholics.

One of those who heard the siren call of the New World was James Donnelly. It is unlikely that Donnelly engaged in idle dreams about an overseas Utopia; the promised land was an unknown quantity almost certainly to be preferred to rack-rents, poverty and famine.

Jim Donnelly in 1844 was in his twenty-ninth year. He was considered handsome—of medium height, dark-haired, heavily-built and muscular. His wife of three years, the former Johannah Magee, was "black Irish"—thick-set and swarthy, by no standards a beauty then or later.

The departure of the family was delayed. It was many long months before the dirt-poor Donnellys could scrape together the money even for steerage passage. Then William, their second son, was born on a blustery January night in 1845. His coming was a sorrow to his parents. Unlike their first son James, born in 1842 and destined like his father to die a violent death, this child was imperfect. One foot was deformed.

With still another potato famine in prospect, the Donnellys fought for space on an immigrant vessel and finally, late in 1845 or early in 1846, set sail for Canada.

There is no record of the ship on which they crossed the Atlantic. If it was like other ships of the "immigrant run," it was a floating pigsty—cramped, foetid and disease-ridden. Designed to transport large numbers of human cattle at the greatest possible profit to the owners, these sea-going charnel houses were periodically subject to outbreaks of "ship's fever" or typhus. The worst of these epidemics occurred in 1847 when it killed unknown thousands of poor Irish immigrants on the sea and after their landing. A memorial on Grosse Ile, a former quarantine station in the St. Lawrence River, records the epitaph of a few of them:

IN THIS SECLUDED SPOT LIE THE MORTAL REMAINS OF 5,424 PERSONS WHO, FLEEING FROM PESTILENCE AND FAMINE IN IRELAND IN THE YEAR 1847, FOUND IN AMERICA BUT A GRAVE.

The Donnellys saw Grosse Ile. It was the unsavoury first experience of every immigrant on Canadian soil. A battery of heavy guns manned by British artillerymen ensured that every newcomer should taste to the full the wormwood of Grosse Ile before encountering the wilderness he had come to see and conquer.

Eyewitness accounts of the moral and physical degradation of the Irish immigrants seem at first glance morbidly exaggerated but there is unfortunately abundant evidence to justify them.

Even travellers case-hardened by exposure to the squalor of nineteenth-century British factory slums grew soul-sick and nauseated at the filth, disease and degeneration shamelessly exhibited on Grosse Ile. They speak of hordes of almost naked, dirt-encrusted immigrants howling in a score of Old Country dialects; the well robbing the sick in spite of the danger of contagion; an old man crawling from his pallet to suck water from a ditch; of wizened children wise from birth in the ways of death sitting by the roadside to die. It is little wonder that when the Right Reverend George Jehoshaphat Mountain, Church of England Bishop of Quebec, visited the island in 1847, he chose to preach upon these words from the 107th Psalm:

> And He gathered them out of the lands, from the east and from the west, from the north and from the south. They wandered in the wilderness in a solitary way; they found no city to dwell in. Hungry and thirsty, their soul fainted in them.

However, the true spirit of those who passed through Grosse Ile is found not in the Psalmist's cry of despair, but in the words of a gigantic Irishman whom one woman writer saw there—a wild, exuberant figure, naked except for a tattered great-coat, flourishing a huge shillelagh in one grimy fist, yelling his challenge to the world from a heap of rocks:

"Whurrah, my boys! Sure we'll be jintlemen!"

The miracle of it all is, some of them did become gentlemen.

II

From the horrors of Grosse Ile the immigrant Donnellys moved by slow stages to the minor horrors of the "immigrant sheds"— minor only by comparison with the gargantuan pest-hole of the St. Lawrence. These sheds were vast, draughty, windowless barns thrown together by government contractors at all major dispersal points for the immigrants.

The Donnellys in their painful journey into the interior would have made compulsory stops at several of these hostels. One was at Kingston, at the eastern end of Lake Ontario, reached from Montreal by St. Lawrence bateaux—huge, slow-moving river barges. Another dispersal point was Toronto, linked with the East by flotillas of busily-shuttling lake boats. The last one was London, then a somewhat hectic frontier village of 5,000 population. The final portion of the journey was made by ox-cart over a bone-rattling corduroy road.

In the very heart of London, much to the disgust of the earlier immigrant population whom two decades of settlement had made respectable, were two of the great sheds. In one clustered the living amid the chaos of their belongings; in the other lay the ill, the dead and the dying. On pallets laid on the dirt floor, or on the floor itself, they lay in rows waiting for death or recovery.

There is no monument in London to those who died; even their number is unknown. They were hauled away, anonymously, in the dead of night in farm carts and buried unceremoniously, shroudless and often unshriven, beneath a few inches of dirt in a gravel pit outside the town. The sheds themselves were later burned to the ground by a public-spirited incendiary, fearful lest the disease spread from the foul-smelling timbers of the pest-house.

While the sheds still stood, area farmers, merchants and manufacturers used them as a cheap-labour market. Standing well back to avoid contamination they scrutinized Ireland's chief export and chose the sound in wind and limb for work in the factory or behind the plough. Many of the men went directly from the immigrant sheds, bare shanks and all, to pound spikes on the railroad then snaking its way across country towards the American border.

Of the thousands who came, the strongest survived. The weak and the single women found: their way into early graves, domestic service, prostitution, the pauper rolls or the prisons.

Such was the introduction of the Donnelly family to their new Canadian home. They were numbered among the survivors. Pestilence was no stranger to them; poverty and degradation of spirit had been theirs from birth; arson and murder had long been night-time companions to them and to their neighbours. Their arrival did not beget these larger and lesser evils; their coming only added to the number of victims.

III

The road north from London to Biddulph Township and the holdings of the Canada Land Company was known as the Proof Line. It received the name by virtue of its having been the road allowance used by an early surveyor to "prove the line" of his survey.

In the spring of 1847 a farm wagon bore the Donnelly family and their few effects north on this road. Family tradition has it that Jim had found employment in London on their arrival but the call of the land finally drew him to the fertile Biddulph acres.

On their journey north the Donnellys passed a line of coach houses, taverns and lesser places of refreshment which had sprung up along this main highway into the Queen's Bush. At Elginfield, where the road after running die-straight due north for fifteen miles makes a slight jog to the north-west, they came to Andrew Keeffe's tavern, where the pitched battle of December, 1845, had been brewed.

The inn was undistinguished architecturally. Geographically it straddled the border between the farmlands held by the Tipperary Protestants of London Township and the Tipperary Roman Catholics of Biddulph. This strategic location made it the natural locale for the rebirth in Canada of the Tipperary feud. Again it must be emphasized that the feud had been regenerated long before Jim Donnelly's cart drew up at the Keeffe inn door. But from that moment the fates of the Keeffes, the Donnellys and the inn itself were mutually and inextricably involved.

From the welter of fact, legend and deliberate fiction which has obscured the Biddulph feud during the passage of the years, the vague shape of the Keeffe inn swims into focus periodically. The shape is evil, and the context of its frequent appearances, invariably violence. It is no coincidence that on the very night in 1897 when Will Donnelly finally went to the reward his enemies had long and ardently wished for him, the hand of an unknown incendiary set fire to the empty shell of the old tavern. As the flame devils feasted on the old, rotten timbers, Will Donnelly and the Biddulph feud died, together.

In the spring of 1847, this was still fifty years in the future. There were many other graves to be filled first.

IV

Jim Donnelly had no money and few prospects. Unable to afford to buy a farm from the Canada Company, he followed the practice of many poor immigrant families—he found a piece of vacant land that appealed to him and settled on it. There is little legal justification for the so-called "squatter's rights," but a great number of Canadian pioneers successfully employed the practice.

The plot Jim selected was the south-east quarter of lot number eighteen on the Roman Line. The lot actually belonged to an absentee landowner. If Jim knew this, and he probably did, it must have given him a perverse satisfaction to appropriate it for his own use. The nineteenth-century Irishman had no love for absentee landlords.

Whatever his faults, Jim was not a lazy man. He worked hard to clear his lot, to throw up a log shanty and to put the rich soil to seed. Johannah worked along with him until the seed stirred in her, too, and she was brought to bed with her third son, John, in the harvest season of their first year in Biddulph. Four more sons followed—Patrick in 1849; Michael in the following year; Robert in 1853 and Thomas in 1854.

Life was not all work for Jim Donnelly. Of a Saturday night he might ride into the village recently renamed Lucan in honour of an Irish peer. Previously it had been called Marysville, after Protestant Jim Hodgins' wife, which made the name socially unacceptable to the Roman Catholics. Here he might indulge in a drop of the "craythur," listen to the loud talk, and now and then take part in a little genteel skull-cracking resulting in an occasional headache but no permanent injury.

Jim shared his bottle with few men. The Donnelly family never made friends easily. They walked alone and mostly kept their own counsel. This caused them to be set apart from their neighbours. Enemies described them as "black Irish—black inside and out." This was a prejudiced viewpoint. There were many who testified later to the kindness and warmth of the Donnellys. There was laughter and fun in them—but they showed this side of their natures only to a few close friends.

Sometimes Jim went down to the Keeffe inn instead. Like the Donnellys, this family had deep and ancient roots in the tortured soil of Tipperary. Like the Donnellys, they were known to be "Blackfeet." Their friendship persisted all through the years of the feud, even in the face of great danger.

Sometimes Jim took his liquid refreshment at Protestant inns. The Tipperary Blackfeet drew no distinctions and patronized Roman Catholic and Protestant merchants alike, in direct defiance of the Whiteboys' oath. From the beginning, Jim Donnelly made no attempt to disguise his position in the Tipperary feud, or to alter his family's principles in deference to the feelings of his Whiteboy neighbours. Indeed, he underlined his stand by subscribing, shortly after his arrival in Biddulph, to the building of St. James's *Anglican* Church.

It would be wrong to imply that the first ten years of Jim Donnelly's residence in Biddulph were without incident. There were fights in plenty and an occasional case of manslaughter. There was much raking over of old grievances and harsh talk about informers, Blackfeet, Whiteboys and the martyred Father Sheehy. The records of the local magistrates are full of assault cases and felonies of one kind and another, the commonest being something called "dogging hogs." A significant fact about these records is that while they contain numerous references to families later to loom prominently in the feud, they are atogether barren of the name Donnelly either as plaintiffs or defendants.

The Tipperary feud at this point lacked direction. It had no pivot, no focus.

The focus was provided in 1856 or 1857 by the sale of Jim Donnelly's lot to a man named Patrick Farrell.

The Blooding of Farrell

"Let there be light!" said God, and there was light!
"Let there be blood!" says man, and there's a sea!

Lord Byron: DON JUAN

JIM Donnelly's murderers claimed it was his informal ownership of Pat Farrell's land that touched off the Biddulph feud. They claimed further that it was Farrell's death in the summer of 1857 at Donnelly's hands that initiated the chain of murders that culminated in the virtual annihilation of the Donnelly family twenty-three years later.

These, like many other statements tirelessly and maliciously circulated by the assassins and their kin, friends and descendants, are at best intentionally misleading, at worst deliberate falsehoods.

In the first instance it has been demonstrated in an earlier chapter that bad feeling existed in the township before the Donnellys ever arrived and that this factionalism had caused at least one death by violence. Jim Donnelly neither started the feud nor did he draw first blood.

The legal aspects of the disputed ownership had been arbitrated by 1857. The disputants had appeared in court and mutually agreed to the bench's disposition of their claims. Donnelly was awarded twenty-five acres. The balance, including some land already cleared by him, went to Farrell. It was often said that the feud would not have begun if the court had not granted Donnelly some of the fruits of his ten years' labour. Surely this is begging the question. It certainly fails to take into consideration Jim Donnelly's fiercely independent nature. Had the court dispossessed him entirely of his hard-won shieling, there almost certainly would have been an immediate blood-letting. As it was, it was Farrell's active and continued enmity towards Donnelly that led to his own death.

Jim Donnelly did not draw first blood in the Biddulph feud, nor even second blood. Farrell's death in that year of violence was unique only in two instances. It was the only crime of that year that could be attributed unequivocally to a member of the Donnelly family. It was also the only death in a long series of deaths by criminal violence for which a penalty was paid by anyone.

The first major crime of 1857 was a cold-blooded, premeditated murder. It was conveniently forgotten by all except the Donnelly family, whose surviving members tried unsuccessfully to revive it at the trials of the Vigilantes in 1880 and 1881.

In the first week in February an English Protestant cattle drover from a neighbouring township passed along the Roman Line on his way to the market at London. He had made the journey many times before and was well, if not favourably, known to the Tipperary settlers. His name was Richard Brimmacombe.

Brimmacombe's return trip ended abruptly on the night of February 6 by the roadside on the seventh concession of Biddulph, three-quarters of a mile north of the Roman Line. His body was found there the next morning by Stephen Cormack, a farmer living near by. There were signs of a struggle and three knife wounds on the body—on the temple, neck and thigh. He had been robbed.

According to *The St. Marys Argus*, a weekly newspaper published in the area, suspicion immediately fastened itself on "a man residing within half a mile from the place where the body was found." The paper "deemed it proper" to withhold his name. Later information identified the suspect as Patrick Ryder, of the Roman Line, and named one Casey as an accomplice.

The death of Richard Brimmacombe went unavenged. There was no trial, no conviction. There was an inquest and an investigation. In keeping with the Tipperary tradition information was given and later repudiated. The Tipperary code was very strict on the subject of informers—the Whiteboys had seen to that. Information given to police officers in moments of anger or indignation was usually retracted on sober second thought. Had perjury been punishable by death, the Irish population of Biddulph would very soon have been exterminated.

It is true there were arrests in the Brimmacombe case. The man Casey was taken into custody shortly after the commission of the crime but escaped from the constable while being taken to the county jail at Goderich, some distance north. Evidence was presented—factual and perjured—in such confusing profusion that the law, as usual in Biddulph, was balked.

There the legal aspects of the case end and local legend takes over. The legend insists that the killers profited handsomely by the violent transaction; that the money was invested in land and cattle, leading to a measure of unexplained prosperity for one of the Tipperary families. The name of that family was Ryder. It will recur many times in this story.

The year that had begun so violently continued bloody. In March, the anniversary month of Father Sheehy's execution, there were two more violent deaths among the Tipperary families, one by accident, one by design. A young man named Shea was accidentally killed by his uncle when the latter's axe flew off its shaft and buried itself in the victim's heart. A Tipperary man named Gleason was murdered near the village of Garranbrook in another township. There was an inquest but no arrest, trial or conviction.

There were many other crimes in 1857 of a more petty nature. Tipperary names like Madigan, Atkinson, Cunningham, Glendenning, Neill, Glavin, Loughlin, Garry, Flannery, Blake and Heenan abound in the records of the courts.

The name Donnelly is conspicuous by its absence.

The truth is, Jim and Johannah Donnelly were far too busy on their pre-empted acres chopping, burning and sowing, bearing and raising children, to engage in any of the more violent Tipperary "sports."

Jim apparently had accepted the court ruling with reasonably good grace. He asked only to be allowed to go his own way. However, Pat Farrell, said to be a distant relative, brooded over the loss of his twenty-five acres. With relish he told his friends repeatedly what he was going to do to Jim Donnelly. The men of Tipperary showed little imagination in their threats. The commonest proposal was an offer to "cut out the black heart of the bejasus bastard and make him eat it."

There is no evidence that Jim Donnelly sought an encounter with Farrell. Even the most notoriously prejudiced accounts of this period of the feud make it clear it was Pat Farrell who went looking for trouble—and eventually found it.

It happened on Saturday, June 27, 1857. A gang of the Tipperary men and some of their women met at a neighbourhood barn-raising. In the communal custom of pioneer Canada the older settlers decided to hold a "bee" to assist a newcomer in erecting the frame of his barn. Custom also decreed that at such events work and play should receive at least equal billing, and a plentiful supply of cheap, potent and raw liquor was accordingly made available.

Unfortunately for all, both Jim Donnelly and Pat Farrell decided to attend. Jim seems at first to have persevered in his efforts to avoid an open clash with Farrell. For once exhibiting some common sense, the other Tipperary men supported Jim's efforts and tried to steer such conversation as there was around the demijohns to neutral subjects. Principally they talked about the railway and its probable effect on the future of the community. A gang of surveyors had recently passed through Biddulph, planning the line of a proposed railroad from the market town of London to the port of Goderich on Lake Huron.

Even on this subject there were two schools of thought in the township—those who saw in it the beginning of a period of unexcelled prosperity for the village of Lucan and those who saw in it a threat to the successful operation of the Proof Line Road, the principal highway artery to the north, and to the prosperity of the chain of hotels and inns that served it, including Andrew Keeffe's wayside shrine to Bacchus.

All efforts to steer the belligerent and by now intoxicated Farrell on to safe conversational ground were in vain. Whatever the topic, he made it the vehicle for a verbal attack on the character and antecedents of Jim Donnelly. Meanwhile, Jim tried to counteract the stings of the gadfly by hard application alternately to the axe and the jug. Presently he gave up the axe.

At last a particularly vicious jibe stabbed through Jim's armour of reserve. He replied in the same vein and Farrell, axe in hand, sprang at him. There is confusion in the testimony concerning Farrell's axe. Some witnesses claimed he threw it to one side before going at Donnelly with his bare hands. Others claimed he flung it at Donnelly but missed his target. Whatever happened in that instant, in the next they were at one another's throats.

By this time both men were thoroughly drunk. The other Tipperary men, feeling that in this condition they could do each other no harm, made no attempt to separate them and settled back to watch the fun.

After a moment or two of clinching and in-fighting Farrell accidentally landed a solid punch which lifted Donnelly off his feet and laid him flat on his back. The spectators closed in. Their object in so doing was to prevent Farrell applying the accepted Tipperary *coup de grâce* to a fallen foe—the technique known as "putting the boots to him." If that was indeed Farrell's intention, he never had an opportunity to perform it.

Donnelly was down but not out. Shaking his head violently in an effort to clear the whiskey fumes from it, he struggled to his feet. As he did so, one hand encountered an iron handspike someone had left lying on the ground. As he staggered to his feet, clutching the piece of iron, Farrell rushed him. He threw the handspike.

The daemon of the Donnellys supervised the flight of the missile. With the inevitability of death it sped true and straight to the left temple of its victim. The next moment Pat Farrell lay sprawled on the ground. It took him three days to die.

It was neither the first time nor the last that a Canadian "bee" ended in death. But never did such a straightforward case of manslaughter lead to such an appalling series of consequences.

The "bee" ended then and there. If Jim Donnelly had taken the advice of his neighbours and given himself up to the law the affair might have been concluded with a minimum of dislocation to the uneasy structure of Biddulph relationships. But this was asking too much of a Tipperary man accustomed to the ways of English Protestant courts with Irish Catholic peasants.

Jim disappeared from his farm and his usual haunts. Township rumour said he was still in Biddulph but only Johannah knew the truth of that statement.

Pat Farrell died on Monday, June 29, and a warrant was sworn out for the arrest of James Donnelly on a charge of murder. It was finally served nearly two years later.

"The Reproach of the Counties"

CHAPTER

We hope the trial of these cases will have the effect of weeding out the few bad birds who have made Biddulph the reproach of the Counties.

The HURON SIGNAL, Jan. 9, 1858

FROM June 27, 1857 until the end of the year 1859 the name of Jim Donnelly must be removed from the list of suspects in the Biddulph vendetta. During part of that time he was a hunted fugitive, and during the balance, a prisoner in close custody.

His wife Johannah can also be eliminated from the list. The burden of operating the farm and rearing her brood of boys left her no time to indulge in arson or manslaughter. The ages of the remaining members of the family—James, the eldest, was only twelve when his father threw the fatal handspike at Pat Farrell—effectively rule out their participation in the events of that period.

In that two and a half years there were at least three major cases of arson and two deaths by violence—all directly attributable to the Tipperary feud. In none of these events was the memory of Pat Farrell or the crime of Jim Donnelly invoked.

There were larger issues at stake.

Even before the Donnelly family arrived in Biddulph a new dimension had been added to the imported Munster feud. Religious intolerance deepened with the introduction of Canadian political bias.

The years between 1857 and 1859 were marked by the utmost confusion in the Canadian political scene. It was a period of unstable government, shifting political ground, and shady backstage deals. As a consequence of political and economic turbulence, the country went through three administrations in two years.

The elections of January, 1858—in the midst of a period of intense economic depression—were contested particularly hotly. This was especially true in Biddulph. But, however confused the political issues were elsewhere, in Biddulph they were clear-cut and deadly. The party labels—Conservative, Reform—meant nothing. In the local riding one candidate was a Roman Catholic, the other an Orangeman. No Tipperary man needed to know any more. This was home ground. With shouts of glee the men of Munster formed up on either side of the invisible line dividing the native Irish from the descendants of the Cromwell planters. The memory of Father Sheehy was invoked and his martyred bones figuratively paraded before the voters.

There was no secret ballot in those days. A man fearlessly or fearfully—depending on his physical strength and the number of his friends present—declared his choice before an avid audience of his peers. There was violence at many polling places in the 1858 election and deaths at some. There were probably clashes in Biddulph but nothing serious enough to engage the attention of the public prints. It was not until the election was over and Cayley, the Conservative champion of the Irish Roman Catholics, was declared the winner over Holmes, the Reformer-Orangeman, that the men of Tipperary began cracking skulls in earnest.

It was inevitable that the setting of the gravest post-election incident was, once again, Keeffe's tavern. Here is how the meeting of the Tipperary Protestants and Roman Catholics was described by a reporter for *The Huron Signal,* published in the Huron County town of Goderich. The date of publication was January 9, 1858:

We are sorry to say that the election in these counties did not pass off without one of those disgraceful rows which Canada has been too noted for. In Quebec two lives were lost—in Guelph one man was killed; and in Huron, it seems, that at least one poor fellow has been beaten within an ace of his life, and will probably be dead before this is in the hands of our subscribers.

Many of our readers who are in the habit of passing along the London road will recollect the toll gate in Biddulph, and a small tavern hard by it. This is Keefe's tavern, rather well known in the neighbourhood as the general resort of the Roman Catholic settlers. Keefe and his friends voted for Mr. Cayley. On the day after the declaration, or rather in the evening, if we are right informed, some sleighs containing Holmes's voters were passing Keefe's and some of them cheered for Holmes, upon this, some parties rushed out and threw some heavy missiles at the Holmes men. —One of them named Calligham had his skull fractured and is not expected to live. The parties who had committed the assault made their escape to the tavern, followed by the Holmes party, which was soon largely reinforced. They failed to capture the aggressors, and becoming all the more enraged at the want of success, attacked the house, smashing in the doors and windows, destroyed the furniture and left the house a mere wreck.

Three men were afterwards arrested, charged with the assault on Calligham, and held to bail by the magistrates to take their trial at the next assizes. The party that attacked the house were committed to gaol, and to the number of three and twenty, were brought in on Saturday last. Many of them protest that they were not of the party, but the magistrates seem to be convinced that they were sufficiently identified. An application was made to the judge of the county court to admit to bail; and upon his order they gave bail to appear at the next Quarter Sessions on the 9th March next; themselves in £50 each and sureties to the amount of £1000.

> We have two of the names of the men charged with the murderous assault, Ryan, Keefe's barkeeper, and Casey, a brother of the man who escaped from the Constable when in custody, charged with assisting in the murder of Brimmacombe. The list of the men held to bail for the attack on Keefe's house comprises most of the well-known Protestant Irish names in the neighbourhood: Stanleys, Hodgins, Callinghams, etc. etc. etc. We hope the trial of these cases will have the effect of weeding out the few bad birds who have made Biddulph the reproach of the Counties.

Records are lamentably scarce with respect to this incident. One thing only can be stated with reasonable certainty. Persons were charged, as this report indicates, with the commission of specific crimes. There were, however, no convictions. Owing to either the laxity of the authorities, or the consistently perjured nature of the evidence, or both, the participants in the feud were allowed to continue to make their own laws and exact their own penalties.

Innkeeper Keeffe was not among those charged as a result of the riot. As a Roman Catholic he had sustained heavy property loss at the hands of the angry Orange mob. As one of the Tipperary Blackfeet, characterized by their enemies as "more than half Protestant," he next incurred the ire of the Whiteboy faction. Perhaps he had given evidence unfavourable to the Cayley supporters in the riot case. Whatever the cause, he was marked out for vengeance.

The reprisal took the familiar form of arson. If any of the evidence in the case can be trusted, it was not the act of a single malcontent but that of a group of Tipperary Irish Catholics working in combination. Behind the scanty facts one can see again the shifting shadows of the secret night meeting, the taking of oaths, the sealing of undying fealty in tumblers of raw whiskey.

The Whiteboys were riding again.

The arsonists may have been surprised at their work. In any event the inn was spared but the wooden stables went up in a sheet of flame, in the dead of night, a funeral pyre for ten horses, innocent of Tipperary blood.

Like the murder of Brimmacombe, the burning of Keeffe's stables became a landmark in the Biddulph feud, a turning-point, the often cited excuse for the later excesses of the younger Donnellys. Will Donnelly was only thirteen at the time of the incident but twenty-two years later, standing by the shot-riddled body of his brother John, he was declaring:

"There were ten horses burned at Andrew Keeffe's about twenty-three years ago ... There was a party arrested and stood trial for it. We were not suspected of burning our father's barns or killing an Englishman on the road. We have suffered as much as others in the neighbourhood."

Lack of records again blurs and fogs this period of the feud. Here and there a newspaper report or a vagrant court record throws isolated incidents into sharp relief. A single paragraph in *The London Free Press* for September 10, 1858, carries the account of the Keeffe arson a step further:

> On Monday last a number of persons were ar-raigned before Messrs. Ryan, Flanagan, Barber, Hodgins, Carter and Kelly at Biddulph, on the information of a person named Hogan. The infor-mation stated that Dennis Twoey, Sen., Patrick Quigley, James Rider, Jun., John Twoey, Patrick Twoey and Darby Twoey had offered him (Hogan) a sum of $30 in May last if he would set fire to the premises of Andrew Keefe. Several other persons were also charged with those previously named, but they were discharged, the others being com-mitted to the assizes. Strange to say the informant, Hogan, has absconded and is nowhere to be found, a course taken most probably at the instance of the accused. Had the magistrates before whom the information was laid performed their duty, Hogan

> would have been bound over to appear; but through
> what appears to be either gross ignorance or negli-
> gence, the principal witness has run off. These gen-
> tlemen are magistrates appointed under Mr Cayley.

This is the first incident of the feud in which political bias
is seen definitely influencing the factual reporting of events in
the district press. The reference to the Cayley appointees is gratuitous and significant. The *Free Press* at this time was a Reform
newspaper committed to the support of the Orange Order. It
was the first time this journal indulged in editorial comment on
the Biddulph feud. It was not the last.

If Will Donnelly's later memory of the event is to be
trusted, some accused person or persons actually did stand trial
for the burning, but nobody's memory carried any reference to
a penalty accruing therefrom.

Even this necessarily incomplete record of events shows
a community wrenched and racked by internal dissension.
Newspapers were few and reportage erratic, yet enough remains even after a century to paint for us a picture of Biddulph
Township in the depression years of 1857–9 as a seething
cauldron of political and religious intolerance.

It was during this period that the priest of the newly-
established Roman Catholic parish of St. Patrick's preached a
fiery sermon to his delinquent parishioners. None of his flock
ever forgot it. Fearless in his faith and the righteousness of his
indignation, the priest did not mince words. No one recalled
exactly what he said, but a quarter of a century later an anonymous letter-writer in *The London Free Press* vividly recalled
the content:

> It is now nearly 24 years since a highly respected
> reverend gentleman said he was afraid the hand of
> God would fall on Biddulph; and if it has not, the
> hands of men and women at least have fallen.

A prophetic, Biblical echo to the priest's Jeremiad came from another part of the township a few days after Christmas, 1859. Only one mutilated and unsatisfactory record can be found of the crime of John Cain. He was only a boy of about nineteen, but he was old enough to kill his man. In a dispute with William Cahalan, of the 11th concession of Biddulph, over some matter now lost to view, Cain brained the older man with a steelyard. A steelyard is a kind of simple balance used for weighing grain and must have been an ugly weapon. Cahalan died a couple of hours later. He left a widow and eight children—two of them blind. The account concludes by stating that Cain had a bad character in the neighbourhood.

A diligent search of the remaining newspapers of the time has failed to reveal a single other statement with respect to this killing, the fourth Biddulph murder in four years.

The Fugitive

"Oh Sairey, Sairey, little do we know what lays afore us!"
Dickens: MARTIN CHUZZLEWIT

JIM Donnelly was a fugitive from justice for almost two years after the death of Pat Farrell. At no time was he very far away.

Biddulph Township in 1857 was at most twenty-five years removed from the first wilderness survey by the officials of the Canada Land Company. A substantial proportion of its 40,308 acres was still forested. The population was small and its peace officers few and overworked.

Jim Donnelly took to the woods.

While the first search for him was being carried out, he undoubtedly kept a safe distance between himself and his Roman Line homestead. As the summer waned and harvest time approached, he sneaked home to help Johannah in the fields.

Help was certainly needed in that grim summer of 1857. It was a "black year" that must have wakened the sleeping fears of the survivors of the Irish potato famine. There was little sunshine, much rain and heavy frosts in July and August. All the farmers had sown wheat—at $2.60 a bushel and with an avid market, who could blame them? To complete the ravages of the frost a blight struck at what was left of the crop. A district farmer got up one morning, looked at his stricken fields and blew out his brains.

To save anything at all from the wreck, to salvage enough to tide them over the winter, Johannah Donnelly needed another pair of hands. Young Jim and Will were the only two old enough to be of any assistance. Jim was fifteen, Will was twelve. The other five sons, ranging in years from four to ten, were too young to be more than an extra burden.

With her fugitive husband to care for as well, Johannah now had ten mouths to feed, for the family circle had been swelled by the unofficial adoption of still another boy—William Farrell, son of the man Jim Donnelly had killed. From the day Pat Farrell died, Jim and Johannah assumed the care of his son, bringing him up as one of their own.

There was nothing else for it—Jim must help with the farm.

The homestead was in plain sight of travellers on the Roman Line, a secondary but well-used route to the more northerly townships of the Canada Company tract. If Donnelly was to work in the fields, obviously he must be disguised to prevent detection.

Johannah produced some spare clothing of her own and Jim became a square-shouldered and compassionate "neighbour woman."

If any of the legitimate neighbours suspected the identity of the bonneted and sweating helper, they held their peace. The near-approach of any visitor to the farm always sent the "neighbour woman" off home on a sudden domestic emergency. It was not considered polite at that time among these people to probe into a proffered reason and so, after the visitors had ingested tea and cakes and departed, Jim would return to his labours.

Periodically visitors came on official business. Such was the efficiency of the bush telegraph that the "neighbour woman" was never in evidence on such occasions. This was not because Jim Donnelly had a plethora of friends; every native Tipperary Irishman had a bounden duty to hoodwink the law whenever an opportunity offered itself.

One never knew when the constables might call; it was unsafe for Jim to sleep in the house. Most nights he passed in the barn, bedded down on the sweet-smelling, new-mown hay. He did not spend all his nights there. Towards the end of his first year as a fugitive another Donnelly was born. She was the last child and the only girl. They called her Jenny.

The summer nights were not too bad; the winter must have been frightful. Jim and Johannah worked out a system of signals. One candle in the window told him it was safe to come into the house for the hot evening meal that kept him going. Two or more candles signalled trouble. Biddulph legend is full of stories of Jim's many narrow escapes from capture and of Johannah's cleverness in helping her man evade the never-ending efforts of the law to trap him. The law knew he was in the township, of course. Too many people were in on the secret.

The winter of 1857–8 dragged to a close. The excitement in late winter and early spring—the riot at Andrew Keeffe's and the later burning of his stables—took the attention away from the missing Jim Donnelly. How he must have hated to miss the brawl at Keeffe's! During the succeeding summer and fall he often worked in his own fields without benefit of disguise.

The baby, Jenny, was born and winter came again. Many an Irish housewife must have passed an idle moment that winter reckoning back nine months on her fingers and giving a knowing chuckle. That Jim Donnelly was a bold one and no mistake.

By the coming of another spring the "bold one" had had enough of the woods. The hunt had died down, the death of Pat Farrell was a stale piece of news and tempers had cooled. Maybe the law's memory too had been softened by the passage of time.

At Jim's behest, Johannah went to see Jim Hodgins. The former Tipperary constable had been, and would remain until his death, the best friend of the emigrant Donnellys. With a nice sense of justice Donnelly had forborne any approach to Hodgins while he was in hiding. Hodgins was a Justice of the Peace. It would have put him in an awkward position.

Jim Hodgins gave Johannah the only advice he could.

"Tell Jim to give himself up."

So Jim Donnelly walked into the village of Lucan (*née* Marysville) and gave himself up to the law. The long masquerade was over.

The trial was held at the spring assizes for the County of Huron in the county town, Goderich. As many Biddulph people as could manage it got themselves subpoenaed as witnesses and had a trip to Goderieh at the expense of the Crown. A good many others actually paid their own way, for it promised to be a good show.

They were not disappointed, but the trial proved shorter than had been expected. Witnesses paraded to the stand to recount the details of the barn-raising and the striking of the fatal blow. The defence did not make as much as it might have of the plea of self-defence, which was strongly substantiated even in the evidence of hostile witnesses.

It was a shock to the Munstermen when the jury brought in a verdict of guilty of murder. Still and all, they murmured to one another, the judge himself could temper justice with mercy. He chose not to do so.

Stunned and unbelieving, Jim Donnelly saw the judge don the ominous patch of black and heard the legal voice drone the awful formula:

". . . there to be hanged by the neck until you are dead."

It was a solemn crowd that made its way back to Biddulph. Johannah was frantic. She went straight to Jim Hodgins. The old man was astonished. He had had no idea the law would take so grave a view of what was essentially a manslaughter committed during a drunken brawl. He advised her to draw up and circulate a petition asking for clemency. On second thoughts he would draw it up himself. He did so—and his was the first name on the list.

During the next few weeks Johannah was everywhere—calling on merchants and farmers and innkeepers for their signatures. Jim's time was running out and the petition was getting longer, but too slowly. She had another conference with Jim Hodgins.

The next Sunday when the parishioners left the wooden church of St. Patrick's after mass there was the entire Donnelly brood lined up along the walk, as if for a royal inspection. They were washed, scrubbed and polished within an inch of their lives and decked out in their best clothes. First in line was Johannah armed with her petition. Then, like the steps of a stair came James, 17; William, 14; John, 12; Patrick, 10; Michael, 9; Robert, 6; Thomas, 5; and the toddler, Jenny.

A plea for sympathy and a determination to help her man shone in Johannah's square-cut, unhandsome Irish face. Silently she held out her petition to the first comer. He signed it. Before she left, nearly everyone had signed it. The friends of Jim Donnelly signed it gladly. His enemies signed it because others were watching them.

Soon the giant screed was ready and Jim Hodgins sent it for her to the appropriate provincial authority. Then came the time of waiting.

The day for Jim's execution was very close at hand when word finally came. After taking into consideration the facts of the case and the petition signed by so many respectable residents of Biddulph Township, the Executive Council had decided to commute his sentence to seven years in the provincial penitentiary at Kingston.

There must have been a fine Irish celebration in the Donnelly log house the night they received the news.

A week or two later, after a brief interview with Johannah, Jim boarded "the cars" with a guard for the long trip to the eastern part of the province.

In those days there was no time off for good behaviour. Jim's sentence was seven years and it was to be seven years exactly before he saw home and family again.

Entr'acte

Let us have a quiet hour,
Let us hob-and-nob with Death.

Tennyson: THE VISION OF SIN

WITH the departure of Jim Donnelly for the provincial penitentiary at Kingston and the death of William Cahalan at the hands of John Cain, the Biddulph feud seems temporarily to have exhausted itself. At least it went underground.

This is not to say that crime took a holiday or that the Tipperary shillelaghs were allowed to collect dust. Roman Catholics and Protestants, Whiteboys and Blackfeet continued to carry on the social customs expected of them, and many a farmer limped out to his fields on Monday morning nursing a bruised head. At no time in the nineteenth century was life in Biddulph permitted to fall into a humdrum pattern.

Tipperary names and the Tipperary feud occasionally cropped up in places remote from Biddulph. The murder of an Irishman named Maher by another named Farrell in Quebec City in 1861 was probably connected, however distantly, with the Munster vendetta. Both were residents of St. Catharines in the Niagara peninsula, a town which attracted many Tipperary residents including, in later years, Patrick, a son of Jim Donnelly.

There were other outbreaks closer to home during Jim's absence. There was no loss of life in these incidents, but a fairly substantial loss of property. In a twelve-month period ending in August, 1865, there were seven major fires, of which at least three were the work of arsonists. John O'Donohue, a close friend of the younger Donnellys, suffered the heaviest loss, in two separate blazes.

No legal action was taken with respect to any of these fires. There does not seem to have been any investigation into the causes.

The Biddulph thirst for blood and action found a more legitimate outlet during the five exciting years of the American Civil War. Like thousands of other young Canadians, many of the Tipperary boys went off to fight in the Union armies. Meanwhile their parents were kept too busy profitably raising beef cattle for shipment to the United States to raise hell at home.

In the last year of the war between the States another mysterious death occurred—a death that is still the subject of whispered comment among the older people of the township.

On September 12, 1865, the body of Pat Ryder, the elder, was found on the tracks of the Grand Trunk Railway near Lucan, mutilated and decapitated. There was undoubtedly an inquest, although no record of its findings has been discovered. Local legend says it was murder and that the old man's sons were in some way involved. This was the same Pat Ryder who, back in 1857, had been a suspect in the murder of Richard Brimmacombe. What connection these two violent deaths had with the feud or with the Donnellys is not clear, but that there was some connection seems evident from the number of times Will Donnelly drew attention to them in later years.

The following year the affairs of the Tipperary men were driven out of the local journals by infinitely more stirring events also connected in a mad way with Ireland. In the spring of 1866 the Canadian authorities learned to their consternation that the Fenian brotherhood was in fact ready and prepared to make its threatened invasion of Canada from the United States. This Irish order, the latest in a long list of secret societies dedicated to the release of Ireland from English bondage, seriously contemplated conquering the British possessions in North America and holding their 5,000,000 people as hostages for the return of Ireland to her "rightful owners."

The whole adventure now smacks strongly of musical comedy at its most extravagant but it did not seem so to the prosperous farmers of the western peninsula who had long dreaded the possibility of an American conquest of British North America once the quarrel between North and South had been settled.

In common with every village and town from Toronto to Windsor, Lucan sent hastily trained militiamen to the Niagara border and formed its old men and teenagers into ill-equipped "home guards." Two Biddulph lads—Thomas Hodgins, twenty-eight, and Charles Piper, sixteen—died while in service and were given military funerals.

In the midst of the national panic over the coming of the "Finnegans" an almost-unnoticed event occurred of much more significance to the Munstermen of Biddulph.

Jim Donnelly came home.

It was a quiet affair. There were no muttered threats, no chairs through store windows, no shouted references to the "bastards" of the outside world. He probably came by stagecoach, leaving it at the Roman Line, south of the village, for the short ride to his home.

They must have met him there—Johannah and the boys. Seven years had effected great changes in the seven tall lads, the work-hardened woman and the little girl who surrounded him.

Johannah had changed the least. She was taller than Jim and always carried herself erect "like a soldier." Her eyes were perhaps steelier and the chin squarer with the effort of "holding up her head" through seven years of social ostracism; her figure was stouter and there were hard lines round her mouth, but he could still recognize her as the Johannah Magee he had married so long ago in Tipperary.

Will, of course, he recognized immediately by the twisted foot, in spite of the strange, twenty-one-year-old face; the rest had to give him their names. There was Jim, a reckless-eyed young man of twenty-four; John, a strapping boy of nineteen with a quick, infectious grin. There was Pat, who already at seventeen showed the sober, industrious nature he displayed throughout his life; Mike, a year younger, a quick-tempered boy with a passion for railroading. And then there were the two youngest boys, Bob and Tom. At the ages of thirteen and twelve they showed plainly the consequences of having passed seven of their formative years without the discipline and example of a father.

Jenny, the girl, a demure eight years old, had to wait until the boys finished pounding their father's back and shouting their greetings at the tops of their voices before she could offer her cheek to the near-stranger who had sired her. He had scarcely known her as a baby; at eight she was less strange than the others.

Then they all piled into the farm wagon to continue their private celebrations at the log house with its sad and merry memories. It was probably there that Jim renewed acquaintance with the eleventh member of the Donnelly household—the boy, Bill Farrell, whom Johannah had cared for in his absence according to Jim's strict injunction.

Uneasy Peace

We have just enough religion to make us hate
but not enough to make us love one another.

Swift: THOUGHTS ON VARIOUS SUBJECTS

JIM's first New Year's Day at home in seven years turned out to be unexpectedly bleak. On the first day of 1867, after some weeks' illness, old Jim Hodgins died. Donnelly was inconsolable. As long as the sturdy old magistrate lived, Jim felt he could endure the hatred of his neighbours, secure in the knowledge that if the worst came, his old friend would somehow stand between him and them, as he had during that grim time after the judge in Goderich had donned the black cap.

Donnelly would scarcely try his Roman Catholic faith so far as to enter the Protestant church for the service, but he and his brood were undoubtedly at the graveside as they lowered into the frozen ground his oldest and dearest friend, Constable Jim Hodgins of Tipperary.

With the typical verbal extravagance of the Donnelly clan, Jim Donnelly had once said of his friend:

"I know who God is and I believe in Him; his name is Jim Hodgins!"

Now he was gone. Who was to tell the Donnellys the right things to do?

As it happened, the next three or four years were reasonably uneventful for the Donnelly family and the other residents of

Biddulph. A deceptive peace settled over the township, but it was the peace of preparation.

The two youngest boys, Thomas and Robert, passed through a turbulent adolescence—wild, wilful and wary, scarcely heeding even the hard hand of their father, paying respect only to the brilliant but erratic leadership of their brother Will.

The family prospered in a modest way. The whole property had long since been cleared and added to, and the annual yield of wheat kept them in bread and a little cash to jingle in their pockets as they stood about the door of St. Patrick's after mass, greeting their friends and turning their backs on their enemies. Like many of the other million and a half Irish refugees in America they may even have been able to send a little money home to ease the continuing poverty of the Irish masses.

It was the fine cellarful of bagged potatoes and the great heavy Clydesdale horses in the stable that convinced Jim he had come into his heritage. To the Irish peasant, these spelled wealth. These things, plus seven fine healthy sons and 100 acres of land, probably represented a greater competence than any generation of his family had enjoyed since bloody Cromwell and his legions had ravaged the hills and fertile valleys of Tipperary.

It was time the older lads were thinking of marriage and homes of their own. Pat may have been the first to leave. Although the Donnelly clannishness was as strong in him as in the others, he does not seem to have shared their relish for the feud. He was depressed by it, while the others, particularly Will, were stimulated to even greater deeds of daring. Pat learned the trade of blacksmithing in St. Thomas, a city thirty-five miles to the south of Lucan. He later moved to St. Catharines in the Niagara district, where he became a respected citizen.

Michael, who could discourse at length on the size of the drive-wheels of the big iron wood-burners that hauled the cars of the Grand Trunk Railway past the village, eventually achieved his ambition and went to work for the Canada Southern Railway that ran between Detroit and Buffalo. Unlike

Patrick, he maintained an active interest in the Biddulph feud and became the first member of his family to pay with his life for that interest.

After its initial resistance to the coming of the railway Biddulph Township had settled down to accept the chugging, horse-scaring nuisance as one of the penalties of progress. The fears of those who made their living through the Proof Line Road Company, its stage-coach lines, toll gates and thickly clustered taverns had not been realized. Biddulph and some of the other northern townships had been attached to the County of Middlesex. Their county town was now London, in place of Goderich. London was booming—a city with a population of close to 15,000—and trade with the north was brisk. The railways carried the heavy freight but there was still plenty of business for the stages. They carried the small freight, the daily papers and the majority of the north-bound passengers. Once in a long while, some person or persons unknown would place a few logs on the Grand Trunk right of way or weaken the underpinnings of a trestle bridge, but these were, in the main, merely "boyish pranks" and not the work of a concerted, adult opposition.

Of course, when anything of the kind did happen, many Roman Catholics could be found who would declare it to be the "work of the Donnellys." If pressed for reasons these people could always cite Jim Donnelly's prison record, overlooking those uncribbed criminals whom luck and perjured testimony left free.

It is no wonder that Jim once declared in a moment of passionate resignation:

"If a stone fell from Heaven, they'd blame it on the Donnellys!"

All this is not to say that the Donnelly boys were lily-white and stainless. Far from it. As the record will show they indulged in, or were implicated in, the commission of many lawless acts. But had the elders of this transplanted community been willing to forget the transfixed head of Father Sheehy and all the blood, misery and guilt that stemmed from that savage execution so long before, there might have been peace between the non-conforming Donnellys and their conformist neighbours. But this the old people refused to do. Theirs is the true guilt.

As the slow years went by, the weight of the vendetta passed from Jim's bowed back to the squared shoulders of Will. From the first his enemies feared and hated Will; they feared him for his savage tongue, his extravagant gestures, his natural leadership. They hated him because he was handsome, because he was popular; but mainly they hated him because his name was Donnelly.

Judging from the handwriting of his many surviving letters, Will probably had a reasonably good education. He may have attended a Catholic seminary. This is probably the basis of later references to him as "a spoiled priest." Perhaps it was there also that he learned to play the violin.

The few years of relative peace only served to set the frame of the feud in immovable lines. Prevented by these invisible boundaries from mixing at will with their Irish-Canadian, Roman Catholic contemporaries, the younger Donnellys were driven into themselves to become a family more homogeneous than is the natural pattern of youth.

They found friends of course—not always the best kind. There were the Keeffes and the Hogans, friends of long standing. Will had others—Bob Corcoran, Pat Quigley, Bill Atkinson, a young man named Denby, Tom Gray, the bartender at the Central Hotel, and Jim Feeheley who had not yet heard the magic jingle of thirty pieces of silver. Some of these were Protestants, for the Donnelly boys were not particular on which side of the religious or political fence they found their friends. They could not afford to be particular. In any event the Donnellys had always counted as many Protestants as Roman Catholics among their friends. Association with the Donnellys was sooner or later to bring every one of these young men into conflict with the law.

The first of Will Donnelly's friends to get into serious trouble was Dan Keeffe. His arrest in the summer of 1871 marked the opening of a fresh chapter in the story of the feud.

It happened one Saturday night in the bar-room of the Huron House at Lucan. In the plain language of the court record, Dan was drunk. The bar was crowded and, in Dan's own words, he was "fooling around." Another patron, Martin O'Meara, took exception to something Dan said or did and a dispute arose between them. Words led to blows and blows to worse. As the weary battlers clinched at the end of an unofficial round, Dan drew a jack-knife from somewhere on his person and gave O'Meara a nasty gash on the neck. The knife work was too much for the spectators and while O'Meara lay bleeding on the floor they set upon Dan, beating and kicking him in a manner described by the reports as "frightful."

O'Meara almost died from loss of blood and it was months before Dan Keeffe could breathe properly without pain from his broken ribs. He had nearly three months in which to recuperate at the county jail in London, before his case came up at the Middlesex fall assizes.

To the obvious astonishment of the presiding judge, the Honourable Justice John Wellington Gwynne, the jury returned a verdict of common assault against Dan. In passing sentence the Justice remarked that he felt the jury was perfectly justified in acquitting Keeffe of the first charge against him, that of intent to murder, but he could not for the life of him understand how they had come to the conclusion that Keeffe had only committed common assault.

"The man O'Meara was severely cut by the prisoner's hand," the Justice said, "and in such manner as the statute calls unlawful wounding."

Here the learned Justice produced a weighty volume and read the law in such matters, then continued in tones of great severity:

"It is melancholy to think that in this county such an offence as his—the cowardly use of the knife against a fellow man—is regarded as only common assault!"

It is only fair to remark that it was the worthy judge's first official visit to London, county town of the sanguine Munstermen. It was a baptism of fire, for he had ten criminal cases to deal with, including two murders (not connected with the Biddulph feud).

He gave Dan Keeffe the most he could—six months' imprisonment in the common jail at hard labour.

During part of Dan Keeffe's pre-trial stay in the London jail he had had company—an old friend from Biddulph.

His name was Will Donnelly.

Mistaken Identity

CHAPTER XII

"Oh Sammy, Sammy, vy vorn't there a alleybi!"

Dickens: PICKWICK PAPERS

WILL Donnelly's first major brush with the law was not of his own making. He could be forgiven some bitterness on that occasion for he spent two weeks in the London jail largely because of an accidental physical resemblance to another man.

It began with a report by Robert B. Orme, owner of a small lumber business in Lucan, that he had been robbed of a cash box containing more than $400 in the early morning hours of Saturday, August 26, 1871. The box had been taken from his room while he slept, he said. He had been awakened by the bold burglar and had given chase, but the culprit had escaped.

The following Thursday two detectives of the London police force arrested Tom Gray, the bar-keeper at the Huron House. Will Donnelly was with Gray at the time and he was arrested as well.

The preliminary examination took place on Saturday in the office of the Crown Attorney at London. Brock Stevens, a Justice of the Peace, presided.

Orme told his story with a wealth of detail. Before retiring on the night of Friday, August 25, he had placed the cash box containing $418 in notes and silver on a chair by the head of his bed beside a lamp which was left burning.

His precautions against robbery seemed thorough enough but at a late hour in the night he was roused, he said, by a sound "as if the box was striking against the door." He called to his brother who apparently was sleeping in another room, but received no answer. He called a second time and then jumped out of bed, pulled on his "pantaloons" and made after the burglar, who was not more than thirty feet from him when he reached the outer door. He claimed to have recognized Gray as the culprit before he disappeared into the darkness.

At this point in his narrative Orme modestly revealed himself as a nineteenth-century Inspector Maigret. He "thought things over." What would be the next step of a burglar in illegal possession of such a considerable amount of money? Obviously, he would leave Lucan as soon as possible. With Orme, to think was to act. Enlisting a friend (name not given) he made for the Grand Trunk Railway station where, according to his deductive reasoning, the criminal would be awaiting the arrival of the next train.

At the station no criminal was to be seen, but the keen eye of Mr. Orme spotted a big granary, the base of which was raised some few feet off the ground by heavy timbers. An ideal hiding-place! With no thought for his personal safety, Orme plunged into the gaping cavern. Sure enough, a man was hiding there. The culprit immediately leaped up to make for freedom. The tell-tale box again struck against an obstacle and Orme distinctly heard the rattle of his money. With an exclamation of triumph Orme plunged after his man, but alas he struck his head against a beam and was momentarily stunned. The burglar escaped.

We are not told what Orme's companion was doing all through this excitement.

At this stage in the examination there came the inevitable question from Magistrate Stevens. Did Mr. Orme recognize the man who had committed the burglary? Yes, he was in the room. Orme pointed at Tom Gray.

What of Will Donnelly?

Donnelly apparently had been picked up by the detectives for good measure. He was with Gray when the latter was arrested and, according to the police officer, "in form and dress the two are very much alike." Orme, the detective reasoned, might have mistaken his man.

At the end of the hearing, Gray was allowed his freedom on putting up $2,000 bail. Will Donnelly had not a hope of raising so much. He was committed to jail.

The case was laid over to the fall assizes, due in a matter of two weeks. The grand jury brought in a true bill and the trial took place before Justice Gwynne on September 15, four days before Dan Keeffe appeared in the same courtroom. A local attorney, Warren Rock, acted for Gray.

After the big build-up the trial itself was anti-climactic. Orme told his story much as he had given it at the preliminary examination, but on cross-examination he failed to identify either the prisoner, Gray, or his alternate, Donnelly, as the man he had seen. Then Rock uncorked a flood of witnesses.

The first was enough. He testified that the night in question was so dark that it would have been impossible for any man, even the eagle-eyed Mr. Orme, to identify another ten feet away, let alone thirty. Furthermore, even on a moonlit night the darkness under the granary would have been too complete for a man to recognize his own grandmother.

At this point the case for the prosecution broke down utterly. With a busy docket before him and no inclination to trifle, Justice Gwynne immediately ordered an acquittal.

Rock was unexpectedly displeased at the judge's decision. He had, he said, a large number of witnesses whose testimony would doubtless have thrown some light on the suspicion freely expressed by Gray's friends that the charge was a trumped-up one.

One of the witnesses was Jenny, youngest member of the Donnelly family. Only thirteen at the time, she had come prepared to testify that the complainant Orme had tried to induce her by offers of money to connect Gray (and presumably her brother) with the crime.

During Rock's cross-examination Orme had admitted that since the alleged robbery his father had been obliged to pay a note of $400 (a significant amount) which he (the father) had endorsed for him.

In concluding its account of the trial the *Free Press* stated that Tom Gray had a good reputation in Lucan, that he had $1,000 to his credit in a local bank, and that it was his intention to take immediate proceedings against his prosecutor for false arrest. No record can be found of any such step being taken. Probably Gray and Will Donnelly were glad enough to be rid of the gloom of the old courtroom without deliberately seeking its atmosphere again.

Besides, Will had more urgent and pressing business of a romantic nature to attend to.

Will previously had not paid much attention to his female contemporaries, but about this time he began to notice the superior attractions of Margaret Thompson, daughter of a near neighbour of his parents on the Roman Line. They had probably gone to school together, for she was only three years or so his junior and her parents had lived in Biddulph for some time.

Their first adult meetings must have been accidental, as their later meetings were clandestine; their social paths could not have crossed otherwise. The girl's father, William Thompson, was anti-Donnelly. From all the available evidence Thompson had a deep and implacable hatred of the Donnelly family. He was a dour, harsh and unbending man who, on a later appearance in court, confessed he could not recognize his own daughter's handwriting and was not even sure of her age.

It must have been a bleak, even unhappy, home in which Maggie Thompson passed her first score of years. She was obviously a girl of some spirit, and the gay, reckless and irresponsible character of William Donnelly must have appealed to her irresistibly. Marriage to him—if her thoughts were set on marriage at this time—must have loomed before her like an escape from prison, a door to a bright new world of love and laughter.

Between her and that happy fate stood her father, hard and unforgiving. The meetings of the lovers became fewer and more difficult to manage. They took to writing letters.

A man with marriage on his mind had to give some thought to the future. It would cost money to set up housekeeping and the elder Donnellys could ill afford to spare anything from their meagre savings.

Will Donnelly had to find a job.

This was not as easy for him as for his six stalwart brothers. A club-foot limits one's choice of occupation. The hearty, back-breaking kind of employment open to tradeless Irish-Canadians was not for him.

Always an admirer of the hard-drinking stage-coach drivers who drummed their sweating horses on to the Lucan main street three times daily, Will immediately tried his luck in that direction. Sitting on the box, controlling the fleet-footed teams, it did not much matter whether a man had a twisted foot or no foot at all. Further, Will had an easy way with people, and that was a good thing for a stage-driver to have.

Traffic was heavy on the Proof Line Road, business was good and Hugh McPhee, owner of one of the stages, had an opening for a driver.

William Donnelly had a job.

Maggie Thompson

It was an amiable weakness . . .

Sheridan: SCHOOL FOR SCANDAL

AT the beginning of the 1870s Lucan was a thriving village with a population of some 1,100, the centre of a flourishing cattle trade dating back to the American Civil War and the site of a busy grain market. Its incorporation as a village was proposed in June, 1871. The appropriate act was passed by the Ontario Legislature and became law on January 1, 1872. The new council met fourteen days later, and as its first order of business issued separate tavern licences to Robert McLean, George Hodgins, John Carroll, W. E. Wilkins, W. Walker, Joseph Fitzhenry and Hugh McPhee.

McPhee, in addition to operating a tavern, ran one of the three stage-coach lines which, in addition to the Grand Trunk Railroad, provided transportation of goods and passengers for the people of Lucan and Biddulph Township. What is more to the point of this story, he was Will Donnelly's employer.

Even considering the relative density of population along the main road from London to the Lake Huron port of Goderich, three stage lines seem too many. Certainly, judging from later events, there was stiff competition among them. Two of the north-bound stages left London daily at the same hour from different locations and a similar redundancy seems to have existed at the Lucan terminal. Times of arrival at their respective destinations depended on the speed of the teams and the endurance of drivers and passengers.

Considering the tempers and characters of the Irish residents of Biddulph Township, such a state of affairs was bound to cause trouble, and shortly did so.

Meanwhile, Will Donnelly was earning his salt as a driver for the McPhee stage and enjoying the feel of silver in his pockets at the end of each week. All would have been well, could he have passed part of his free time with Maggie Thompson. However, her father had found out what was going on between them and Maggie had been as thoroughly cloistered on the Thompson farm as a nun in a convent.

Love, as always, found a way and the Donnelly–Thompson correspondence flourished. Maggie's surviving letters are curiously stilted and full of the clichés of the Victorian lower middle class, but they none the less breathe the authentic air of romance.

Will had not seen his love for some time and in the spring of 1873 he wrote begging her for a photograph. Her reply finally came, bearing the date of April 22:

> Dear William:
>
> I address you these few lines hoping they will find you in good health as they leave me enjoying the same blessing at present. Dear William I was a long time about getting this picture for you. You can keep it now, in hopes you think as much of me as I do of you. At the beginning of another term of our future summer, which we can look back upon with pleasure I desire to bear testimony to the faithfulness with which you have laboured for my benefit and the kindness which you have ever shown towards me.
>
> Yours truly
> Maggie Thompson

Will's reply must have been prompt; Maggie acknowledged it on the thirtieth. Will was self-conscious and disturbed lest his frequent writing be construed as softness. In the rough-and-tumble of the Biddulph feud no charge was more destructive to a man's standing in the community than that which accused him of being "soft."

Maggie reassured him.

Dear friend,

I take the pleasure of writing you these few lines, hoping they will find you in good health as they leave me enjoying the same blessing at present. I now wish to inform you that I have made up my mind to accept your kind offer, as there is no person in this world I sincerely love but you. This is my first and only secret, so I hope you will let no person know about it. But I cannot mention any certain time yet. You can acquaint my parents about it any time you wish after the 1st of November next. Any time it is convenient to you will please me if it is in five years after the time mentioned. If it does not suit you to wait so long you can let me know about it, and I will make it all right. Do not think that I would say you are soft for writing so often, for their is nothing would give me greater pleasure than to hear from you, but no matter now. I think soft turns is very scarce about you. If you have ever heard anything of the kind after me I hope you will not attribute it to a desire on my part to give you pain, but regard it as thoughtless behaviour of youth; and that the blessing of God may ever attend it the sincere wish of your affectionate friend.

Margaret Thompson

In its mixture of formality and tenderness this letter is particularly touching. The reference to November 1 would seem to mark some special milestone, most likely a birthday, probably her twenty-first. If she knew the date and year of her birth, she was considerably better informed than her father. Reading between the lines, it is quite apparent that poor Maggie was having a rough time.

Will had been careful with his pay; the following month he took a major step forward in his business career—one destined to hasten perceptibly the ultimate fate of the entire family. With the help of his older brother Jim and a neighbour, Pat Whelan, he bought out his former employer, McPhee, and began operating the Lucan stage himself.

The departure of the first Donnelly stage from Lucan must have been a tremendous occasion for the family. They were all there, every single one of them. Will had delayed the official inauguration until May 24, the official holiday which marked the birthday of Queen Victoria, then in the thirty-sixth year of her long reign. He had done so in order that Pat and Mike, the absent members of the family, could get away from their work to attend the celebration.

Old Jim's heart must have swelled with pride as he contemplated the freshly painted and polished vehicle, the well-groomed horses and the newly oiled harness. He and Johannah must have been close to tears as their thoughts went back over the years to the days of penury and distress in Tipperary. What a long way they had come. There could now be no regrets, no lingering thoughts of return to the homeland, no fears for the future.

The Donnelly diligence—to use that delightful nineteenth-century synonym for stage-coach—was successful from the start. The Donnelly boys were quick, clever and courteous, and their coach soon rivalled in popularity the official mail stage which had been running since 1838. The other local enterprise, the Hawkshaw stage, soon began to suffer from the aggressive salesmanship of the Donnelly brothers. Finally, in October, 1873, Hawkshaw sold out to a partnership of two district merchants who then ran the line as the Flanagan and Crawley stage. John Flanagan, member of a Mayo County, Ireland, family which had settled in 1844 in the neighbouring village of Clandeboye, was a big, burly man determined from the beginning to drive his opposition into the ground. Crawley, an adherent of the Church of England, seems to have been the silent partner.

The fast-paced events of the summer of 1873 gave momentary pause to the correspondence between Will Donnelly and Maggie Thompson. With the coming of fall and a seasonal decline in the stage-coach business it was apparently resumed—with dire consequences. A member of Maggie's family must have intercepted one of Will's letters or perhaps surprised her reading one. Anyway, her father learned of the correspondence and there was a dreadful family scene. Maggie, who seems to have filled the post of domestic drudge in the solemn Thompson home, was immediately packed off by her father to the home of her elder brother, William, who lived eight miles away in McGillivray Township, there to assume the same unpaid-domestic role.

The magic date of November 1 came and went and found Will and Maggie no closer to the consummation of their desires. Indeed, her father gave it out that she was shortly to be married to a young farmer of the vicinity. From the surviving evidence it is not clear whether Will, Maggie or even the anonymous farmer had yet been informed of this decision.

About this time, Will either met or called on old man Thompson to put the matter plainly to him.

Thompson said no.

Will said he would have her in spite of the "old people."

Thompson said he would rather have Maggie burned at the stake than married to a Donnelly. And that was the end of that.

Until Christmas Will was kept in the dark with respect to Maggie's whereabouts. The family's conspiracy of silence was complete. So far as Will knew, she was still at home. He took to frequenting the neighbourhood of the Thompson farm in his off hours, vainly hoping for a glimpse of her.

A day or two after Christmas he got a letter from her, hastily scrawled in a country post office on Christmas Eve. In spite of the circumstances under which it was written, the letter exhibits the same stilted formality as her earlier epistles. The opening salutation, however, showed some agitation. The rest of the letter is sheer tragedy—the desperate cry of a woman abused and loveless, held actual prisoner by her own family.

Dear friend,

I address you with these few lines to let you know I am well, and hopes you are enjoying the same blessing. I wish to let you know a little about the performance I had to go through since I came up here. My friends heard all about me writing letters to you, which caused an awful storm so that I could not attempt to ask to go anywhere and on that account you will please excuse me for not writing to you. Dear William I would rather be in the grave than home at present for the way my people abused me on your account hinders me of ever forgiving them. I will never have anything like a chance of fulfilling my promise of marriage with you except you come and take me away by force, and if you think as much of me now as you did always I trust you will relieve me before long, and if not you will please send me my letters to Offa P.O. and I will try to put up with all. I burnt your letters when they commenced to abuse me about you, for they would surely get them if I did not do something with them. Excuse my bad writing for I am in an awful hurry, as it is in the office I am writing. No more at present from your

Loving friend
Margaret Thompson

Will's reaction was drastic, impulsive and foolish. He was bursting with the importance of his new role in the community and arrogant in his new wealth and the friends it had bought for him.

He was also twenty-nine years old and in love.

During the holidays he talked it over with the Keeffe brothers, Dan and Jim; with Bob Corcoran and Bill Atkinson and Pat Quigley; and with his harum-scarum brothers, Tom and Mike. Dan and Jim did not give a damn for the law anyway; the others were more cautious about taking part in an actual abduction.

There was a lot of excitement on the Roman Line a day or two after New Year's when a fire of accidental origin did considerable damage to the brick church of St. Patrick's which had recently replaced the old wooden building. The only unusual thing about this fire is that it was blamed on a defective heating appartus and not on a member of the Donnelly family.

There could be no question, however, about the events of the night of January 9, 1874.

That was the night Will Donnelly and his friends went looking for Maggie Thompson.

The Failure of Lochinvar

Oh, come ye in peace here, or come ye in war?

SCOTT

M AGGIE'S father must somehow have learned of her letter
to Will from McGillivray Township, for he promptly whisked
her back home, openly and obviously. Then under cover of
darkness, he sent her off to stay with a friend in another part of
the township. The friend's name was Toohey—another family
long on bad terms with the Donnellys.

Will and his friends fell nicely into the trap. Shortly after
dark on January 9, 1874, they rode up the Roman Line towards
the Thompson farm, bent on the rescue of Maggie.

*. . . I will never have anything like a chance of fulfilling my
promise of marriage with you except you come and take me away by
force and if you think as much of me now as you did always I trust
you will relieve me before long. . . .*

Will's friends probably considered the whole thing a romantic lark. His brothers, Tom and Mike, were with him. Then
there were his two old friends, Jim and Dan Keeffe, of the inn-
keeping family, Pat Quigley, Bob Corcoran and Bill Atkinson.

They rode boldly up to the Thompson farmhouse in a cutter
pulled by a team of the Donnelly horses. Will stayed in the
cutter. The rest went up to the house. Somebody pounded on
the door and somebody else shouted:

"Open, in the Queen's name!"

It was open sesame—a favourite Biddulph device, frequently used throughout the feud. The door opened to reveal Thompson, Senior. Eight young men politely stamped the snow off their feet and entered. William Thompson, Junior, was there and also a younger brother, Michael. The boy was sent for chairs for the guests. They all sat down. All except two of the newcomers had the lower parts of their faces covered with scarves. There was silence for a moment, then one of the visitors said:

"We'd like something to eat."

"You could probably get something at the tavern," Thompson replied shortly. "It's only a mile away. There's no woman around here."

At this, significant glances were passed. Somebody cleared his throat. This was more difficult than they had expected.

"Could we borrow an overcoat?"

"I've hardly enough clothes for myself," Thompson snapped. Another pause.

"Could we stay the night here?"

"You cannot."

The abduction was not going at all the way it should. The old man had said Maggie was not here. He could be lying.

"We have a warrant for a horse thief."

"Show it," Thompson demanded promptly.

"No. We're not allowed to."

"Then read it to me."

A long pause.

"It isn't a horse thief you're looking for, but my daughter, Maggie!"

"That's right, Thompson."

"Well, she isn't here."

That seemed to be that. There was an uncertain shuffling of feet and clearing of throats and uneasy glances at one another.

"Well, I guess we'd better be going."

With that, the amateur kidnappers got up and left.

So far, the evidence is trustworthy. For what happened next, we have only Thompson's word:

About five or six minutes afterwards, I went south to my next neighbour's Mrs. Widow Fogarty to tell her what had happened. I came up to the sleigh. The men were just starting in an easterly direction. When they saw me, they turned around in the way that I was going and followed fast. When I got near the house they were close on me and I hollered as loud as I could. One or two jumped out and caught me within a few yards of the fence and one of them put his hand or a handkerchief across my mouth so that I could not holler Fogarty. I struggled and got away and called for an axe. At this they fired two shots in the direction of where I was. I went into the house and had the door partly shut when they came and pushed it open and caught hold of Mrs. Fogarty. They searched the house and said they were looking for my daughter and would have her wherever she was. One of them stepped up to me and reached out his hand and struck me a blow over the eye with his fist which cut me and knocked me down.

The evidence of Ellen Fogarty differs in some significant particulars from that of the irate Mr. Thompson. She heard no shots, as Thompson claimed. Her notice was first attracted by a voice shouting her name. Then she heard the same voice calling for an axe—surely an unusual weapon. She recognized the voice on the second calling as that of her neighbour. She then opened the door to Thompson and his five or six pursuers, who then searched the house. She can be forgiven for asking:

"What do you want?"

One of the Donnelly brothers—Thompson said it was Tom—addressed his reply to Maggie's father:

"We want your daughter."

"That, Donnelly, you will never get!"

This was the point at which Thompson claimed he was struck and knocked down. The "Mrs. Widow Fogarty's" recollection of the incident was terser and probably more accurate:

"The old man got a box on the ear."

That was the end of the incident at Ellen Fogarty's. Everyone went home. As far as the law was concerned, nothing was said of the incident until nearly a month afterwards.

Will Donnelly was not content to let the matter stand, unfortunately. Three days after the affair at Thompson's he wrote a long, confused, contradictory and altogether extraordinary letter to the girl's father. It read:

Dear Sir:

I address you at present in a more polite manner than that which you received on Friday night, of which I am the occasion. To make matters a little plain to you I wish to let you know I was in the crowd myself, and my sole business was to have satisfaction for some of your mean, low talk to your daughter that never deserved it, at least she never deserved it on my account. And now, Dear Sir, I want you to understand that I will have my revenge if it cost the lives of both families, which I am sure it will not, for I can get crowd enough in almost any town to carry out my design without any trouble, except a little law from you, but I do not care for that, as I have plenty of money to pay my way through all. Dear sir, in the first place I will show you who were wrong in saying that there were letters passing from your daughter to me, as I defy her to say that anything of the kind ever happened; and secondly you were wrong in saying that I was a son of a bitch; and that you had sons could back you up in saying so. As far as your sons are concerned there is one of them I would for ever wish to be in friends with; but any time you feel inclined to have them or Mr. Toohey try their muscle, you will please drop a line to me, or some of your humble servants, and will try to accommodate you. But, my dear sir, my opinion is that in all the friends that hangs around, either by birth or marriage, there is but two has got a principle. At present I will not mention names, but will simply say you are not one of them.

For the long length of time your daughter was in Biddulph, I defy her or anyone else to say there was one word of marriage passed between us and for that reason I would like to know what you abused her for and talked of me in the manner you have done, which a letter I have in my possession will plainly show. Dear friend, I hope you will be prepared to receive me and my adventurers before long again, and if you should succeed, as you say you will, in sending that crowd to Kingston, I have another ready to follow the same track until the job is completed. And, old friend, I want it impressed on your mind that if the business must be done on the way to church I can get any amount of men to do it, so you may just as well stop getting yourself into trouble first as last. Your son William used some talk lately I shall never forget, and if he wants to dwell in peace on the Roman Line you had better tell him to be a little cautious, as I have a little money and plenty of good boys to see me through all my undertakings. Give my respects to your daughter. Answer if you like.

Yours,
W.D.

Coupled with the protestations of love and broad implications of a marriage offer contained in Maggie's letter, this is indeed a strange document. It may be that Will, denying and confessing the correspondence in practically the same breath, was merely trying to protect Margaret Thompson from the wrath of her family. If so, he chose an odd means of doing so.

Shortly after the date of this letter, William Thompson, Junior, married Mary, daughter of Michael Carroll, an old Roman Line pioneer, and took his bride to his McGillivray Township home. To Will Donnelly and his friends, this provided an opportunity of making another reconnaissance in force under the guise of a well-accepted but rather violent back-country social custom—the "shivaree."

The shivaree, more properly charivari, was originally a noisy pioneer celebration by which the newly-married couple were welcomed to their new home by their friends and neighbours. Like many pioneer customs it became perverted in the second generation of its observance. In its final form it was a thoroughly disreputable excuse for rowdyism and drunkenness, and was often a thinly disguised means of making completely miserable the lives of an unpopular couple. It was with this object in mind that Will Donnelly and his friends descended on the home of the junior Thompson on the night of January 30. It was obviously their hope that in the general hubbub of the shivaree Maggie would make her presence known, if she was indeed there.

The shivaree was a masterpiece. It set a standard for such affairs that was not soon matched. They broke nearly every pane of glass in the house; they used the chimney as a target for pistol practice until the whole thing came tumbling down; they pitched sticks and stones at everything that moved and they used up every bit of ammunition they had left firing at, over and around the house. Finally they tore down part of a rail fence, heaped the timbers near the house, set fire to it and whooped round the bonfire like wild Indians. Then when Maggie had still not appeared, they departed.

The next day the two Thompsons rode into London, told their separate tales first to the police magistrate and then to the *Free Press,* and demanded the arrest of the miscreants. The warrant named William, Michael and Thomas Donnelly, James and Daniel Keeffe, Robert Corcoran, Patrick Quigley and William Atkinson. The *Free Press* accepted the Thompsons' story in its entirety—the brutal attack on the old man, the shots which "whistled around his head like hail," the poor, trembling daughter hidden out from her diabolical tormentor—the whole "despicable" tale.

With the exception of Pat Quigley and Jim Keeffe the whole lot appeared in the magistrate's court in London on February 14. Two Justices of the Peace were on the bench: Lawrence Lawrason and Will Donnelly's old friend, Brock Stevens. The senior Thompson told his story. When he reached the climax, the place where he was struck on the face and stunned, he stated:

"To the best of my belief, it was Dan Keeffe who struck me." Dan was on his feet in a flash.

"You're a liar! When a man is on his oath he ought to tell the truth."

"You're not allowed to use such language in this court," said Magistrate Lawrason sternly. "The witness will continue."

At this point Thompson produced the letter he had received from Will Donnelly; the defence attorney Warren Rock, not to be outdone, produced three of Maggie's letters. Thompson declared he did not know the handwriting; on cross-examination he admitted he would not recognize her handwriting in any case; he was not sure of her age; he had never prevented Donnelly from seeing his daughter; his daughter had told him she would rather suffer death than marry Donnelly; when he had heard his daughter was "looking after" Will Donnelly he brought her home for safe keeping; he would sooner see her go to her grave than marry Will Donnelly; he did not know where his daughter was; he would not swear he did not know.

With Victorian niceness, the bench prevented further examination on this point; it "did not think it would be proper to press for an answer." Propriety forbade insistence on the young lady's presence in court but it made no bones about having her private correspondence read, the letters the *Free Press* in a headline termed "spicy."

The Thompson sons, Bill and Mike, were no great help to their father's cause. Mike became so confused in trying to remember his story that his examination was abandoned.

No evidence whatever was offered with respect to the shivaree. William Thompson, Junior, had withdrawn his charges on the payment of fifty dollars.

Despite the obviously conflicting testimony offered by the prosecution, the magistrates laid the case over to the June sessions of the county court. On June 11 the grand jury returned a true bill of assault against five of the defendants, and a week later the case was tried. Ellen Fogarty's "no-nonsense" testimony seems to have been the deciding factor.

The jury returned a verdict of not guilty and the accused men were discharged.

This was the official end of the case of Maggie Thompson. So far as the lovers were concerned, it was also the end of their romance. We can only guess at the young woman's feelings at having her "first and only secret" rudely paraded before the world to the lip-smacking delight of sensation-hungry newspaper readers. She would have been more than human if she had not exhibited some displeasure at Will Donnelly's callous behaviour in producing her letters in court. Certainly she would not have accepted his plea that his attorney considered it necessary.

The private distress she showed at her lover's action, however, was nothing compared to the public grief she demonstrated when her father, true to his promise, married her off to the man of his choice.

Until a few years ago there were still some old residents of Biddulph who could remember that marriage—the silent, sullen bride who managed to retain some degree of composure until the priest spoke the crucial words removing her forever from the world of Will Donnelly. Then came the most embarrassing scene of all; a wildly weeping girl being hurried out of the church by her husband and her family, off to a new home and obscurity.

Assault and Arson

There is nothing like being used to a thing . . .

Sheridan: THE RIVALS

THE first half of 1875 was quiet. Then in mid-September the stage-coach feud erupted in full fury. The long-expected incident occurred on the Proof Line Road a few miles north of London. Will Donnelly was driving his stage when it was in collision with one of the Flanagan vehicles. Will claimed the accident was deliberately caused by the opposition driver. Whatever the facts were, the Donnelly coach was overturned and the passengers spilled ignominiously on to the highway. Two women, Martha and Louisa Lindsay, were injured.

Probably as a direct result of this incident, a big brawl took place near Lucan on September 17, involving among others Tom Donnelly, some of the Keeffe family and two Lucan constables, Joseph Berryhill and James Curry. Berryhill later claimed Donnelly bit off part of his nose in the engagement.

At nine o'clock on the evening of October 1, the barns and stables of John Flanagan, telegraph agent at the village of Ireland, a few miles from Lucan, were set on fire and totally destroyed with all contents. Flanagan was a relative of Pat Flanagan, the Donnellys' chief competitor. Pat's turn came three days later, at one o'clock on the morning of October 4. His stables were completely consumed and a larger fire prevented only by hard work on the part of the now thoroughly practised Lucan fire brigade.

On November 24 Tom Donnelly was arrested by a Detective Enoch Murphy of the London police force and three charges laid against him as a result of the fracas in September. In addition to the assault charges preferred against him by James Curry and Joseph Berryhill, he was accused of relieving the former of $7.75 on the same occasion. The case dragged on until the middle of December and ended with Donnelly being convicted of the attack on Berryhill and fined $20 or two months. One cause of delay was the drunkenness of George Alloway, of Lucan, a witness. He had made a valiant effort to reach the courtroom, but had passed out on the stairs.

More of the Donnelly stage-coach profits were dissipated in December when an assize court jury awarded a verdict in favour of the Misses Martha and Louisa Lindsay against Will Donnelly for injuries received in the September accident, which they declared was due to the "careless driving" of the defendant. The jury awarded Louisa $20 and Martha $15.

The stage-coach feud had entered a hectic period. If whoever set fire to the Flanagan stables in October had hoped thereby to put him out of business, he was badly mistaken. According to the following item from *The London Free Press* of December 4, Flanagan was still in business and had new stables and horses. He had his problems, however:

At an early hour yesterday morning a murderous attack was made at Lucan upon a man named Patrick Flanagan who drives one of the stages between this city and that village. As was his wont he had gone to tend the stage horses before daylight. No sooner however did he open the stable door than he was set upon by an unknown man who, with what he believes to be a club, knocked him to the ground, splitting his head open and rendering him insensible for some time. Medical assistance was obtained and the wounds inflicted dressed; and it is believed that, although severely injured, he will recover. Whether the fellow had any ill-feeling towards Flanagan or not is unknown, as from the suddenness of the attack and the darkness of the morning Flanagan is unable to give any clue as to who he was and the scoundrel had decamped before any alarm could be given to the authorities, who are now however on the alert for him.

It may be assumed, the *Free Press* notwithstanding, that the attacker did, in fact, harbour some "ill-feeling" against Flanagan. Although authorities were "on the alert" nothing seems to have come of the incident so far as the courts were concerned.

In the midst of all these battles Will Donnelly was inviting fresh trouble. The case of Maggie Thompson had taught him nothing. On the rebound from Maggie, he was courting the daughter of another of his family's intransigent enemies.

Her name was Nora Kennedy.

The Kennedy courtship was the same old story over again. The girl's family was bitterly against the proposed marriage. Like the Donnellys, the Kennedys were an old native Tipperary family of considerable prominence in the Irish county in the halcyon days before Cromwell. Like the Donnellys they had fallen on evil times and had been ground between the upper millstone of the Catholic persecution and the nether millstone of rack-rents and tithes. Unlike the Donnellys they were so-called "good" Catholics and, so far as the Canadian courts were concerned, had kept their noses relatively clean. For the cause of their enmity with the Donnelly clan, one would have to go back into Tipperary history, to the days when the Whiteboys rode the County.

Whatever the remote cause of the bitter feeling, Will Donnelly's proposed marriage to Nora Kennedy brought the whole ugly mess boiling to the surface. Of all the Kennedys, none was more opposed to the match than Nora's brother, John. He threatened to prevent it by any means in his power.

Nora Kennedy had none of the meekness of Maggie Thompson. The happy couple set their wedding date for early in the new year.

The Vigilantes

I am not determining a point of law; I am restoring tranquillity . . .

Edmund Burke

THE year 1876 witnessed the first appearance of the most sinister element in the whole history of the Biddulph feud—the Vigilance Committee. The name was borrowed from the organization set up to protect the law-abiding citizens of San Francisco in the days of the 1849 gold rush. However, in practice it was nothing more than a revival of the Tipperary Whiteboys.

During the three abortive trials of the alleged murderers of the Donnelly family, consistent attempts were made by the defence attorneys to portray the Biddulph Vigilantes as a semi-legal association of honest and reputable citizens earnestly and sincerely concerned with putting down crime in their township.

It may be argued that in the remote areas of the western portion of the continent legitimate reasons can be advanced for the creation of such associations. In communities newly settled and temporarily without the formal processes of law, citizens may find it necessary to constitute informal courts.

No such argument can reasonably be advanced where the Biddulph feud is concerned.

South-western Ontario at this time had been settled for nearly three-quarters of a century. Adequate courts of law had been set up as early as 1792. For judicial purposes this fertile peninsula, with a population in the 1870s exceeding half a million, was divided into fourteen counties, each with appropriate legal machinery. There were several cities with populations of more than 10,000. There were many industries. The economy, while not booming, was sound.

Short of complete failure of the legal system or widespread corruption, of which there is absolutely no evidence, there could be no excuse for the formation of the Biddulph society. The acts these men committed were lawless acts; the deaths they caused were murders, not executions. Their actions, on the evidence, were more brutal and more savage than the most extreme of the criminal activities they were allegedly organized to suppress.

As has been previously said, the Donnelly family was not blameless. There can be no reasonable question that on some occasions they committed acts of lawlessness and even brutality. It is equally certain that they did not commit, nor could they have committed, all the illegal acts with which they were charged by their enemies. It is commonly said to this day in Biddulph:

"Many things were done by others which were blamed on the Donnellys."

Admittedly such statements are easy to make and more difficult to prove in a community where perjury was a normal practice. Nevertheless, older residents of Biddulph can still cite examples, and some of them are backed up by legal documents.

There was the case of James Chisholm, for instance. This young man, member of a respected Western Ontario family, lived with his parents in Lucan. He fell in with a gang of what we would call today juvenile delinquents. They apparently had no connections with either the Donnelly family or the opposite faction. They engaged in lawlessness out of boredom and meanness. Chisholm died in 1882 at the age of twenty-six. On his death-bed he is said to have confessed that he and his companions had been responsible for many of the local crimes that had been conveniently blamed on the Donnellys.

Local tradition and a few court records point also in the direction of a family named Levitt which in this same period lived south of Lucan on the Proof Line Road. Members of this family are alleged to have made banditti-like attacks on solitary travellers returning from the London market with bulging wallets. These activities, too, were blamed on the Donnellys.

The plain facts are that there was an astonishingly large criminal population in the township and that the existence of the feud provided a ready-made cover for the commission of crime for profit.

There was, however, no apparent profit motive in the first two major offences against "the peace of our lady the Queen, her Crown and dignity," as reported in January, 1876. The following item from *The London Free Press* is given in its entirety, including the three-decker Victorian headline:

THE NORTHERN KU-KLUX
Diabolical Outrages Near Lucan
Narrow Escape of an Express Train— A Stage Coach Sawn in Pieces

On more than one occasion lately, we have had occasion to refer to outrages of an ugly character perpetrated in the neighbourhood of Lucan. Only the other day an attempt was made to set fire to a stage-coach; in a day or two after a farmer's barn, within a few miles of the village, came under the torch of the incendiary; and numerous other outrages were perpetrated. The latest diabolical outrage was attempted at a late hour on Wednesday evening when some fiend or fiends attempted to saw down the wooden posts and trussel-work of a bridge on the Grand Trunk Railway. This bridge is but temporary and will be removed when the masonry of the stone bridge is completed. The rascals had apparently intended to complete the work and saw the woodwork entirely down thus demolishing the bridge, in which case the most dire disaster would have been the result. As it was, the structure was rendered sufficiently insecure to render it impossible for any train to pass over it without being precipitated below, a distance of many feet. Fortunately, the attempt was discovered early on Thursday morning and the bridge was sufficiently propped up before the arrival of the express, which passed over in safety. But for the discovery our readers can imagine the sad loss of life which would have inevitably resulted.

It is believed that the same parties—and they have doubtless their own reason for so acting—who destroyed Crowley & Flanagan's stage near Lucan village last Sunday morning, were parties to the outrage recorded above. Rowdyism and flagrant outrages have, however, become so prevalent at Lucan that the discovery of crime appears to create but little stir among the inhabitants who live in a sort of "reign of terror." Several previous attempts were made to destroy Crowley & Flanagan's stage, but the effort on Sunday morning was crowned with complete success. The stage was drawn about a quarter of a mile up the road and sawed into pieces as small as stove wood. It is needless to say that no one knows who perpetrated this most disgraceful outrage, but the surmises are numerous; and doubtless the destruction of this stage, together with the fact that traffic on the LH & BR is increasing so much, will be put together and a clue afforded. It is a chance for a clever detective. Who will put a stop to this extraordinary state of affairs? Matters have now reached such a crisis in Lucan that nobody thinks of going out at night without a revolver and the person who goes on another person's premises after dark goes at the risk of his life, for if the owner happens to be a nervous man, he may shoot first and make inquiries afterwards. Something should be done and done speedily, to stamp out the rowdyism which has been practised in the village named with impunity for the last year or two, or the prospects of the village are not worth much.

From the nature of the two reported offences, it is plain that some person or persons was trying to reduce the amount of competition in the passenger trade between London and Lucan. As the account states, the amount of traffic on the nearly completed London, Huron & Bruce Railroad was increasing rapidly. Nervous travellers would undoubtedly prefer rail travel to the exciting vagaries of the four stage-coach lines.

The identity of the culprits was never legally established. It is reasonably safe to assume that Flanagan did not destroy his own coach. It is also safe to assume that one of his rivals did, and suspicion points strongly to the Donnellys, but once again it is an open verdict.

The day following the announcement of these crimes, evidence of a third was found north of Lucan. A large hardwood tree was discovered carefully laid across the LH & BR tracks in the Township of Morris, between Lucan and Goderich.

Meanwhile the sixteen-mile stretch of the Proof Line Road between London and Lucan was witnessing almost daily Donnybrooks. In mid-January Mike Donnelly charged Peter McKellar, one of Flanagan's drivers, with threatening to shoot him. The case was dismissed by a Lucan magistrate.

On January 25, McKellar turned the tables by having Mike arrested on a charge of "threatening to kill." At the same time Mike was charged by Henry Brien, a former county constable, with "using grossly insulting and abusive language." Mike was tried on the Brien charge two days later in the London police court and fined. The McKellar charge was changed to one of perjury and laid over for a month.

The following day a county constable named Rhody Kennedy got off one of the evening stages in Lucan. He had a warrant in his pocket for James Donnelly, Jr., on the old Berryhill assault charge. The first person he saw was Jim. For what happened next, here is the *Free Press* account:

Kennedy jumped off the stage, read the warrant and took the man in charge. He was not to be so easily captured however. Drawing a revolver, he threatened to shoot his captor if he did not let him free. Kennedy, who it may be stated has but one arm, bravely held to his prisoner, but of course was powerless either to take the revolver from him or to draw the one which he had in his possession. Observing this, the prisoner again drew the revolver and commenced to beat the constable most brutally on the face and head—so much so until, as stated by an unwilling spectator to our reporter, the revolver was covered with blood and the face of the constable was scarcely recognizable. He called to the crowd for assistance—demanded in fact, that they should "help him in the Queen's name"—but although some 40 or 50 men had assembled, no one offered the slightest assistance, and of course the constable had to allow his prisoner to escape. What next?

Let us not lightly condemn the forty or fifty unwilling and immovable spectators for not helping the constable. A cursory search of a month's files of any metropolitan daily paper will produce at least one contemporary account of a similar nature.

It will be noted that this news story speaks only of Jim Donnelly. By the time the case came to court there were witnesses by the score willing to Swear that the entire Donnelly family and most of their Tipperary relatives participated in the assault on the one-armed Kennedy.

Mike Donnelly appeared on the McKellar perjury charge in London on February 14. The usual aggregation of witnesses showed up to give evidence pro and con. One said the stage-coach feud had become so bitter that all drivers went armed, and another witness gave his occupation as guard for the stables of one of the coach lines. Mike's lawyer, John Taylor, contended there was not sufficient evidence to send the case to trial. The bench thought otherwise. The case was laid over to the court of assizes and Mike was granted bail.

It was John Donnelly's turn next. Peter McKellar was again the complainant. John, he said, had beaten him up. John made an appearance and was granted bail. His sureties were William Penny and Alfred Panton. The case was called on February 18, but without benefit of accused and his two bondsmen. All three recognizances were estreated. At the same session Mike Donnelly's name was called to answer a charge of using abusive language towards William Kennedy, brother of Will Donnelly's new light of love, Nora. Mike was also otherwise engaged and a warrant was issued for his arrest.

Mike received further attention from the courts on February 22, when he was the defendant in a civil case brought by John McLeod, one of Flanagan's drivers. The issue was tried in the Middlesex County Court. Mike had previously accused McLeod of "maliciously colliding with and damaging" the Donnelly stage in the incident in which the Misses Lindsay had been injured. A London Township magistrate had ruled McLeod guilty and awarded Donnelly $35. McLeod appealed the conviction and had it quashed with costs by the county court judge. The complainant's attorney was Edmund Meredith, of whom we shall hear later; Mike's counsel was Warren Rock.

The case was tried on Tuesday. On Thursday night, February 24, the Donnelly family attended in force the wedding reception of a friend, Tom Ryder, at Fitzhenry's Hotel in Lucan. This hotel, on a Lucan side street, was known locally as the "Catholic hotel." It was apparently a common place of resort for the Roman Line families.

The murderers of the family would have us believe that the Donnellys were by this time moral and social outcasts, ostracized by all respectable persons. Contrary to this view the presence of the Donnellys at the Ryder wedding does not seem to have prevented the attendance of a large and enthusiastic gathering which crowded the little tavern to the bursting point.

It was obviously known to others that the Donnellys would attend. At a highly inappropriate hour—at the very height of the festivities—three uninvited guests appeared. They were county constables. They shared a common first name—John. Their surnames were Reid, Bawden and Coursey. The three Johns had a warrant for the arrest of John and James Donnelly. The charge was assault on the person of Rhody Kennedy. As Kennedy convalesced from his injuries his memory continued to improve and all the persons he remembered were surnamed Donnelly.

As to what happened in Fitzhenry's Hotel we have a choice of accounts. The one that appeared in *The London Free Press* was highly editorial in tone and obviously originated with a source inimical to the Donnellys. The report preserved in the diary of the Lucan postmaster, William Porte, is, on the other hand, admirably factual and neutral. It states:

> Thurs. Feb. 24, 1876: At Tom Ryder's wedding at Fitzhenry's Jno. Bawden, John Reid and Jno. Coursey went to arrest Jim and Jack Donnelly. They were resisted by them and Bill Donnelly and Bill Farrell. Jno. Reid was shot twice in the body by Farrell and it is said that Bill Donnelly shot twice at Bawden but missed him. The end is not yet. Jack and Jim Donnelly attested this evening.

There was never any question about the shooting of John Reid. The constable was seriously wounded but eventually recovered. Nor was there any doubt about who fired the shots that struck him. Farrell is identified in the *Free Press* account as "a son of the man who met his death some time since, as the result of an old family feud." William Farrell, whose father Jim Donnelly Senior had killed nearly twenty years before, had so far adopted the cause of his foster family as to take up arms against their enemies.

There is a great deal of doubt about Will Donnelly's part in the affray. There was a wild mêlée in the "parlour" of the tavern, in which an unknown number of shots were fired. Some witnesses claimed to have heard only the two shots which wounded Reid. Others claimed to have heard three additional shots, fired, they were willing to swear, by Will Donnelly. Still others portray Will as a madman with a shillelagh in one hand and a loaded and cocked revolver in the other, proclaiming death to the invaders. One of the most trustworthy accounts states that he did indeed have a weapon in either hand but replaced the undischarged revolver in his pocket in favour of the more familiar shillelagh. The Donnellys were not overly fond of firearms and on the few occasions when they did use them, proved to be wretched marksmen. Perhaps it is just as well.

While some of the wedding guests tended the wounds of the constable, the entire Donnelly family piled into a sleigh driven by a close friend, Bob Keeffe, and headed for home. There John Donnelly awaited the arrival of the peace officers. Jim Donnelly, Junior, went to earth at the nearby home of Dan Keeffe. The constables found him there hiding between two feather beds.

Young Jim and Jack Donnelly were now in jail at London and there was a warrant out for Will. Tom was arrested on March 1 on a charge of burglary and Mike was picked up the same day, charged with the Flanagan arson case of the previous fall. Will gave himself up to the London authorities on March 15—Sheehy's Day. Five of Jim Donnelly's seven sons were now in the toils of the law.

The events of the first two and a half months of 1876, set down in factual detail, point strongly to the existence of a deliberate pattern. This sudden rash of warrants, arrests, revival of old charges and opening of old wounds, breathes powerfully of design. The design appears nakedly, but almost accidentally, in a news story which appeared at the beginning of March. The account read, in part:

> On Saturday last a young man named Denby from this city visited Lucan in company with Mike Donnelly and spent the Sunday with him—in a manner best known to themselves. During the evening it became noised around that Denby was if not an active member of the Donnelly gang, at least an ardent sympathizer and on Tuesday morning the *Vigilance Committee* interviewed Denby and escorted him out of the village limits, reminding him of the consequences should he be found inside the bar of the toll gate in future—at least until the excitement had died out. . . . Denby took the hint and has not been observed in the neighbourhood since. [Italics mine.]

This is the first public reference to a Vigilance Committee in Biddulph. With this report, the pattern of previous events becomes clear. Nothing in the whole Biddulph story approaches the secrecy of the operations of this organization. For a society ostensibly devoted to the preservation of public order, it was remarkably shy of the light of day. From elusive references in the court records it appears that the committee some time in February, 1876, hired a Hamilton detective, one Hugh McKinnon. His job was to build the various cases against the Donnelly family. McKinnon's methods were crude and lusty.

One day late in March, McKinnon and a number of others including Henry Collins, David Atkinson, James Atkinson, Thomas Atkinson, John Bawden (the constable), Arthur Gray, Albert McLean, Alexander Reid, James Hodgins and Jacob Palmer, seized Will Donnelly's friend, Bill Atkinson, and took him outside the village. Their purpose was to "question" Atkinson about the Flanagan stable-burning case. First they fastened a noose round his neck and threw the free end of the rope over a low tree limb. When the threat of lynching failed to produce the right answers, they tightened the noose and gave a few tugs on it. When this too, failed to achieve the proper results, the inquisitors tried a more direct form of torture.

According to Atkinson's later statement, they then attached cords to his thumbs and suspended him in this manner from the limb. Only when it became abundantly apparent, even to "Detective" McKinnon, that their guest was no longer interested in answering any questions, did the gang release poor Bill Atkinson. When he recovered Atkinson left Lucan and was not seen in Biddulph for several months.

By fair means and foul the Vigilance Committee now had five Donnellys and several of their friends in jail and the rest of their friends either driven out of the community or afraid to open their mouths. The fruits of their efforts were harvested at the Middlesex Spring Assizes, which opened on March 23. It was almost exclusively a Biddulph docket. This is the list:

The Queen versus Thomas Donnelly—arson.
The Queen versus William Donnelly, John Donnelly, William Farrell, James Keeffe and William Denby—assault.
The Queen versus William Farrell—shooting with intent to kill.
The Queen versus William and John Donnelly—assault.
The Queen versus William Donnelly—shooting with intent to kill.
The Queen versus James Donnelly—assault.
The Queen versus John Donnelly—assault.
The Queen versus Thomas and James Donnelly—arson.
The Queen versus Thomas Donnelly—larceny.
The Queen versus James and William Donnelly—assault.
The Queen versus James and Patrick Donnelly and James Keeffe—assault.

With the inclusion of Patrick Donnelly in their round-up, the net of the Vigilance Committee had all the younger Donnellys with the exception of Robert. His turn came later.

The trial of the cases took more than a week. The results were not entirely satisfactory to the Vigilantes.

"Poor Jimmy Howe" XVII

Accidents will occur in the best-regulated families.

Dickens: DAVID COPPERFIELD

THE Donnelly cases came up at the spring assizes in London in March, 1876. The grand jury returned thirteen true bills and the trial of the cases began on the thirtieth of the month. The most sensational case—the charge against William Donnelly for "shooting with intent to kill"—was the first heard. The curious were out in force, the courtroom was packed. The Crown's case, as presented by F. Davis, Q.C., was summarized by the *Free Press* as follows:

> Having warrants to arrest John and James Donnelly for assaults committed some time previously, Constables Coursey, Bawden and Reid proceeded to Fitzhenry's Hotel on the night in question. A wedding was taking place there, at which John, James and William Donnelly were present. James Donnelly had previously broken away from Coursey and this was the reason they determined to arrest them at the wedding. The constables exhibited their warrants at the ballroom door, a general row took place and in its course William Farrell, a friend of the Donnellys struck Reid over the head with a stick; the latter then relinquished his hold upon

John Donnelly and made after Farrell, who in the scuffle shot at him, two of the balls taking effect in his intestines. Reid returned the fire, Bawden and John Donnelly being still engaged in desperate struggle. While this was going on, William Donnelly came up to Bawden and said "You—, let him go or I'll shoot you." Bawden did not do so, however, and thereupon William Donnelly flourished a stick over his head which disabled him, and he had to let his prisoners go. This took place in the bar room, near the ballroom and it was alleged that William Donnelly, who was flourishing the revolver in one hand and the stick in the other, fired two shots at Bawden, which, however, did not take effect but lodged in the wall opposite. Farrell got away by the help of the crowd, who refused to help the constables, and has not yet been arrested; the prisoner also ran off but was subsequently caught.

The evidence of the three constables was heard, and was corroborated by William Ryan, a young man who apparently accompanied the peace officers. The next Crown witness, Joseph Fitzhenry, owner of the hotel, gave evidence which was at variance on some critical points. He had heard one shot only; it was not fired by William Donnelly; after threatening to shoot Bawden, Donnelly had put the revolver in his pocket and "used his stick."

After reporting the Crown's case in some detail, the *Free Press* dismissed the defence evidence, as led by David Glass, Q.C., with a short paragraph pointing up a statement by John Donnelly that the pistol carried by the defendant was broken and could not have been fired, even if he had wished to use it. The witness, however, was unable to account for the weapon being loaded.

The jury was out for some time and returned with a verdict of guilty on the third count of the somewhat complicated indictment—assault with intent to maim. Will's counsel, probably on his client's suggestion, asked that the jury be polled. This was done, without changing the decision. Sentence was reserved until the following day.

A miniature drama in the jury room was revealed prior to the passing of sentence by Mr. Justice Morrison. George Randall, the foreman, handed in a letter stating that the jury had understood the third count of the indictment to have been that of common assault, not the more serious charge with which their verdict had been credited. The Justice said the matter would have his consideration. Shortly thereafter he committed Will Donnelly to nine months' imprisonment. His brother John later received three months for assault in the wedding case and James got nine months on the long-standing charge of assault on Joseph Berryhill.

The following day, April 1, the Will Donnelly jury was in the news again, with the publication in the *Free Press* of a letter written by another member of the panel. The letter read:

> In your report of the Queen vs. William Donnelly it is stated Mr Randall, foreman of the impanelled jury in the above case, sent a communication to the Judge that the jury intended in finding the prisoner guilty of the third count in the indictment, was guilty of the offence of common assault. It was distinctly understood that the prisoner was guilty of shooting with intent to maim, which was the third count in the indictment, and such finding was thoroughly understood by each juror in the jury room; and we were not consulted in said communication in any way by the said George Randall.
>
> (Signed) ONE OF THE JURY

It is obvious from David Glass' request for the polling of the jury, the foreman's unusual communication to the Judge, and its rebuttal by another member of the jury, that more factors were involved here than meet the eye or can now be discovered. It is possible to arrive legitimately at one reasonably sound conclusion: the nature of the Biddulph troubles was known beyond the confines of the township and had partisans.

A state of exhaustion seized both factions in Biddulph following the climactic events of March, which events had suitably marked the 110th anniversary of the death of the martyred Father Nicholas Sheehy. The Vigilance Committee had failed in its attempt to put the Donnelly family behind bars for long terms. Arson had a brief holiday; assault became an accidental concomitant of the normal Saturday night libations rather than a *modus vivendi*.

It was a deceptive calm, the calm found in the eye of the hurricane.

The storm broke next with seeming irrelevance in the nearby city of London. The elements were simple and deadly: the presence in one place of a number of residents of Biddulph Township of varying allegiances. The incident claimed the life of a young man named James Howe and added still another factor to the feud.

It happened on the twenty-fourth of May—a day celebrated by the Canadian nation as the birthday of Queen Victoria, and by the inhabitants of Biddulph as the anniversary of the day Will Donnelly started running his London-Lucan stage in 1873.

Charles W. Kent, a member of a long-established London family, had hired a number of the Tipperary Irish that day to prepare a field of his for the spring planting. His choice of men was unfortunate; there were Orangemen, Whiteboys and Blackfeet among them. No one seemed to remember later exactly how the fight started, but in the mix-up Kent struck Howe two or three blows with a spade. Howe's skull was fractured. He died six weeks later and Kent was charged with murder.

The case was a sensation in London. The Kent family was one of the city's most respectable. They had been residents of the area since 1820 and were extensive landowners in the city and county. Charles Kent fought the case with all the resources at his command, and fought it successfully. At the fall assizes the grand jury refused to accept the indictment and Kent was freed of any further criminal action.

At first glance the introduction of Charles Kent into the Biddulph feud seems a digression. The thing is dramatically untidy. He is like the red herring introduced unfairly by the amateur mystery-story writer to confuse the reader. Here we have a respectable resident of a city sixteen miles distant from the seat of warfare becoming accidentally involved in a quarrel not of his own making, nor indeed known to him.

However, early in the study of the Biddulph cases one learns that the accident of circumstance has little or no place in this unparalleled record of violence. Charles Kent and his family were not strangers to the people of Biddulph. His brothers John and William both owned property in the township and ran farms there. William Kent was a friend of the Donnelly family. Furthermore, Kent was related to one of the principal participants in the brawl, Edward Collins, the Lucan tinsmith. Among the other persons connected with the fatal incident were Rhody Kennedy, the one-armed erstwhile constable who had been so mercilessly beaten by "Young Jim" Donnelly, and a member of the numerous Hodgins family, long-time friends of the Donnellys.

The Donnellys themselves were not present on this occasion, but Orangemen, Blackfeet and Whiteboys were—and once again, death was the outcome.

Jimmy Howe's death did not go unavenged. Before the end of the year all that was inflammable on the properties of the Kent family in Biddulph Township had been burned to the ground.

The spectre of Tipperary vengeance continued to stalk the unhappy Charles Kent. At the height of the excitement surrounding the murder of the five members of the Donnelly family, in 1880, he received a threatening letter signed "Vigilance." It read in part:

You murdered poor Howie [sic]. It was a cold blooded murder. You bribed Lawyers and Doctors and Jurimen . . . Give a hundred dollars to Bishop Walsh for the repose of the soul of poor Howie . . . Do this before the 24th of May poor Howie's death day . . . When we have settled you we intend to go for Drought, another murderer. . . .

At the close of the year 1876 the Vigilance Committee was nursing its grievances, sullenly and secretly. Its year of decision had not been an unqualified success. The Committee had got its hooks into three only of the seven Donnelly brothers. It was true the three had been sent to jail, but only for short terms, and by the end of the year the redoubtable family had been reunited.

Furthermore, by December, 1876, the Committee's stock had sunk so low that one of its victims, William Atkinson, actually dared to take action against them in the courts for the wrongs he had suffered at their hands earlier in the year. Several members of the Committee and their hired "detective," Hugh McKinnon, were named in the charge. The trial took place in the county magistrate's court just before Christmas. Atkinson did not make out his case. The jury brought in a directed verdict of acquittal, but the Committee's power had been challenged and shaken.

It is a curious fact that throughout 1876 the London newspapers almost invariably referred to any of the Donnelly family in the news as a member of the "Lucan Ku Klux Klan." Yet the reporters and copy-writers seemed entirely to have missed their opportunity in reporting the details of the kidnapping and torture of William Atkinson. Certainly the action of the persons who strung Atkinson to a tree while they "questioned" him bore a much closer resemblance to the techniques of the infamous Klan than did any activity of the Donnelly family.

In a way, 1876 *was* a year of decision; by its conclusion the involvement of the people of Biddulph in the feud was complete. Sides had been chosen; there were few if any neutrals.

Much the same might have been said of the wider geographical field in which the feud was set. The people of the County of Middlesex knew, at least in a general way, what was going on. The officials of the county, the legal fraternity and the judges were well aware of the scope and nature of the Biddulph troubles; their bulging briefs attested to this.

Even at this late date a determined stand, some positive legal action, could easily have prevented what was to follow. The appointment of a commission or, failing that, the naming of three or four good, well-trained constables from outside the county, might have halted the spread of the infection. Even if these things had not been done, a firm stand by the bishop of the Roman Catholic Diocese of London or the bishop of the Anglican Diocese of Huron, or both, along with a reasoned, non-partisan campaign for law and order by the editors of the London daily newspapers, might have had permanent influence for good on the inflamed tempers of the Biddulph Irish.

Reign of
Terror—Fire

*Where their worm dieth not" and the fire is not
quenched. . . .*

ST. MARK ix. 44

IN 1876 the Vigilance Committee had failed in its efforts to
dispose of the Donnelly family through the courts. From that
time on they resorted to more direct methods.

It is only fair at this point in the story to draw attention to
some of the conditions that caused residents of the county to
endorse and even encourage this extra-legal group.

There was a great deal of lawlessness in Biddulph and its
immediate area in no way connected with the Tipperary feud.
Indeed the feud, with its periodic outbreaks of violence, served
as a perfect cover for the commission of illegal acts either for
profit, private vengeance or the perverted pleasures of sheer
vandalism. A robbery on the highway, a case of break-and-
enter, or the brutal beating of an enemy or the destruction of
his barns, could always be blamed with reasonable impunity on
the Donnellys or, if you happened to be a friend of theirs, on
the Thompsons or the Kennedys or the Mahers or some other
of their foes.

Since this is an attempt to paint a true picture of what
happened in Biddulph Township over a period of fifty years, it
cannot all be done in pure blacks and pure whites. While the

Biddulph story has many of the aspects of a modern "horse opera" it fails in the classic simplicity of a television western. The "good guys" and the "bad guys" are not marked by characteristic headgear. It is impossible to draw a line and place on one side of it the members of the Donnelly family, their friends and kin, and identify them as the put-upon heroes of the piece, and place on the other the remaining residents of the township with the label "villain." It did not work out that way. It is true that, at any given period in the history of the feud, one can point to a group of Biddulph families and say, "These were the friends of the Donnellys in June, 1876." A year later, this might not be true.

In the faction opposing the Donnellys in the 1870s were probably some who sincerely believed they were at the root of all the Biddulph troubles and wished to put them behind bars or at least to restrain them legally. It is equally certain that there were many others, opposed to the Donnellys for religious or political or personal reasons, who were prepared to use law, if it served, or naked force if it did not, to drive them from the township for good and all. These are the men whose names appear, not once but many times, as members of the Vigilance Committee from 1875 to the bitter and bloody end.

Then there were the uncommitted, who formed the bulk of the population of the township. Their opinions shifted, their allegiances altered. They belonged first to one faction, then to another, or refused their support to any. It is in the nature of the Irish to take sides in a quarrel. A French traveller, Alexis de Tocqueville, visiting Ireland in the early years of the nineteenth century, has left us a vivid picture of the results of this tendency. His picture bears a startling resemblance to the events of a half-century later in Canada. He attended a sitting of the assize court in Waterford in 1835 and reported it as follows:

> Sixteen murder cases. All these affairs turned out to be manslaughter or homicide by negligence. But in all of them, I believe, men had been killed. These assizes gave us

the strong impression that the lower classes in this county are very prone to quarrels and fights, and that almost every village forms a kind of faction with a code name. Factions which started nobody knows when, and which continue nobody knows why, and which take on no political colour. When men of different factions meet, at a fair, a wedding or elsewhere, it is exceptional if they do not come to blows just for the love of fighting. These quarrels very often end in someone getting killed; generally speaking, human life seems of little value here.

In only one thing were the Biddulph Irish united—hatred and distrust of English law and fear of the law courts. This was the rock on which foundered the numerous attempts of the courts to establish order. A weekly newspaper published in an adjacent township summed up the situation in an editorial comment in mid-1877:

> Those quasi-respectable people of that neighbourhood, who petted the gang of scoundrels who infest it, winked at their crimes and were the means of their escaping punishment, may live long enough to repent of their folly; and should they themselves become the victims of the spite of these ruffians, we hope they will not expect sympathy. At the present and for some time past, Lucan has been a most dangerous place to live in. The slightest difference between employer and employee, or between neighbours, was often sufficient to cause murderous midnight attacks, incendiarism or other destruction of life and property. And the trouble is that popular feeling does not set itself against these outrages and their perpetrators. Even when the law is invoked, the person who invokes it is made a martyr of by the townspeople, he stands a double degree of danger to life and property, and after all, the law is rendered powerless by the exertions of prominent citizens in behalf of the ruffians.

The events which elicited this blast from *The Parkhill Gazette* reached their peak in May, 1877, with an inevitable earlier climax in March—Father Sheehy's month.

The most reliable contemporary source for a factual record of the events of the first half of 1877 is again the diary of William Porte, the Lucan postmaster. In his own laconic style this rural Evelyn reported the details of what must have been an insurance agent's nightmare:

> Fri., March 9.
> Pieper & Hoggs' flax building and about $3,000 worth of flax and seed and one horse burned between the hours of 8 and ten o'clock this evening.

> Tues., March 13/77.
> Jas. Moloney's Waggon Shop and all contents burned down on the Robins Corner between 12 and one o'clock this night—midnight.

> Sat. March 17/77.
> Fire broke out in Collins' and Donnelly's Stable about ½ past 11 o'clock P.M. tonight. Fatally consumed one horse, burned Harness, Hay and grain belonging to stage.

From this entry we observe that the Donnellys were now associated in the operation of their stage-coach with a member of the Collins family. Their partner, whose name was Henry, was probably related to the tinsmith Edward Collins, who was involved in the events leading up to the death of Jimmy Howe. From the above entry we may also detect the new and more sinister design of the Vigilance Committee.

The usually meticulous Mr. Porte neglected to mention one alleged case of arson in mid-April, either by accident or design. This was a curious case, reported in *The London Free Press* in its somewhat partisan style:

CHAPTER XVIII
REIGN OF TERROR—FIRE

INCENDIARY FIRE

Some time during Wednesday night, one of Mr Watson's London and Lucan stages was burned, while standing in the driving shed of the Montgomery House, Proof Line Road. From the traces of coal oil found in the immediate neighbourhood of the burning coach and other indications of inflammable ingredients, Mr Watson is led to the belief that the stage was set on fire by an incendiary, probably in the interests of parties whose names need not be dragged into print just at present.

On the following Monday the same newspaper printed a letter over the signature of Thomas Donnelly, which stated:

Sir: I notice in today's issue of your paper a news item headed "Incendiary Fire," wherein you state that "one of Mr Watson's London and Lucan stages was burned while standing in driving shed of the Montgomery House" etc.

I beg you will have the kindness to correct an error which has crept into the above paragraph whether intentionally or not on the part of the informant I am unable to say. The stage in question did not belong to Mr Watson, nor has he any interest whatever in it. It belonged solely to your correspondent, neither Mr Watson nor any other person having the slightest claim thereto except myself. Owing to this fact, I am of the opinion that Mr Watson will not turn many stones in order to find out the perpetrators of the dastardly act.

A slightly acrimonious editorial note was appended to the letter stating that the information on which the *Free Press* story was based was "handed in by a responsible person. It matters not to us who was the owner of the stage, the act was one which should deserve condemnation."

We are left to puzzle out for ourselves the vexed matter of the true ownership of the destroyed stage. What of William Donnelly in all this? He had been released from the county jail three months earlier, although there is an indication that other charges may have been pending against him, including one of perjury allegedly committed about a year previously. Had he transferred his interest in the stage to his brother Tom prior to his committal, or was Tom in this instance speaking in behalf of the whole family?

On April 25 William Porte noted another fire: "Jim McMahon's Barn and outbuildings with all the contents including five horses burned last night. Loss about $1,000 over and above insurance." On Friday, May 11, the diarist himself fell victim to the arsonists:

> All McLean's stables and my own burned up about 2 o'clock A.M. this morning. And all the contents. McLean lost three valuable horses. Cannot say the value of amount lost. No insurance on my own building. Think McLean must have lost $1,000 above an insurance of $600 on the premises. Drought's house and cabinet shop burned same time. Don't know anything as to loss, or amount of insurance.

There is no indication that Porte had been specifically marked out for retribution by the feudists. The proximity of his buildings to those of McLean would seem to have been the more or less accidental cause of his loss.

The following day, May 12, an even more destructive fire swept a hardware storehouse belonging to Bernard Stanley, a prominent Lucan merchant. Porte estimated the loss at $1,500; Mr. Stanley told the *Free Press*, $4,000.

There occurred that same night an incident reported with aggravating lack of detail. Apparently the Lucan business men, alarmed (as well they might be) by a wave of arson, hired a painter named George Gear and another unnamed person to patrol the village and act as fire-watchers. It appears that Gear surprised some vandals who had just thoroughly ransacked the interior of a Lucan barber shop and was fired upon, a bullet entering his right leg from the rear. From the direction of the shot we are led inescapably to the conclusion that the painter was in the act of discovering the superior virtues of discretion over valour. We are not told if he returned the fire.

Three days later Porte made this entry in his diary: "Tuesday, May 15, 1877—James Donnelly died today." This was "Young Jim," eldest child of James and Johannah Donnelly. The burning question is: Of what did he die?

Donnelly family tradition is evasive on this point. Their friends will tell you only that Jim "died in bed." This, for a member of that much-persecuted family, was indeed something worthy of note.

Other Biddulph families are not so reticent. They will tell you, as a matter of record, that Jim Donnelly died of gunshot wounds. They will tell you circumstantial stories about where he was wounded and what he was doing there at the time— three different versions, in fact. He was shot by a fire-watcher while trying to steal grain from the elevator at the Grand Trunk Railway station. He was shot by George Gear while making his escape after the vandalism at Bervy's barber shop, referred to above. He was shot by a temporary constable named Delmage during an attempt to fire the Queen's Hotel.

The last story, which is also the most popular version, can easily be disposed of with the help of the calendar. The incident in question, to be dealt with later, happened almost a month after Jim's death.

The grain elevator story cannot be checked. The elevator was robbed so many times by so many different persons that the events were not considered worthy of the attention of the columns of the London newspapers, or even of William Porte's careful diary.

If James Donnelly did indeed die of gunshot wounds, the barber shop case seems the logical setting for the incident in view of the timing.

The manner of Jim's wound is also circumstantially attested to by village tradition. He was struck in the stomach. The family of William Porte persists in a macabre but probably apocryphal story that the attending physician attributed the death of his patient to "lead poisoning." Another account names the physician, a Dr. Sutton, and states that he was a friend of the family and on the death certificate listed the cause of death as "acute appendicitis."

There is no mention in any reputable record extant today of any previous illness suffered by James Donnelly. Few people in Biddulph, aside from supporters of the Donnelly family, seem to have given consideration to the fact that acute appendicitis was in those days an often fatal ailment as likely to strike a strong, well-built man like Jim Donnelly as a sickly weakling.

Jim Donnelly may have died, and probably did die, a perfectly normal death. However, in the absence of a death certificate and further corroborative evidence we must leave the matter of Jim's passing as it stands, shrouded in impenetrable mystery.

It was the first break in the family circle. The silent and secret enemies of Jim and Johannah Donnelly and their seven stalwart sons could now pass the word up and down the Roman Line: "One down and eight to go."

The only mystery about the remaining events of the spring and early summer of 1877 is the assignment of culpability. We return to Mr. Porte's diary for a record of the next few incidents in what was truly called a "reign of terror."

Tues. May 22/77 — 3 horses belonging to William Walker butchered in Tim Carey's pasture last night, two of them found dead, and shot the other one.

Thurs., May 24/77 — Fire set in Goodacre building behind Photograph rooms this morning about 12:15 A.M. but providentially discovered before doing any harm.

Sat., May 26/77 — Attempt made to burn Oddfellows Hall.

Fri., June 8/77 — Whalen Corners Post office burned last night.

Thurs., July 5/77 — Fitzhenry Hotel occupied by Jas. Moloney, together with Stable, Shed and Mr Gleeson's Stable burned this morning between one o'clock A.M. and daylight. Loss to Fitzhenry about $900. Gleeson stable about $200.

Mon., July 9/77 — Ben Blackwell's house occupied by Mike Donnelly burned about one o'clock A.M. this morning. Completely gutted. Shell left standing. Origin of fire a complete mystery.

The files of *The London Free Press* fill in some of the details William Porte left unsaid, as well as recounting instances of crime and violence which the diarist did not bother reporting. For instance, in its issue of May 23, under what must have been a "standing head"—KU KLUX IN LUCAN—it adds some gruesome facts to the story of the Walker horses:

> ... During the last week or two several thousand dollars' worth of property has been destroyed by fire, the origin of which, to the minds of all who reside in the neighbourhood, was clearly traced to incendiaries. In addition to this some 15 horses, principally belonging to Messrs. Walker and Watson stage owners, have perished, either by being burned alive or otherwise. The latest outrage, which appears to be the most fiendish of the series, was perpetrated between last (Monday) night and this morning. It appears that Messrs. Walker and Watson having as stated, lost several valuable animals by the burning down of stables,

etc. were afraid to keep their horses in the stables over night and so put them out to a field. They did so, as usual, on Monday night, Mr Walker putting three good animals and Mr Watson one into a field adjoining the village. During the night, horrible to relate, some fiend or fiends in human form, visited the pasture and cut the throats of the whole of the dumb animals, at the same time frightfully mutilating their bodies. Finding it difficult to cause the death of Mr Watson's horse by the process named, the scoundrels disembowelled him. The whole of the animals were found in a dead state this morning. These outrages have caused a great deal of indignation in the neighbourhood and threats to lynch the miscreants, should they be discovered, are freely indulged in. The authorities should lose no time in offering a reward for their arrest and conviction.

For some unknown reason the diarist made no reference to the two attempts to fire the Queen's Hotel in June, although both incidents were played up in the *Free Press*. The first occurred on Sunday night, June 3. One of the fire-watchers, of whom there were now several, all armed, saw two suspicious-looking persons lurking at the rear of the hotel. He called on them to halt, whereupon they began to run. A second demand to halt bringing no response, both men fired, apparently without effect. In the morning traces of human blood were found. The newspaper commented on a village rumour that a suspected person "was missing from his accustomed place in the village yesterday, as a solution it being supposed that he was the person wounded."

The second attempt took place in the middle of the same month. On this occasion a fire was set, but a resident at the hotel spotted the blaze and succeeded in extinguishing it, having first fired a few shots at the arsonist.

Two other incidents in June were omitted by William Porte. The first was the arrest of Robert Donnelly for participation in the famous "wedding" case. The second was the appointment, on June 12, of a Constable Butler of the village of London East as chief of police for Lucan.

This has been a bald narrative of the events in Lucan and its neighbourhood in the first six months of 1877—one of the most hectic periods in the history of the feud. In those six months there were twelve fires showing evidence of arson, two attempts at arson, one case of vandalism and one of mutilation of animals.

While it is impossible now to assess responsibility for these crimes, some significant facts can be pointed out. Of the twelve fires, the Donnelly family and their friends were the victims in five instances—the fire at James Moloney's wagon shop on March 13, the destruction of the Donnelly stables on the 17th, the burning of Tom Donnelly's stage-coach (if it *was* his) on April 15, the burning of Fitzhenry's Hotel on July 5 and the gutting of the house occupied by Mike Donnelly on the 9th of that month.

It would be naïve categorically to deny some measure of Donnelly complicity in the other fires during the period under review. They had been injured; they would have been denying their Tipperary heritage had they not at least contemplated retaliation.

It would seem unlikely that they had any connection with the burning of Bernard Stanley's buildings on May 12. The Stanleys, Hodgins and Armitages—all Tipperary Protestant families—appear always to have been on reasonably good terms with the members of the Donnelly family. In the state of mind of the Roman Catholic people of Biddulph at this time, that in itself may have been sufficient cause for the destruction of Stanley's property.

It is worth noting particularly that seven of the properties attacked during the six-month reign of terror were owned by Protestant merchants or institutions; three belonged to the

Donnellys or were occupied by them or their friends. The Donnellys were known to be on generally good terms with the Protestant merchants of Lucan, to be tolerant of Protestant institutions (even including the Orange Order), and to be staunch Liberals. The Vigilance Committee membership was 100 per cent Roman Catholic and Conservative (generally considered at this time to be the Catholic party).

Why then has the Donnelly family been burdened in the public mind with the guilt of these crimes for more than eighty years? The answer is simple. After February 4, 1880 there were few Donnellys left to answer the lies of their traducers.

While it is not this writer's intention either to promote or to attack other works bearing on the Biddulph feud, attention must be drawn, in simple justice to a family long bitterly maligned, to a chapter in a book by one Thomas P. Kelley.

In Kelley's work the fire of March 17–18 is made to occur at the home of the elder Donnellys on the Roman Line. We are then treated to a melodramatic scene in which James Donnelly and his boys address the assembled population of Lucan, warning them of the wrath to come. There then follows a list of sixteen cases of arson and six cases of the poisoning and mutilation of cattle and horses—all attributed to the Donnelly family. The names of the sufferers are given in all cases.

Not one of the twenty-two cases in the Kelley list coincides in any of its particulars with those of official record. If we are to assume Kelley's list to be accurate, then we must also assume a degree of inaccuracy so extravagant as to be ludicrous on the part of *The London Free Press, The London Advertiser, The Parkhill Gazette* and William Porte, postmaster of Lucan.

Strychnine for
Breakfast

They love not poison that do poison need.

Shakespeare: RICHARD II

THE sudden death of John Regan was not directly related to the Biddulph feud, although many of the persons involved in the court case arising from that death were also involved in the feud. The matter served to prove that the township was the most lawless community in Canada.

In the Regan household there were the old man, his wife, James Hogan, her son by an earlier marriage, and the couple's own son, William Regan. William Porte's account of John Regan's demise was admirably terse. Under the date of August 10, 1877, he reported: "Old John Regan died suddenly this morning after partaking of a hearty breakfast."

By noon the manner of the old man's death had aroused sufficient suspicion to result in an investigation, and by 7:30 p.m. an inquest jury summoned by a Dr. John Gunn of Ailsa Craig had determined that the deceased "was poisoned by some parties administering strychnine."

This is the only recorded use of poison by the contentious Irishmen of Biddulph. The persons eventually charged with the commission of the crime escaped punishment—as usual.

One of the witnesses at the inquest was Michael Carroll. The following day Porte's diary contained this entry: "Michael Carroll's Barn, Stables, two horses and his entire crop, the growth of two farms, consumed by fire about 2 o'clock a.m. this morning. Incendiary, so says Mr. Carroll."

Carroll seems to have been a particularly important witness in the case, as appears from a later, cryptic entry in the Porte diary: "Tues., Feb. 18, 1876—Wrote Mr D. Glass today in re Hogan trial. M. Carroll the man, as near as I can tell."

Mary Regan, James Hogan and William Regan were indicted for murder and allowed bail. Hogan seems to have broken the terms of his bond on at least two occasions, thereby delaying the trial of the case until November, 1878.

This was standard procedure among the Tipperary people. The theory seemed to be that the longer the trial of the case could be put off, the dimmer would become the memories of the witnesses and the law alike, and the greater the chances of escaping punishment. Jim Donnelly had tried the system, without marked success. His emulators did much better. No one ever paid a penalty for the "breakfast murder" of old John Regan.

Through the troubles of the Regan family we are introduced to a new character with an important role to play in the climactic act of the Biddulph feud. This was the new chief constable of Lucan Village, Samuel L. Everett.

Everett appears suddenly on the scene in the fall of 1877 and in short order establishes himself as a bold, colourful and profane addition to the cast of the drama. One of his first acts was to make a bitter enemy of the village Pepys:

> Fri. Oct. 5/77 — Council night in the new lock-up chambers. Mr Everett . . . displayed his powers of Billingsgate to myself because of an effort to make him do his duty. Also made an attack upon Mr John O'Donohue for no earthly reason whatever . . . [it] shall not be forgotten. Salted down.

For weeks thereafter William Porte's diary is full of detailed references to the anti-social and, on occasion, criminal activities of the new constable. If Porte's account is to be trusted, Everett was a very peculiar peace officer. In November Porte accuses him of having blackmailed a prisoner out of $10; of assaulting the Donnellys' long-suffering friend, John O'Donohue, at the Queen's Hotel; and finally, of having allowed the village "bad boy," James Chisholm, to escape arrest by giving him advance warning in order "to make money out of the transaction."

Sam Everett may not have been properly carrying out his duties with respect to current crime, but he was most conscientious in the prosecution of old and half-forgotten offences. On December 19, 1877, at his instigation, Joseph Berryhill of London Township preferred an assault charge against James Keeffe of Biddulph Township for an offence allegedly committed on September 15, 1875. This was the celebrated stagecoach riot which had been periodically in the courts ever since its occurrence.

A careful examination of Everett's activities during the first few months of his term of office reveals some interesting facts. Whether or not he was guilty of the offences noted by William Porte, he seems to have shown a great lack of enthusiasm for the discharge of most of his duties. In one respect only he was most assiduous, and that was in his determined pursuit of the friends of the Donnelly family. John O'Donohue, the Keeffes and later the Donnellys themselves felt his heavy hand again and again, while James Chisholm, Arthur Gray, the Levitts and other notorious disturbers of the peace were left almost entirely unmolested.

It is not unreasonable in these circumstances to assume that Everett's appointment had been sponsored by the Vigilance Committee, as in the later and more fatal case of Jim Carroll. If this was so, the plan of the Committee's operations during this period seems to have been aimed at the intimidation of the Donnellys' friends, giving the family itself a short breathing space.

Of Jim Donnelly's seven sons, two only were now living at home—John and Tom. Will and his bride of a little over a year were established in a home of their own. Will had turned farmer. He seems to have given over the active operation of the stage-coach to Tom. Will's farm was located in the adjacent township of Usborne; he is referred to in a record of the period as a "respectable farmer" of that township.

Bob Donnelly was working in the village of Glencoe, some forty miles to the south-west of Lucan. Mike was a brakeman on the Canada Southern Railway but, as we have seen from the "fire record" in the previous chapter, he had rented a house in Lucan from Benjamin Blackwell. Mike was now married to Nellie Heins (or Henes) whose brother, Edward, was a house painter in Lucan.

Pat Donnelly was now thoroughly established in the business life of the town of Thorold, not far from Niagara Falls, where he seems to have held an enviable position in his community, well liked by all.

There was little hope of suitable marriages for Tom and John. The family had been the targets of a well-planned campaign of defamation. A girl of respectable family might lose her community standing by being seen with one of the Donnelly boys, and the proud Donnellys could not contemplate marriage with any other kind of girl.

An incident will illustrate the degree of social ostracism to which the Donnelly boys were subjected at this time.

Miss Murphy, nineteen years old, with a wealth of red hair, came to teach at a one-roomed log schoolhouse in Biddulph at the height of the feud. She was Irish-Canadian, pretty and 300 miles from home, among strangers. Soon after her arrival she went to a local dance. Her daughter tells what happened:

> The Donnellys landed in; the women sat like statues. No, no, they would not dance with the Donnellys. My mother felt there was going to be trouble if they were snubbed. When William came to her and asked her to dance she said: Yes, sure she would dance—much to the amazement of both men and women. . . .

The Donnellys were partial to schoolteachers, in the sense that they had a deep respect for their learning. The school on the Roman Line was only a few hundred yards north of the senior Donnellys' homestead and was commonly called the "Donnelly School." Occasionally a teacher boarded with them; but whether they lived there or not, Johannah kept a sharp eye out for their welfare. One story that received wide circulation, even among those who were no friends of the family, was retold in a pamphlet published by *The London Advertiser* in 1880:

> One very wet morning a lady school teacher was passing the house of the Donnellys, when the old woman hailed her. "Good morning, Miss—. Come in and dry yourself before going to school." "Thank you, Mrs Donnelly, but I haven't time," responded the teacher. "Sure your feet are all wet! Come in till I get you a pair of dry stockings." The teacher however, hurried on. Mrs Donnelly then passed into the house, and calling one of the passing scholars she gave her a pair of dry stockings to carry to the teacher. "Tell the teacher to change her feet," was the quaint but good-natured direction of the murdered woman.

In spite of everything the Donnellys had now achieved a measure of prosperity; the stage-coach business was probably largely responsible. The Roman Line homestead was well stocked with cattle and fine Clydesdale horses. The original log structure had been framed over. Will owned his own farm and everybody had a job. The "boys"—meaning in this case probably those still living at home—had even bought a piece of property near Bad Axe, Michigan.

There is a good deal about this transaction in the Porte diary. William Porte seems to have acted as their agent. The purpose of the purchase is obscure. It does not seem to have been a speculative venture. In view of numerous later references to family discussions dealing with the advisability of removing from Biddulph, it may be that they planned to give up the unequal fight and start a new life in Michigan.

If this was their intention, nothing came of it. On the Dominion Day holiday in 1877—the tenth anniversary of the confederation of the Canadian provinces—Jim Donnelly and William Porte took advantage of special excursion fares on the railroad to attend an Odd-fellows' celebration at Point Edward on the Canadian side of the St. Clair River. While there, they went across to Port Huron on the United States side to negotiate with a firm of solicitors there, apparently with a view to the sale of the Michigan property.

This step may have been forced upon the Donnellys by the losses they had sustained in the first half of the year by the acts of incendiaries, and by the costs of young Jim's funeral. Thus it may be that those who were working hardest to drive the family from Biddulph Township were actually responsible for them staying.

The number of their friends had been drastically reduced by the actions of the Vigilance Committee. John O'Donohue, Martin Hogan, John Purtell, one or two of the Feeheleys and the members of the Keeffe family, were all they could really count on. They had, it is true, the friendship of many of the Protestant merchants of Lucan, but this was of little assistance to them in the hate-filled atmosphere of the Roman Line.

Some members of this narrowing circle of friends were not of a type to boast about. Jim Keeffe got himself into trouble with the law regularly, and *all* the incidents cannot have been the fault of someone else. John Purtell, by all accounts a very dim-witted fellow, had an encounter with the law in the fall of 1877, when he was charged with stabbing a man in the nearby county of Perth. However, in spite of this, the Donnellys persisted in a warm, big-hearted kind of affection for Purtell. An outstanding feature of their character as a family was their unfailing sympathy for the outcast and the underdog.

The Donnelly circle was fated to shrink even more. The Vigilantes were hot after Jim Keeffe; they would soon dispose of John O'Donohue; they would eventually "get through" to John Purtell and the Feeheleys.

It was only a question of time now.

"I'll Tell Ye of a Plot..."

No! No! Sentence first—verdict afterwards.

Lewis Carroll: ALICE IN WONDERLAND

THE tantalizingly brief entries in the diary of William Porte for the first week of January, 1878, give us a sharp picture of the degree to which the Biddulph troubles had embroiled even so level-headed a business man as the Lucan postmaster and telegraph agent. The first reads: "Tues. Jan 1/78—Our beast of a town constable made a regular blackguard of himself today at the Central Hotel. Drunk and insulting everybody who did not think as he did. . . . But hark, I'll tell ye of a plot, Baitherskin!" The following day we read: "Weds. Jan. 2/78—O'Donohue, Feeheley and Jimmy Keeffe in town today. I know for what."

If the diarist knew "for what," he kept it strictly to himself. There is no record of any disturbance on that particular day. Revenge on Everett for his attacks on O'Donohue would seem to have been the obvious object. If so, it was not achieved on that occasion.

The first two months of the new year were relatively quiet. The factions were building up their strength for the annual outburst in March, the month sacred to Father Sheehy and St. Patrick. The first gun was fired by a local weekly, *The Parkhill Gazette*, in an article by its Lucan correspondent attacking Constable Sam Everett for shirking his duty, getting drunk on the job and committing other misdemeanours. From internal and other evidence it appears the writer of the article was William Porte.

On March 6 *The London Free Press*, in an article strongly commendatory of the village constable, informs us that Everett had entered an action for libel against the *Gazette*'s editor. On March 15 *The London Advertiser* reported that the constable had withdrawn his suit. It further stated that as a result of charges made by Everett against Porte, the London postal inspector had gone to Lucan to investigate the diarist's operation of the office there. The inspector must have found everything in order, for no more is heard of the incident.

On the morning of St. Patrick's Day, which fell on a Sunday that year, the barn and other out-buildings belonging to William Haskett, an officer in the Orange Order, were burned to the ground. According to the *Advertiser*, there was no doubt about how the fire originated, "as the tracks of horses could be discerned around the building."

The state of mind of the people of the village and township was demonstrated in a ludicrous manner the following evening during a performance in Lucan by the celebrated Cool Burgess and his travelling company of comedians. With a particularly macabre sense of humour the ventriloquist of the troupe, making his voice seem to come from outside the hall, shouted "Fire!" A near panic resulted. The *Advertiser*'s correspondent reported on the actions of two of the villagers:

> The lawyer and banker who slept in the adjoining rooms, hearing the cry as they supposed, coming from the street, ran in all directions; the former pounding the doors opposite with a view of awaking the McCosh Bros., and the other making his way to the bank, in order to stand by the vaults in case of emergency.

What happened around midnight that night, the 18th of March, was no laughing matter. Piecing the story together from several sources of information, this is what occurred:

Constable Sam Everett, returning home late (probably from the Burgess entertainment), rapped at the door of his house to secure admission. While waiting for his wife to let him in, he stooped to pat his dog which had come to meet him. At that instant he heard a loud snap in the still midnight. Turning in the direction of the sound, which seemed to come from a woodpile some fifty feet away, he saw the flash of a weapon discharging. A fraction of a second later he heard the vicious "thonk" of ten pieces of buckshot embedding themselves in the door near him. (The *Advertiser* says "a foot from his hand;" the *Free Press*, "three inches from his breast.")

With commendable, if foolhardy, courage the unarmed Everett made for his hidden assailants. As he ran toward the woodpile, three figures burst from behind it and ran across the fields; they were in their stocking feet.

At this point a neighbour, aroused by the sound of the shot, joined Everett in the pursuit. It was a bright moonlit night and the chase was a long one. However, the would-be assassins finally shook their pursuers in the shadows of some buildings in the village and Everett returned to his home, to examine carefully the scene of the ambush. That it was planned and deliberate was shown by the number of footprints in the snow (cold work, in stocking feet), and by the fact that a rest for the proper aiming of the shot-gun had been improvised from pieces of wood.

The *Advertiser* confined its report to a brief statement of the facts of the incident itself; the *Free Press* added a comment from Everett to the effect he was convinced that the person who fired the shot "is one of the gang who were interested in the recent rescue of a prisoner from the lock-up." No other reference to this incident can be found in surviving records.

Unfortunately, the *Free Press* did not let it go at that, but indulged itself in editorializing on the incident in what must be considered an inflammatory manner, in view of the known existence of the Vigilance Committee:

> The merchants and businessmen of Lucan have frequently remonstrated against the publication of items reflecting upon the conduct of certain individuals in this village who have, by their wanton disregard of the laws of the land brought disgrace upon the name of the village and its law and order-loving inhabitants and injured materially the business interests of its denizens. The fault does not lie with the newspaper as is wrongly supposed. Were a man, or any number of men to commit a crime similar to that chronicled below, in any other place, the facts would be given to the public, just as they are in this case. Until the neighbourhood is rid of such base characters the village cannot be expected to prosper. The remedy is in the hands of the Lucanites themselves and it behooves them to act promptly, yet judiciously, in any effort looking to the extermination of the members of a gang who do not scruple to outrage the feelings of a community by attempting the assassination of a peace officer after the manner following. . . .

Then follows an account of the shooting, substantially as it has been abstracted above from various sources. The *Free Press* adds that the constable's wife, opening the door a fraction of a second after the shotgun blast, had a narrow escape. Then the *Free Press* again drives home its earlier message to the people of Biddulph:

> The Constable may have made enemies while discharging his duty, but any man, or set of men, who could deliberately stand by and see his fellow man shot down like a dog, simply because his, or a friend's toes had been trodden upon, *deserves to be lynched on the spot.* . . . [The italics are mine.]

Both newspapers, in their issues of March 21, reported that Sam Everett knew who fired the shot. Five days later everybody knew who his suspect was when he arrested Bob Donnelly and popped him into one of Lucan's new jail cells.

The arrest of Bob Donnelly threw the village into an uproar. Rumours persisted that an attempt would be made to release him, so a heavy guard was placed round the lock-up. The *Advertiser* reported that a young man named Haines was arrested and tried during the day by two local magistrates on a charge of "tampering" with the prisoner—whatever that may mean. Bail was provided by Jim Donnelly and a man named McGuire or Maguire. The man "Haines" is undoubtedly Edward Heins, brother-in-law of Mike Donnelly.

Urgently desiring to get his prisoner out of Lucan, Everett took him to the nearby village of Clandeboye with the intention of taking him to London on the mixed train of the London, Huron and Bruce Railway, which left Clandeboye at 3:30 p.m. They missed the train and had to return to Lucan.

That evening Everett arranged to plant two spies in the cell next to Bob Donnelly. The testimony of the informers, one of whom was George Gear, the painter, was to have an important influence on the outcome of Bob's trial.

To Everett's relief, there was no attempt at a jail-break and the following day he took his prisoner to London where he was committed to trial at the spring assizes then taking place.

On the afternoon of March 28 an incident occurred in Lucan for which we have three accounts, remarkable for their unanimity. Since this is one of the very few occasions on which such agreement existed, the reports are given here in substance.

The *Free Press*, unable to resist the opportunity of a reference to its contemporary, reported:

> On Thursday afternoon one of the Donnelly boys and Constable Hodgins met upon the street and entered into conversation about an item in the 'Tizer, to the effect that a rescue of the prisoner Donnelly would be attempted whilst he was lying in the lock-up here. Words grew pretty warm between them, the result of which was that they

> challenged each other to go out and fight. They then withdrew to one of the back streets and went at it in true pugilistic style. They were surrounded by some 100 or more spectators and allowed to pummel each other for a length of time, to the disgrace of the onlookers. One of the spectators conspicuously displayed his revolver and intimated that he would shoot the first man who interfered until either party cried "Hold, enough."

The *Advertiser*'s account was briefer:

> On Friday Constable Hodgins and one of the Donnellys deliberately retired to Kenny's blacksmith shop and for the space of 30 minutes pounded each other in a brutal manner. Probably the most disgraceful part of the proceedings was the fact that nearly one hundred of the villagers attended the fight and looked on without any effort being made to part the combatants, the fight coming to an end by one of the pugilists crying enough. . . .

It is to William Porte's diary, however, that we must turn for a full identification of the principals: "Thurs., March 28, 1878—Row between Jack Donnelly and Constable Wm. Hodgins this afternoon; had a fight down near the foundry and Jack Bawden showing fair play with his revolver."

We are left lacking only one piece of essential information: who won the fight?

On March 30, Bob Donnelly came up for trial in London. His was the last case in a crowded docket that had included two charges of murder. Representing the Crown was Charles Hutchinson, Middlesex County Crown Attorney. Henry Becher represented Everett, and David Glass, Q.C., was defence attorney. The judge was Mr. Justice John Wilson.

The case had attracted considerable attention. Bob Donnelly was well known, particularly in the south-western part of the county, where he had been working in the village of Glencoe. According to Jim Donnelly's evidence he had returned to Lucan only some four or five weeks prior to the attack on Everett.

Appearing as witnesses for the prosecution were: Samuel L. Everett; Malcolm McIzar (or McIsor); Richard Tapp; John Broadwood, whose occupation was given as hostler; George Gear, painter; William Hodgins, constable; Jacob Palmer, carpenter; Edward Hodgins, mason; and Mrs. Margaret Neil. All were residents of Lucan.

For the defence, the following witnesses were called: Patrick Whalen, James Donnelly, Sr., John Donnelly, James Keeffe, Michael Gary and John O'Donohue, all of Biddulph Township, and William McBride, a carpenter, of Lucan.

A critical feature of the Crown's case was the evidence of the spies placed in the lock-up cells at Lucan to obtain incriminating evidence. The spies, Gear and Palmer, testified that Robert Donnelly had said: "If the gun hadn't missed fire he would have blown Everett's heart out." Bob was also quoted as saying that if he ever got out he would lay half of Lucan in ashes.

In an effort to impugn the evidence of these rather unsavoury witnesses, Glass questioned them closely. He was endeavouring to prove that the spies had long been enemies of the Donnellys and their friends. Through the defence's attack, a corner is lifted of the veil of mystery surrounding the fate of William Atkinson, one of the first of the Donnelly faction to be submitted to the attention of the Vigilance Committee. The *Free Press* stated: "Witnesses George Gear and Jacob Palmer were queried by the defence as to the hanging of a man named Atkinson. Gear denied, Palmer admitted being indicted for it, but denied killing him; said he was still alive; Mr Glass got him to run away."

It is apparent from this startling little bit of by-play that David Glass was fully aware of the dangerous character of the

Vigilance Committee. It was not named during the trial but its shadow lay over the whole proceedings.

The defence limited itself to an attempt to prove an alibi for the prisoner. On the opening day of the trial Glass sought a postponement on the grounds that a material witness, one Thomas Hodgins, was missing, or at least could not be found. The plea was refused.

The defence's available witnesses went into the box, one by one, to give a detailed account of the events of the evening of March 18 at the Donnelly homestead. We are given a homely picture of the comings and goings of the various guests of the family. We catch a glimpse of Bob Donnelly emerging, yawning, from a bedroom, shirtless and in his stocking feet after a post-prandial nap. This was at nine p.m. Unfortunately for the defence, none could give eyewitness proof of his whereabouts between the critical hours of eleven p.m. and one a.m. The household had retired by that time.

Jim Keeffe as usual made a bad witness and left a most unfavourable impression on the court. He was more used to facing a jury as a prisoner than as a witness, and guilt shone from every scrubbed feature of his feckless Irish face.

At this stage Glass must have longed most fervently for the appearance of his missing witness. Tom Hodgins, a member of a large and respectable family, would have been worth three Jim Keeffes in the witness box. However, Tom was not available. So important was he to the defence's case that one cannot help wondering if his absence was due to premeditation on someone's part.

The case went to the jury late on Saturday night, March 29. They brought in a verdict shortly before midnight.

The indictment, as in the trial of Will Donnelly, was in four parts. The jury found Bob guilty on the first count of the indictment which read assault "with intent to kill and murder." On hearing the indictment read into the record, the foreman of the jury, S. H. Craig, of London, objected; they had not intended to find the accused guilty of an attempt to murder. On this occasion the jury agreed with its foreman.

Judge Wilson then had the four counts of the indictment slowly and carefully read to the jury. Finally, on consultation with one another and with the assistance of the learned justice, they decided that what they really meant was that Bob was guilty on the fourth count in the indictment: "Assault with intent to do grievous bodily harm."

It was by this time ten minutes past midnight on Sunday morning. Judge Wilson accordingly refused to accept the verdict at that time and ordered the jury locked up over the week-end, with instructions to bring in their findings, as amended, first thing Monday morning.

David Glass objected to this hardship being imposed on the jury and offered to accept the verdict as it stood in spite of the time element. The Judge, however, wisely refused to lay himself open to reversal on appeal on technical grounds. The jury sullenly went off to be locked up. Promptly at nine o'clock on the morning of April Fool's day they returned the same verdict, following which Judge Wilson delivered sentence.

Both newspapers spoke in glowing terms of the Judge's kindness in dealing with the defendant. Justice Wilson was in his way as colourful as any character who ever appeared before him. He had in his youth defended himself on a charge of murder arising out of the last fatal duel to be fought in Canada, of which he was the surviving principal. While he was not known for a particularly kindly attitude towards the Irish, he probably knew something of the nature and character of the Biddulph feud through long years of practice as a lawyer in this very city of London before his elevation to the bench.

In sentencing Bob Donnelly to two years in the Central Prison at Kingston—the lightest term he could give on the charge—the Justice delivered himself of some general remarks on the prisoner and his family. *The London Free Press* and *The London Advertiser* reported him in almost identical terms. The *Advertiser* account read:

> Mr Justice Wilson then proceeded to pass sentence. In doing so, he said it was very true that no charge had heretofore been brought against the prisoner; but still it seemed from the evidence that he was infected with the spirit that seemed to be the bane of the neighbourhood of Lucan. Now he (the learned Judge) believed there were some good points in the Donnelly family. He had no doubt they were generous, warm-hearted and would make warm friends. But there was no doubt they were bad enemies. He did not wish to refer to any distressing family matters, but he could not help referring to the fact that the prisoner's father was once under sentence of death. And he could tell the prisoner that had the shot taken effect and killed Everett, Donnelly would most assuredly have been hanged.

It seems to me that the reference to Jim's early trouble with the law on the part of the Judge was gratuitous, the very kind of remark calculated to keep banked the fires of resentment in the breasts of the Donnelly family.

There remains still unanswered the big question: was Robert Donnelly really guilty? One must view with some suspicion the evidence of the two spies, proven enemies of the family and their friends. The Judge accepted their evidence with some show of repugnance; he indicated that it was only the forethought shown by Constables Everett and Hodgins in providing two witnesses, one to corroborate the other, that led him to place credence in their statements.

The Donnelly family and their friends always claimed that Sam Everett had made a reasonable mistake in his identification of Robert Donnelly as one of the three assailants who had lain in wait behind the woodpile in their stocking feet. Their story is that Everett recognized Bob Donnelly not by his face but by his clothing; they further claim that this clothing had earlier been stolen, for that very purpose. This seems a very slim and far-fetched explanation.

The search for a motive on Bob's part for the attack on Everett also presents certain difficulties which are not cleared up by the published accounts of the trial. Are we to picture Bob Donnelly, returning home from a protracted stay in a village many miles distant, becoming incensed by John O'Donohue's tales of Constable Everett's many assaults on him and then preparing this elaborate and murderous ambush? It may be so. The Irish temper is always trigger-happy when confronted with injustices, real or fancied.

There was one peculiar feature of the trial noted by the newspapers, but probably misinterpreted by them. During the long procession of witnesses to the box, Bob Donnelly seemed completely unconcerned, sitting at his ease in the prisoner's dock with a broad grin on his face. From time to time he cast an expectant look towards the rear of the courtroom, as though waiting for someone or something. The newspapers interpreted this as the prisoner's foolish expectation of a mass invasion of the courtroom by a posse of his friends, determined to free him. Bob Donnelly was not a romanticist; surely this is a far-fetched explanation of the prisoner's actions.

It is barely possible that Bob Donnelly was innocent of the actual commission of the crime; that he continued, to the end of the trial, in the hope that the missing witness, Tom Hodgins, would appear and provide the needed alibi.

Let us remember Everett's evidence that there were three persons hiding behind the woodpile and let us also recall the two entries from the diary of William Porte which were quoted at the beginning of this chapter; the entry in which he tells that he knows of a plot, followed by the second, written on the succeeding day: "O'Donohue, Feeheley and Jimmy Keeffe in town today. I know for what."

Politics, Beaks, and Bobbies

When constabulary duty's to be done
A policeman's lot is not a happy one.

W. S. Gilbert: PIRATES OF PENZANCE

IT has been pointed out earlier that in Canada the Tipperary feud had a political, as well as a religious, basis. This was so from the very beginning. It was a dangerous combination. By 1878 it had involved, to an alarming degree, persons and institutions far removed in importance from the simple but contentious yeoman farmers of Biddulph Township. The combination led to the enrolment, as active combatants in the feud, of the Protestant and Roman Catholic churches, the two great Canadian political parties and their news organs.

In particular, it had involved the two leading daily newspapers in the City of London.

The London Free Press, founded in 1849 by William Sutherland as an organ of the Reform, or Liberal, party became, a decade later and under the ownership and editorship of Josiah Blackburn, an outspoken supporter of the Conservative party.

The London Advertiser, founded in 1863 by William Cameron to meet the avid demands of district newspaper readers for news from the battlefields of the American Civil War, was a staunch supporter of the Reform, or Liberal, party.

The Conservative party during these years, and especially under the leadership of Sir John A. Macdonald, supported and sponsored the political aspirations of Canada's Roman

Catholics. The Reform party, under its great leader George Brown, championed the cause of the Protestant element and particularly the Orange Order, then politically powerful. In later years the two parties reversed their positions.

The Whiteboys of Biddulph naturally embraced the policies of the party that supported their church; the Blackfeet endorsed the Reform or Protestant party despite the fact that it represented Orangeism.

Thus the battle lines were drawn up, clearly and inexorably.

On the one side were the Conservative party and its local organ, *The London Free Press*, the Roman Catholic Church, the parish priest, the Vigilance Committee and the Whiteboy families of Lucan Village and Biddulph Township.

On the other side were the Reform party and its local organ, *The London Advertiser*, the Orange Order, the Tipperary Protestant merchants of Lucan and the Blackfeet Roman Catholic families of Biddulph Township, whose acknowledged leaders were the younger members of the Donnelly family.

As in all the affairs of men, the lines of demarcation were never as rigidly drawn as this line-up would imply. There was a "twilight zone," a frequent shifting of allegiances which, however, did not affect notably the broad general pattern.

When it is noted as well that 1878 was the year of a critical federal general election, one is the better prepared for what is to come.

The Biddulph battle centred on the two candidates for the riding of North Middlesex. Timothy Coughlin stood for the Conservatives, Colin Scatcherd for the Reformers.

The election took place on September 17. Coughlin and Scatcherd had been stumping the constituency for weeks. The Roman Catholics of Biddulph knew their duty—a vote for Coughlin was a Catholic vote. However, just to be on the safe side, the Vigilance Committee had coined its own campaign slogan which was passed up and down the concession roads in conspiratorial whispers:

"Vote Coughlin or your barns burn!"

The confusion that has long existed in the public mind as to the real causes of the Biddulph feud is admirably illustrated by the popular legend that attributes this phrase to the Donnellys and their supporters.

The Donnellys and their Blackfeet neighbours voted the Protestant ticket in this election, as always. It would not be over-simplification of the case to state that it was for this reason, and for no other, that in time the Vigilance Committee coined another slogan to be passed up and down the Roman Line:

"The Donnellys must die!"

Whether it was due to Timothy Coughlin's eloquence or the Vigilantes' vigilance, the Conservative candidate was a shoo-in in Biddulph. In Lucan, 130 voted for Coughlin and only 28 for Scatcherd. In the township, Coughlin gathered 378 votes to 167 for Scatcherd. As Biddulph went, so went the nation, and Sir John A. Macdonald was triumphantly returned to power.

This was before the day of the secret ballot. Considering the known temper of the village and township, it required no small degree of courage for those 195 men to stand up and declare for Colin Scatcherd.

The balloting unmasked Sam Everett as a Reformer, much to the surprise of both London daily papers, each of which had previously assumed him to be a Conservative. Then, a few days after the election John O'Donohue went before a Lucan magistrate and charged the constable with the theft of a bar from a mowing machine. A warrant was issued with some alacrity and Everett was arrested, committed to stand trial and allowed bail.

The constable himself then promptly set off for London where he applied to Magistrate Peters for a warrant for the arrest of John O'Donohue on a charge of conspiracy.

The Lucan correspondent of *The London Advertiser* (now more leniently inclined towards the peccadilloes of the revealed Reformer) drew facetious attention to what is surely a farcical aspect of O'Donohue's charge. "What," he asked, "would the constable want with a mower bar?"

The *Free Press* correspondent, on the other hand, avowed that two respectable merchants in the village could attest to the truth of O'Donohue's charge. It is difficult to tell which of Everett's alleged crimes aroused the deepest horror in the *Free Press*—the theft charge or his political duplicity:

> WANTED—a precedent for the action of the Village Council in keeping a public official in their employ, and in receipt of his salary, while at the same time he stands committed to take his trial for a criminal offence. Seeing that the said official showed the cloven foot during the last days of the election campaign, may I ask if Gritism has anything to do with his retention of office.

From this item and other evidence it appears that the cunning "Grit"—a common nickname for a supporter of the Reform or Liberal Party—had successfully stated his case before the village council and had been retained in office despite the herculean efforts of his nemesis, William Porte, also a member of council.

Whatever the truth of the O'Donohue case, neither charge seems to have come to the attention of the court of assizes; at least no further records dealing with it can now be found. Everett was suspended from his duties for a very short time; O'Donohue disappeared from the narrative altogether save for one last, oblique and tragic reference some two years later.

On September 25 a barn got burned, but not for political reasons. During a thunderstorm on the morning of that day, a barn and its contents including a threshing machine was burned to the ground on the farm of Edward Ryan (Porte calls him "Ned"). Ryan said it was lightning, but one Patrick Sullivan said it was Ryan. Sullivan's interest, he explained to a magistrate, lay in the fact that the threshing machine had belonged to him. He believed that Ryan had done it for the insurance money.

This case and its repercussions continued for some time to serve as an *obbligato* to the more sombre major motifs of the Biddulph feud. Ryan and Ryan's friends and Sullivan and his friends (he was a member of the Vigilance Committee) pursued one another in and out of the courts and up and down the side roads for some time. On Christmas Day, 1878, Sullivan was arrested for firing three shots out of a revolver at James Meagher, apparently a friend of Ryan's. All three shots missed their target. Fortunately, the Munstermen were much better marksmen with a shillelagh or a half brick than with a fire-arm, else the Biddulph feud death toll would have been even greater.

With a few marked exceptions the conduct of the feud during 1878 had been remarkably good-natured. There was an inclination on the part of the participants to make fun of it and themselves. There are indications that the people of Biddulph had come to experience a somewhat rueful pride in the horrendous reputation their township enjoyed in the Province of Ontario. They continued to take to the courts on the slightest pretext and gloried in the defeats they registered against judges and juries.

The Regan poisoning case is a good illustration of this.

After many delays, the charge against Mrs. Regan and James Hogan was finally heard at the fall assizes in London in November. When the case was called Hogan failed to appear. The bench was told he had vanished about a month previously while being brought to London by one of his bondsmen. The bail money was accordingly estreated and the remaining defendant was brought up for trial on November 7.

The prosecution contended that John Regan died of poisoning by strychnine; that James Hogan had purchased strychnine from a Lucan druggist, W. H. Moore, to "kill some rats"; that a cat belonging to a neighbour had eaten some of the remains of John Regan's breakfast and died within the hour; that Mrs. Regan had scoured all the utensils used in the preparation of that meal prior to the official investigation; that Mrs. Regan and her husband had been on bad terms "due to his drinking" and that they had separated on many occasions during the thirty years of their marriage.

The defence (led by David Glass, of course) spent a great deal of time examining the financial affairs of John Regan, establishing pretty clearly that no one stood to profit in any great way from his death, and dwelt with loving care on the condition of a side of meat hanging in the Regan kitchen from which the old man had made his last meal. (O shade of Lizzie Borden!)

After the case had been stretched out for three days, Glass moved for a dismissal of the charge on the grounds that the Crown had failed to prove motive. The bench agreed and Mrs. Regan was freed. James Hogan later came to trial but was acquitted, and to this day no one knows who put the strychnine in Mr. Regan's breakfast.

Meanwhile the Donnelly family name had been conspicuously absent from the records since Bob had gone off to Kingston Penitentiary in April. Their truce with the law came to an end in mid-October, 1878. This time their name is coupled with that of their most fatal enemy, James Carroll.

Carroll, who was later described as a farm implement salesman, appears first in Biddulph in the year being reviewed, although other members of his family, including his brother William, had been residents of the township for some years. No amount of research seems capable of revealing exactly what happened on October 14, 1878, between the Donnellys and James Carroll, and no lapse of time seemed capable of erasing it from the memories of the family.

Like the late Will Rogers, all we know for certain is what we read in the papers. The gist of what we read is this:

On October 21 Jim Donnelly put in an appearance before Magistrates McCosh and Crunican in Lucan, charging that Carroll had presented a revolver at him on the 14th of the month, "making threats to use it with intent." According to the *Free Press* correspondent, the prosecution "showed plainly that the act had been committed, with sufficient provocation."

Nevertheless the two magistrates discharged the prisoner on the grounds that the act was done in self-defence.

The following day, employing Sam Everett's procedure, Carroll haled old Mrs. Donnelly into Squire Samuel Peters' court in London, charging her with "using abusive and insulting language." Carroll swore that Mrs. Donnelly called him "a blackguard, thief and rogue." Two of the Donnelly boys (which two we are not told) deposed that their mother called Carroll a blackguard only. They also testified that Carroll had pointed a revolver at her, saying at the same time "he would just as soon shoot her as one of her sons."

On this appearance of Mrs. Donnelly—one of the very few she ever made in a court of law—there has been built by the family's detractors a whole body of false legend picturing her as the evil genius of the family, a backwoods Lady Macbeth implacably urging her browbeaten husband and sons on to ever greater and ever more outrageous deeds of rapine and cruelty. The portrait is absolutely without basis and an unspeakably vicious and wanton tampering with the facts. Its purpose is not hard to discover—her despicable murderers felt a pressing necessity to obscure the foul nature of their act.

In the last week of 1878 both London daily papers referred to a petition going the rounds in Biddulph Township praying for the release of Bob Donnelly from prison. Both newspapers referred to the fact that "a number of respectable persons" in the township and also in the city of London had lent their signatures to it. The *Advertiser* listed a score of the names.

They were, with few exceptions, Protestants.

Enter Father Connolly

The Padre said, "Whatever have you been and
gone and done?"

W. S. Gilbert: GENTLE ALICE BROWN

IN appointing Father John Connolly as parish priest of St. Patrick's, Biddulph, the Most Reverend John Walsh, Bishop of the Diocese of London, undoubtedly believed he was doing the right thing. The previous incumbent, Father Bernard Lotz, and his predecessor, Father Joseph Gerard, were non-Irish. Bishop Walsh, himself an Irishman, probably reasoned that a priest of their own national extraction would have better luck managing the wayward parishioners of St. Patrick's than a "foreigner."

This impression is borne out in the comment made by the Lucan correspondent of the *Free Press* in the issue of that daily for February 7, 1879:

> Father Connolly, late of Quebec, has received the appointment of parish priest of Biddulph, vice Father Lotz, who has been called to London. The people of Biddulph speak in laudatory terms of Rev. Mr Lotz as also of Rev. Mr Logan whom they say, came as near the right thing as possible, the only regret being they were not Irishmen; but this, of course, they could not help.

The results of the appointment did not bear out the bishop's sanguine expectations. The degree to which Father Connolly was involved in the criminal events of the years 1879 and 1880 always has been and probably will continue to be a disputed point. Extreme statements have been made on both sides of the matter. The truth lies somewhere between.

It can, however, be said that the choice of an Irish priest was the worst possible solution to the Biddulph problem. By the very nature of his faith and his national allegiance Father Connolly was caught up at once in the vortex of religion, politics and family vendettas that represented the everyday life of St. Patrick's parish. He was an elderly man of strong convictions, eager and zealous in the promotion of his faith. He was also human, prideful of his cloth and at times intransigent in the defence of his Church against those he considered its enemies. He was often dangerously uncritical of those of his flock whose profession of Christian virtues blinded his eyes to their secular activities.

Above all, he believed those who first brought their tales to his ear. The first to do so were members of the Vigilance Committee. As a result, he believed the Donnelly family to be responsible for all they were accused of; he believed that they were the principal architects and perpetrators of the reign of terror that had held Biddulph in its grip for a generation. He believed his greatest enemy in the parish to be William Donnelly, nor could he later be shaken in this belief.

Will Donnelly had been absent from the news for some time. He had been busy around his farm in Usborne Township, with little time to spare for the intricacies of the Biddulph feud. He was, however, not forgotten. On a night late in February, he was host to three unexpected visitors. The local newspapers all reported the incident. The following account is from *The Exeter Times:*

On Friday night last (February 28th) about eleven
o'clock three men entered the dwelling of Mr Wm
Donnelly, a respectable farmer of the Township of
Usborne, adjoining Biddulph, and before he was
well aware of the fact, proceeded to his bedroom,
and securely bound his hands with what was evidently a piece of train bell-cord. Upon having asked
their intention the robbers replied they knew there
was $400 in the house, that they wanted it, and in
case of refusal, would bum the house down. Mr
Donnelly tried to impress upon them that there
was no money in the house, upon which they fired
two shots from a revolver over his head, the balls
of which lodged in the wall in rather close proximity to Donnelly's head. Evidently this was only done
to intimidate him, because they could not have
missed him if otherwise disposed. They then up-
set the contents of two trunks in the bedroom, but
found nothing therein to satisfy them. From thence
they proceeded to another bedroom, occupied by
Mrs Donnelly and a servant girl, who by this time
were screaming loudly, having been alarmed by
the shots. They threatened to shoot the women
unless they covered their heads. In this room was
another trunk which they approached and after a
diligent search, found in it a leather pocket-book,
which one of them immediately took possession of,
remarking that this was what they were after. The
pocket-book contained $132, the proceeds of some
sale notes which Donnelly had recently collected
and which gave rise to the report that there was
money in the house. Mrs Donnelly was in a delicate state of health, having been recently confined,
and the shock received has resulted in a very serious prostration. The robbery took place about one
mile from where a similar occurrence was enacted
about a year ago, a man by the name of Jones being
the victim to the amount of $200 and a watch. Don-
nelly can give no description of the burglars (they

> being heavily muffled up) further than that one of
> them was about six feet high, the other about five
> feet seven, very stoutly built, and the third dwarf-
> ish in appearance. There was a further sum of $38,
> belonging to the servant girl, lying on the stand at
> the head of the bed, but it remained untouched.
> A Mrs Fogarty was also robbed of $240, a short
> time since, by men of a similar description. There
> is work for a detective in that vicinity.

Whoever the bandits were, they were never apprehended, nor was any determined effort made to lay them by the heels.

The newly elected Lucan village council was now the cynosure of all eyes. The election had been fought on the issue of "Everett or no Everett." The faction opposed to the retention of Sam Everett as chief constable had won, but according to the disaffected had as yet "done nothing."

St. Patrick's Day, 1879, was a big day for the township. There were three rival attractions—a grand ball at the Queen's Hotel in Lucan, a lecture by Father John Connolly in St. Patrick's Church on his visit to Rome in 1877, and the burning of "Gully Ned" Hodgins' house.

Something happened the following night. The only clue we have to the incident is a paragraph from the *Free Press,* remarkable as one of the very few instances in print of a reference to the origin of the feud:

> We understand that the Lucan village council has
> ordered an investigation touching the conduct of a
> certain village official on the night of Tuesday, the
> 18th instant, commonly known as Sheelah's Day in
> Tipperary.

The official was Sam Everett. The writer of the item was more than likely William Porte, a lifelong Conservative, who began to contribute to the paper about this time. The reference, together with one or two others, shows that Porte, although a King's County man, had some acquaintance with the background of the Biddulph feud. Unfortunately his knowledge was second-hand and his ear inaccurate, so that "Sheehy's Day" becomes "Sheelah's Day" and the date is altered from March 15 to the day following St. Patrick's Day.

Whatever happened in Lucan on March 18 had immediate and far-reaching repercussions. On April 3, Constable William Hodgins arrested Tom Donnelly on a charge of robbery preferred by Edward Ryan. This was the "Ned" Ryan who had been accused the previous year by Patrick Sullivan of burning down his own barn for the insurance money.

The following day William Porte wrote in his diary: "Fri., Apr. 4/79—Row at the Queen's between Everett and Constable W. Hodgins. The usual slang—and other choice language. No investigation as usual."

On Monday Tom Donnelly came up for his hearing before Magistrate McCosh. The incident precipitated a general Donnybrook involving Everett, Hodgins, Tom Keeffe and James Carroll. The upshot of it all was that Tom Keeffe was arrested for an assault on Carroll, Carroll was charged with an assault on Keeffe, Everett was arrested and jailed for an assault on Hodgins, Tom Donnelly was acquitted of the Ryan robbery and W. H. Hodgins, Reeve of Lucan, tendered his resignation.

Who can blame him?

The next day Porte wrote: "All quiet on the Potomac today. After a storm comes a calm, an adage truly verified. The only talk on the street today was the resignation of the reeve."

In mid-April the dispute between Sam Everett and the village council came to a head. Porte had managed to bring most of the council round to his way of thinking, and Everett was dismissed from his $365-a-year job. Lucan was left without a chief constable.

In May the talk was all politics again, a provincial election having been set for the following month. In North

Middlesex Riding the candidates were J. McDougall for the Conservatives and John Waters for the Liberals. At least two meetings were held in the "Donnelly schoolhouse," a few rods from the family homestead on the Roman Line. To the delight of the Donnellys and the confusion of their enemies, John Waters polled 1,917 votes to McDougall's 1,685. The family's espousal—not for the first time—of the Protestant party was duly noted and remembered.

That the Donnellys' political preference had been especially noted by Father John Connolly there can be no doubt whatever. There had been little overt criminal activity in the township since early in April. The election campaign in Biddulph had been remarkably quiet. Yet shortly after the election the priest of St. Patrick's parish decided on a step that was to brand his name forever.

There was no murder in Father John Connolly's heart. He was probably the victim of circumstance, the dupe of false witnesses, but in the eyes of the law and, it may be, of God Himself, ignorance and pride of faith are insufficient excuse.

There is now no way of telling who or what first proposed the idea to the priest. There is good reason to believe he knew of the existence of the already-organized Vigilance Committee. It may be, as he himself declared on one occasion, that his purpose was to obtain control of this extra-legal group and by his influence to direct its activities to good uses. Whatever his intentions, the end product was unmitigated evil

In the quiet of his study in the huge rectory then but recently built, north of the church, Father Connolly drew out a cheap oilcloth-covered brown notebook, some pages already filled with priestly notes in Latin. He hesitated but a moment over the book and then in a quick, nervous scrawl scribbled across the two centre pages of the notebook the fatal words that were to haunt him all the remaining days of his life. The writing read:

We the undersigned Roman Catholics of St. Patrick's
of Biddulph solemnly pledge ourselves to aid our
spiritual director and Parish priest, in the discovery
& putting down of crime in our mission. While we at
the same time protest as Irishmen and as Catholics
against any interference with him in the legitimate
discharge of his spiritual duties.

The following Sunday he placed the book, open at the oath, inside the front door of the church with pen and ink beside it.

The evidence differs widely as to what he said from the pulpit that day. Some say he spoke merely of lawlessness and the need to curb its authors; others say he blamed the Donnellys, by name, and cursed them.

The book remained at the church for two or three Sundays. A total of ninety-four men appended their names to the oath, for it was regarded as such. The first was James Gleeson. The name of Patrick Breen, acknowledged to be chairman of the Vigilance Committee, was there, and that of James Carroll and that of James Feeheley. Not a single member of the Donnelly family signed the document, nor was any asked to do so.

When the list was complete, the book was filed away in the rectory. Less than six months later it saw the light of day again when still another hand marked on it "Exhibit H," in the trial of the Queen versus James Carroll and others.

The priest on numerous later occasions was to deny that his action was directed against the Donnelly family or that he ever mentioned them by name in the pulpit. Yet by his own admission he did, in his capacity as parish priest, declaim publicly against certain crimes popularly ascribed to that family. Also, in an interview with a reporter from *The London Advertiser* in February, 1880, he made a statement which plainly indicates his personal bias against the Donnellys. The interview read, in part:

Hearing of the many rumours concerning the Vigilance Committee, in connection with which the name of Father Connolly, the parish priest, was mentioned, an *Advertiser* reporter interviewed him on the subject. He was cordially received by Father Connolly, who is an elderly man, with a pleasing, open countenance and of medium stature. He appeared to be in great anxiety, and expressed fears of being arrested. He assigned as a reason for his fear the bitter hatred which the Donnelly boys, and especially William, had against him. From the statement of Father Connolly it would appear that in June last, in consequence of the great number of depredations which had been committed, his people, upon his advice, signed an agreement in a book which he produced. The form of the agreement was very simple, and purported to be made between the Roman Catholics of the parish of Biddulph resolving themselves into a body "for their own mutual protection and assistance in bringing to justice the perpetrators of the deeds which were being perpetrated by unknown parties." The rev. father explained that the purpose which he intended to carry out was this: The Donnellys had been in the habit of committing depredations and stealing things from their neighbours. These articles or goods which were stolen they would leave with a neighbour, who would thus be brought into the mess, and for fear of personal violence to themselves and injury to their property they would not disclose the crime or their knowledge of the theft. The Donnelly boys by thus entangling different parties each time a depredation was committed by them, were enabled to gather a number of friends around them, who, although hating them in their hearts, were obliged publicly to befriend them, and were also afraid to give evidence against them. This state of things continued for a long time. Some time ago Thomas Donnelly was arrested upon a charge of robbing a neighbour named Ryan of

> $80 in money. The case was investigated, and after
> several adjournments Donnelly was discharged
> by Squires W. K. Atkinson and McCosh. Although
> Thomas was acquitted of the charge, a feeling of
> bitter hatred was engendered by them against Ryan,
> which showed itself in several ways....

Unless the *Advertiser* reporter made up his yarn out of
whole cloth we must consider this an extraordinary interview
for a parish priest to give a day or two following the brutal
and callous murder of five communicants of his church by
an unspecified number of fellow-parishioners. On what evidence did he base his charge that the Donnellys were "in the
habit of committing depredations"? Do we detect the authors
of these allegations in the further statement that the stolen
goods were left with otherwise innocent neighbours who
were thus made receivers, according to their stories? On what
authority did he—a resident of the township for a year only—
declare that their friends actually "hated them in their hearts"?

There is more. In this interview the Reverend Father a
dmitted his knowledge of the existence of the "other" Vigilance
Committee:

> It afterwards came to my knowledge that a num-
> ber of the Vigilance Committee which I had
> formed banded together, without my knowledge
> or consent, and formed a committee of their own,
> the members, although not taking an oath in a
> theological sense, making a solemn declaration,
> and without using the form "So help me God,"
> kissed the book.

This is ecclesiastical sophistry—as if the omission of the
invocation to the Deity could possibly dissolve the stain of Cain
from one murderous hand.

In a fatally garrulous vein the priest went on, still further to reveal his all-too-personal bias against the family, and against William in particular:

> It is not true that I have excommunicated or placed the Donnellys under the bann of the Church. Some time ago I received a letter from William, which contained some very impertinent remarks, and I then said I should have nothing more to do with them. . . . A few days after Thomas was arrested for robbing Ryan, John Donnelly came to me to confession. I refused to confess him, and told him I thought he intended to confess to an untruth, in order to free his brother and implicate others. He then went away.

Here surely was the unkindest cut of all. Even the most bitter secular enemy of the Donnelly family admitted John to be an honest, true and religious young man. Yet he was sent away unshriven to die a few months later, a great gaping wound in his breast and a grubby piece of holy candle spasmodically clutched in his hands.

The interview concluded:

> So far as I am concerned I am perfectly innocent of any connection with, or knowledge of, the movements of the second Vigilance Committee. I expect to be arrested, as I know that from the bitter hatred which William Donnelly bears me he will do all in his power to have me arrested.

The priest's fears were never realized. Throughout all the proceedings subsequent to the massacre of five members of his family, William Donnelly not once raised his voice against Father John Connolly. He persistently refused to implicate the priest in any way despite much pressure, and spoke always in the highest terms of the priest's sincerity and good intentions.

"Boney over the Alps"

He was a fiddler and consequently a rogue. . . .

Swift: JOURNAL TO STELLA

THE leaders of the anti-Donnelly faction—the forty persons who formed the core of the Vigilance Committee—were now committed to a single objective, to rid the township of their enemies. It is perhaps unlikely that at this stage they were contemplating murder as the *only* means of achieving their aim, but they were certainly prepared to use anything short of it.

Many attempts were later made to confuse the history of this body, to blur its outlines. References were made to two or three such committees with the object of making it appear that each of these was a loose association, sporadically and periodically thrown together under the pressure of unbearable persecution, to mete out rough justice in specific cases of iniquity where the law seemed incapable.

The evidence does not bear this out. Research shows the active core of this secret society to have been composed from the beginning of the same group of men. The same names occur and recur. They met in and out of season complete with officers, secret oaths and all the trappings of the lineal ancestor of their organization—the White boys of Tipperary.

The concession road immediately east of the Roman Line also had a local nickname. It was called the "Swamp Line." It is now part of Highway 7. A few hundred yards from where this highway intersects Highway 23 a dip in the road marks the former presence of a large cedar swamp. Some distance north is the schoolhouse of School Section Number Four, built in 1874, and inevitably called the "Cedar Swamp schoolhouse."

This was the meeting-place of the Vigilance Committee.

Father Connolly claimed the Committee had no officers, no rules and regulations and no set meeting time. The weight of other evidence is against him. Constant references were made to Patrick Breen as chairman; judging from the experience of some of the friends of the Donnellys who tried to attend meetings, there was a sergeant-at-arms; it was generally known that the first Friday of each month was their regular meeting time and, according to a story published in *The London Advertiser*, the Committee even had a sort of executive group to draw up agendas and plan the tenor of the meetings. This account reads, in part:

A statement made this morning, by a party who professes to know, would fully bear out the remarks made by Father Connolly yesterday . . . anent the doings of the Committee, to the effect that they had deviated from the simple rules laid down by him for their guidance. This authority says that the Committee NOW NUMBERS OVER ONE HUNDRED MEMBERS; that the old and respectable members alluded to by Father Connolly have mostly fallen off, and do not attend the meetings; that those who still remain organized have bound themselves under an obligation to carry out any measures which were sanctioned by a majority at the meetings. As is usually the case when such illegal doings are being enacted, some parties are generally found who do not strictly adhere to the requirements of their obligation, and through this means some of their proceedings have become known. It would appear

that there were thirteen of the members selected from amongst their body whose duty it was to prepare and bring before the meeting any questions which required to be discussed or voted upon. There was a back or ante-room adjoining the schoolhouse, and to this room twelve of those parties would repair to consider and prepare any subject which was destined to come before the members for disposal, and by a preconcerted arrangement between the thirteenth man and the twelve who retired, he harangued the parties as if by accident upon the very subject intended to be brought before them by the conclave in the ante-room, and by the time the question came up their feelings became so excited that they were ready to
VOTE THE CARRYING OUT OF ANY DEED,
no matter how much at variance with the Christian rules laid down by his reverence for their guidance.

This is not the pattern of a casual association. It shows planning and leadership. The only accidental factor was the introduction into the situation of the well-intentioned but misled parish priest of St. Patrick's.

It was undoubtedly Father Connolly's interference in the case of Ned Ryan that hastened the day of reckoning.

Ryan claimed that Tom Donnelly had on March 5, 1878, robbed him of an amount variously reported as $70, $75 and $80. The case had been in and out of the courts ever since that time. In magistrate's court at Lucan and again in London the case had been thrown out, but Ryan still persisted.

It was claimed—and there was probably some truth in the claim—that the Donnelly family in retaliation had threatened dire consequences to anyone who helped Ryan to harvest his grain that fall. Ryan tried to engage one Michael Curtin, who did custom threshing with a machine. Curtin hesitated to take the job.

At this stage Father Connolly entered the picture. This is his account of what happened next, as reported by *The London Advertiser:*

> Thomas Donnelly heard of this and gave Curtin warning that his machine would be destroyed if he attempted to thresh for Ryan. Upon this threat Curtin refused to do any threshing for Ryan, who, reduced to extremities, appealed to me. . . . I went to Thomas Donnelly and asked him as a personal favor to me to allow Curtin to thresh for Ryan. After hesitating, he said he would ask John. I went to John who promised to give me an answer before Sunday, and I went away, fully believing that they would oblige me. I waited patiently, but when Sunday came and I saw nothing of John I felt that my efforts and advice had no weight with them. The Vigilance Committee had met, and, upon Mr Ryan's application, guaranteed to Curtin the value of his machine and any loss of time he might have. Curtin then threshed for Ryan, but they found that the sheaves had been filled with iron, harrow pins, horseshoes, stones, etc., which greatly damaged the machine. This aroused great excitement among the friends of Ryan, and shortly afterwards Ryan's barns were burned. I felt it to be my duty then to declaim the burning of the barns from my pulpit, telling my people about it, but never once mentioned the Donnellys.

This statement by the reverend father repays careful examination. The priest always insisted there must have been two Vigilance Committees—the one he set up at the church and a second, the activities of which were kept a secret from him. He speaks here of a committee convened to discuss the Ryan threshing matter. Since he knew of its action, presumably he is here speaking of his own Vigilance Committee. Yet from other evidence it is quite clear that the meeting in question was held by the same committee that had been in existence since 1876.

In the statement quoted above, Father Connolly implies that Curtin's machine was wrecked by the presence in the sheaves of grain of a great number of hard objects. Under oath at a later date, a member of the Committee admitted that the damage to Curtin's machine was caused by five objects, some of them iron, lying on the ground. There were no objects in the sheaves themselves. Further, at a subsequent meeting of the Committee held to adjudicate on Curtin's claim for damages, payment was refused on the grounds that he had set the blades of his machine too close to the ground.

With respect to the burning of Ryan's barns, it is a peculiar fact that William Porte, usually so meticulous a journalist of the events in his neighbourhood, makes no mention of such a fire, nor is it reported in any of the local papers. The only occasion when a recorded fire occurred on Ryan's property was in September, 1878, when he was accused of setting the blaze himself for the insurance money.

The number, dates and purposes of the earlier meetings of the Committee can be only dimly discerned from the surviving records. From the late summer of 1879 on, it is possible to assign a date and an agenda to most of them. There had been a meeting to guarantee Curtin against damage to his machine. There had been another to adjudicate his claim. The next was called for an even more frivolous purpose.

A cow was missing from the farm of William Thompson, Junior. Thompson was Maggie's brother and long a bitter enemy of Will Donnelly. A cow was gone. It belonged to William Thompson. The Donnellys hated the Thompsons. Therefore the Donnellys had stolen the Thompsons' cow. Q.E.D.

An emergency meeting was convened at the Cedar Swamp schoolhouse. Many people knew about it. Will Donnelly's friend, Martin Hogan, went along to see what was up. He was refused admission.

The meeting was a long one. There may have been a division of opinion. While the total membership at this time may have been over one hundred, as the *Advertiser* stated, the active membership was more than likely limited to two score.

This is the fatal number. They were the inner group, the charter members, the forty patrons of death. It was they who carried out the decision arrived at by the executive committee of thirteen. They were becoming bold; this time they planned to operate by daylight.

It was about nine o'clock in the morning when they arrived at Jim Donnelly's homestead. Some of them were armed with sticks, cudgels and shillelaghs. They let out a shout and called for Jim. Jim was there, and Johannah and John and probably Tom. Bridget Donnelly was there too. She was a niece of Jim and had recently arrived from Ireland. There was great distress at this time in the Old Country and Father Connolly had been taking up collections at the church for Irish relief. Jim Donnelly had taken a step that seemed more practical to him; he had sent for his niece to come and live with him.

Jim came out and stood on the step and asked the crowd what they wanted. Bridget hid behind the door and peered through the crack. The conversation that followed was crisp but not notably elegant.

"What do you want?" Jim asked.

"We're looking for Thompson's cow," replied James Heenan, who seems to have been nominated spokesman for the Committee.

"You won't find it here," Jim said.

Heenan's reply seems to have been profane as well as expressing some doubt as to the accuracy of Jim Donnelly's statement. Somebody else said they were to search for the cow. None of the Donnellys apparently thought of asking if they had a search warrant. They had not.

Jim Carroll and John Kennedy started for the stable. John Donnelly was there with Edward Henes, Michael Donnelly's brother-in-law. Old Jim called after them:

"Don't leave a straw unturned; you won't find the cow here."

Several voices assured him they didn't intend to leave any stones unturned. Jim added:

"Search and be damned!"

James Maher ran up to young John and shouted:

"Who shaved our horses' tails?"

"I don't know."

"It was either you or Tom, and I will have revenge if it takes twenty years!"

At this, Jim Donnelly ran up to Maher and said:

"If you don't like us, you can go to hell!"

Jim Carroll had a witty reply to this:

"How would you like a few kicks in your ribs this morning?"

The old man scornfully looked him up and down and replied:

"I've seen the day I could give you a few kicks in the ribs."

Feeling the need to raise the standard of the conversation and emphasize the seriousness of their task, Jim Heenan said:

"We are bound to put down this work."

The Committee's Greek chorus, recognizing their cue, replied in unison:

"That's right, Jim, that's right!"

The pleasantries dispensed with, the Committee settled down to the work. They took Jim at his word; they did not leave a straw unturned. When they had searched the stable and the barn and the woodlot, they searched the house as well for good measure. They turned Johannah's neat little home upside down and broke a few articles in the process and when they did not find the cow, they went away.

It was ten o'clock or later when they showed up in front of Will Donnelly's house at Whalen's Corners, three miles away. Will later said there were forty of them, most of them armed:

Some had sticks. Michael Heenan had a piece of scantling. James Heenan had a stick. Martin McLoughlin had a blackthorn. Most of them had sticks in their hands. Kennedy and Ryan came a little ahead of the others. They sat down opposite my house and were pointing at my house and buildings. The rest of them sat down a little further down the road.

Not one of the forty set foot on Will's property. After staring at them for a minute or two, Will went back into the house and returned with his violin. Smiling at his audience he struck up "Boney over the Alps." His explanation given later for playing the Napoleonic air was that "it seemed to suit the gang."

If on this occasion music did not soothe the savage breast, it at least baffled its hearers. After some fifteen minutes of indecision, the Vigilantes left. Before leaving the vicinity, however, they called on Edward Sutherby, the local blacksmith, known to be on friendly terms with Will Donnelly. John Dorsey was the spokesman this time. When Sutherby asked what he wanted, Dorsey said they were looking for a stolen cow. Sutherby told him that in his opinion they would "look better at home ploughing or cutting thistles." At this Dorsey called to the others who crowded close to the blacksmith, by now thoroughly frightened. Martin McLoughlin was the one who spoke:

"We will visit you at all hours of the night, when you least expect it."

With that the forty left. Singly and in groups they returned to their homes delighted with the day's work. They had proved their bravery. They had baited an old couple, turned their house upside down, offered them many indignities and escaped scot-free.

They were not so happy about Will Donnelly. He had routed them with a fiddle. There was something uncanny about that. He was probably in league with the devil. Had not Father Connolly, himself, said he would have nothing more to do with him?

Their big success, however, was with Ed Sutherby. Before the end of the year he sold out his business and left for the United States. When he was asked the reason he said:

"I was afraid."

As for Thompson's cow, the beast rather spoiled the effect of the Vigilance Committee's demonstration of force by turning up a day or two later in a woodlot near the Thompson home, where it had strayed.

Jim Donnelly sought redress from the law. He applied to Squire Peters in London and warrants were issued for the arrest of thirteen of the Vigilantes. Those named were: Jerry McDonald, Patrick Breen, Michael Blake, James Carroll, James Flanagan, Peter Dewan, John Kennedy, John Heenan, B. Ryan, John Ryan, John Dorsey, James Maher and James Kelly. They were charged with trespass, the destruction of property and assault on James Donnelly.

The family did not have a chance of making the charge stick. A long line of defence witnesses—some accounts say forty—went before the beak and denied on oath that they were engaged on any other mission than the peaceful one of searching for a lost cow. The cudgels, scantlings and other weapons they carried were described as "walking sticks." However, what really killed the case was the honest testimony of old Jim Donnelly in the witness stand that he had said to his tormentors:

"Search and be damned!"

The law properly construed this as an invitation on the old man's part to inspect his premises and all the charges were thrown out.

It was now obvious even to the most cowardly Vigilante that they had nothing to fear of the elder Donnellys and the niece, Bridget. The rheumatic old man, the care-worn old woman and the frightened girl were easy pickings. It was the sons they had to fear and particularly that club-footed spawn of the devil, Will Donnelly. More drastic measures were necessary. There was another meeting at the Cedar Swamp schoolhouse at which a document was drawn up and sent to the county authorities in London. It read:

> To William Elliot Esquire Judge of the County of Middlesex. The humble prayer and petition of the undersigned inhabitants of the Township of Biddulph sheweth as follows:
>
> Whereas for some time past certain evil-minded persons in the Township of Biddulph have been violating the laws and acting in such a manner as to endanger the persons and property of the peaceable portion of the inhabitants thereof.

And whereas from there being but a few constables in said Township it is difficult and often impossible to have warrants or other process of the local Justices of the Peace executed and in consequence thereof compelling injured persons to either refrain from taking legal proceedings for the redress of wrongs or go to the expense of laying complaints before Justices of the Peace in the City of London. And whereas your petitioners are of opinion that much of the above re-cited inconvenience would be obviated by the appointment of James Carroll of said Township as a constable therein,

Your petitioners therefore pray

That the said James Carroll be appointed as a constable in and for this County and your petitioners will ever pray—

There were fifty-six names affixed to the petition, headed by Patrick Breen, president of the Vigilance Committee.

Who was James Carroll and what were his qualifications for the post of county constable?

He was a farm implement salesman aged about thirty. He had been a resident of the adjacent County of Perth until 1878 when he moved to Biddulph with his younger brother William, a lad of eighteen or nineteen. There are numerous pen pictures of the brothers as their contemporaries knew them. James had a dark lowering face, the lower half of which was concealed by a bushy, jet-black beard. William was a shorter, stouter carbon copy of his brother.

The brothers were related to several of the Roman Line families and were unrelenting enemies of the Donnellys, as their ancestors had been, probably for generations. In the eyes of the Vigilance Committee these were good and sufficient reasons for naming Jim Carroll their instrument of vengeance.

That Carroll wanted the job there can be no reasonable doubt. That he wanted it for the purpose of personal revenge on the Donnelly family there can be equally no question. This, of course, was not the case presented by the fifty-six petitioners named in the document as "the inhabitants of the Township of Biddulph." They were in their manner and presentation God-fearing, law-loving taxpayers and the worthy judge accepted them at their own valuation and appointed Jim Carroll a county constable, effective September 20, 1879.

The appointment was well publicized in London and Lucan. A second appointment made on the same day was not. One William Casey of the Roman Line was named a Justice of the Peace. Casey was a charter member of the Vigilance Committee, one of the inner circle of forty.

Some months later, in court, Casey first denied categorically that he was ever a member of the Committee, then amended his statement to declare that he had been a member at one time but had withdrawn subsequent to his appointment as a magistrate. Of his qualifications for the post he said under oath that he "knew nothing about magisterial duties at all."

Casey's memory was as faulty as his qualifications for the magistracy. He said he had been a member of the Vigilance Committee for a short time only. He did not know that the first Friday in each month was the regular meeting-time. He had been at the meeting about the Thompson cow. The meeting lasted more than six hours but he could only remember the names of two persons who had been present William Thompson and Michael Carroll. He did not remember James Carroll being there; he did not remember that Carroll had been sent to Lucan to get a warrant to search the Donnelly farm; he did not remember that Carroll had returned without a warrant. His memory of that search itself was a little better and he recalled several names Anthony Heenan, James Heenan, Martin Dorsey, John Kennedy, Martin McLoughlin, Patrick Breen, John Heenan and one of the Ryders.

Two of his statements in the witness-box are particularly difficult to reconcile. He said he had given up his membership in the Committee on his appointment as magistrate "because I didn't think I had any business going around looking for stolen things when I was a Justice of the Peace." He also declared he had attended two or three meetings of the Committee, the first of which was the one about the Thompson cow. Since that meeting was held only a week or so before his appointment we are forced to the conclusion either that the Committee held one or two further meetings in rapid succession—for which there is no evidence—or that Casey lied under oath.

This then was the new order of things in Biddulph. These were the men who had sworn to uphold the dignity of the Queen's justice—a constable with a personal grudge and an unqualified magistrate who was either a dolt or a prevaricator or both.

Carroll's first act as constable was to arrest Tom Donnelly for the Ryan robbery, a charge for which Tom had already been acquitted in magistrate's court at Lucan. Carroll took his prisoner to London where he was bailed to appear before Squire Peters. At that hearing he was bound over to stand trial at the fall assizes for the County of Middlesex. His bondsmen were Sam Everett and Jim Keeffe.

During the last week-end in September a severe electrical storm swept through the township and caused a good deal of damage. Lightning struck William Kent's house, burned down Thomas Courcey's barn and stables and smashed Jim Donnelly's "double buggy." In the midst of the storm the home of a Mrs. Hogan caught fire from the explosion of a lamp and was destroyed. *The London Free Press* correspondent reported she was ill and expected to die, but did not further identify her.

The storm must have caused some of the older and more superstitious residents of Biddulph to recall, uneasily, the prophecy made twenty-two years before by a priest of St. Patrick's that the "hand of God" would smite this lawless community. It must also have given the Vigilance Committee some satisfaction in that most of the sufferers were Protestants and/or friends of the Donnelly family.

Tom Donnelly's case came before the grand jury, which found a true bill, on October 9. The day before saw the final disposition of the long-drawn-out Regan poisoning case with the acquittal of James Hogan on a charge of murder.

Tom's case never came to trial. A letter written a year later by the Crown prosecutor, Matthew C. (later Sir Matthew) Cameron, explains why:

Ryan and a young lawyer in London came to
me and represented that Ryan had been robbed by
Donnelly—that the J.P.s were afraid to act and would
not send Donnelly up for trial and that justice could
not be obtained otherwise than by going directly
before the grand jury. With a good deal of hesitation
I sent the bill before the grand jury. I afterwards
discovered that the case had been investigated once
if not twice by the J.P.s and dismissed. Under these
circumstances I did not feel inclined to proceed. I
think the lawyer's name was Blake but am not sure.

So far as the processes of the law were concerned, that was the end of the alleged Ryan robbery case. A day or two later a brief paragraph in *The London Free Press* presents a complete mystery. In its entirety the item reads: "A large number of men are in pursuit of one of the Donnellys. At one time they had him surrounded in a piece of woods but he escaped."

Which one of the family was it? Was it Tom? Who were the men pursuing him? Why were they hunting him? These are questions that cannot now be answered. William Porte makes no reference whatever to the incident in his diary which, however, does record the case of a criminal assault on a Lucan merchant two days later: "Thurs., Oct. 16/79 R. B. Orme robbed on Johnny the Bull's side road on his return from London this evening about 8 o'clock p.m. of $87.00. Two men jumped into the wagon, knocked him down, gagged and tied him, and left him so until his team arrived home."

A significant feature of this case is that no one apparently thought of accusing the Donnelly family. Orme was a Protestant.

November was quiet, at least superficially, but December brought tragedy again to the Donnelly family.

On the evening of December 9 Mike Donnelly entered the bar-room of Slaght's Hotel in Waterford, a town in Norfolk

County some seventy miles south-east of Lucan. Mike had finished his day's work as a brakeman on the Canada Southern Railway which ran through Waterford, and planned a quick drink before supper. Another C.S.R. employee was already there—William Lewis, a navvy and former resident of Biddulph Township.

Mike got into a dispute with another occupant of the bar whose name is not mentioned in the surviving records of the case. Apparently Mike was disturbed about the stranger's treatment of a dog. Lewis came up and interfered. Mike promptly whipped off his coat to teach Lewis a lesson. Lewis fled behind the bar and Donnelly followed, pinning his victim with both hands by the coat collar and pushing him into a corner. Then as Mike released one hand to deliver a haymaker, Lewis produced a knife from somewhere on his person and plunged it deep into Mike's groin. Mike at once turned round, walked to the end of the bar and cried out:

"Boys, I am gone!"

Someone caught him before he fell and stretched him out on the floor, where he died within two minutes.

With somewhat astonishing sang-froid Lewis at once went home to his boarding-house, where a constable found him putting away a hearty supper. Two days later an inquest jury found him responsible for the death of Mike Donnelly.

At this stage in the account of the Biddulph feud it will come as no surprise to learn that William Lewis escaped all punishment for his crime. Within the month he was back in Biddulph, no doubt receiving the congratulations of the members of the Vigilance Committee, who could now amend their score against the Donnelly family to read: three down and six to go, for Bob was still in the penitentiary. Within three months Lewis would be bragging in a Port Huron, Michigan, bar that he had watched four other members of the Donnelly family fry in their own juice.

From later evidence it is by no means certain that this man's name was actually William Lewis, although he certainly used this name in Waterford. He later claimed to have been one of the Vigilantes but no such name appears on any of the lists. He was one of the "mystery witnesses" who were to plague the work of the Crown's detectives.

Mike's body was brought back to Biddulph for burial in the family plot in St. Patrick's churchyard. The funeral was held at 11:30 a.m. Friday, December 12. A great many people attended and extended condolences to the family. Porte noted it briefly in his diary. The last sentence of his account has great significance: "A large funeral, the majority Protestants."

Mike left a wife and two children then living in St. Thomas.

The feud was now nearing its gory climax. The Vigilance Committee was growing stronger, more determined and more bloody-minded day by day. They now owned their own constable, Jim Carroll, and their own Justice of the Peace, William Casey. Before the end of the year they added another magistrate, with the appointment of Martin McLoughlin, a member of the inner circle.

There were two deaths in 1879 in the Lucan neighbourhood that did not rate a line, either in the local press or in William Porte's diary. They received no publicity until after the fatal fourth of February, 1880—and then the references are elusive and unsatisfactory. One was the death of Daniel Clark, laid by their enemies at the door of the Donnellys. The other was the burning alive of a man whose name is given as O'Donagan; this was charged to the Vigilantes.

A single newspaper reference to the Clark case states that there was an inquest at which the cause of death was determined to be "excessive drinking and over-exposure." The body was found in Alex Levitt's stable in Lucan. Of the "O'Donogan" case there is no explanation. Considering the Tipperary habit of mutilating surnames it is barely possible that the anonymous writers of the two or three letters dealing with this case meant O'Donohue. John O'Donohue was a good friend of the Donnelly boys. His fate is unknown.

"A Deacent Man"

Shut up your doors . . .
He is attended with a desperate train,
And what they may incense him to, being apt
To have his ear abus'd, wisdom bids fear.

Shakespeare: KING LEAR

ABOUT four o'clock on the morning of January 15, 1880, the barns and stables on the farm of Patrick Ryder, Senior, Lot 16, Concession Seven, Biddulph Township, were burned to the ground with the loss of all their contents, valued according to William Porte at about $4,000.

In spite of the early hour a great many people gathered at the scene. Before the ashes had cooled Pat Ryder was declaring the fire had been set. The Vigilance Committee did not need to ask by whom. Before the sun had set that day warrants had been prepared for the arrest of old Mr. and Mrs. Donnelly.

Until the case of the Thompson cow and the appointment of James Carroll as constable, all the hatred of the Vigilantes had been directed against the Donnelly boys; now it was returning on the old people. James Carroll was doubtless responsible for this. He hated the whole family and on several occasions declared he wanted to see them driven out of the township, root and stock. If those who heard him make these statements are to be believed, he sometimes put it more strongly than that.

Whatever the supposed basis of the charge, the Donnelly boys were not named. They had been attending the wedding of a daughter of Robert Keeffe until a late hour; there were too many witnesses to attest to their presence and provide a strong alibi. The old folks had been home alone with the niece, Bridget. The three could only corroborate each other's story with no independent supporting evidence.

Even so, Carroll knew he was going to have a hard job making out a case against the elder Donnellys. The Ryders and the Donnellys had lived within a few hundred yards of one another for thirty years without any major differences. There was no obvious motive and very little evidence, either true or perjured.

Nevertheless, the warrants were served. Jim seems to have been home but Mrs. Donnelly was staying with her daughter, Mrs. Currie, who was then living at St. Thomas. It is more than likely she had gone there to help Jenny with the care of the widow and the orphaned children of Mike. These sentimental considerations did not of course carry any weight with the saturnine Jim Carroll who went there on the eighteenth to arrest her.

Whether it was because his brave Tipperary heart quailed at the thought of travelling thirty-four miles alone in the company of the redoubtable Mrs. Donnelly or because he feared being compromised by the chunky fifty-six-year-old Johannah, Carroll asked Chief of Police James Fewings of St. Thomas for a policeman to accompany them. The chief obliged with a Constable Sissons and the one-day journey back to Lucan was safely accomplished.

The preliminary hearing took place before the Vigilance Committee's own magistrate, William Casey, at the village of Granton. Previous to Casey's appointment, such hearings had had to be held in Lucan before magistrates known to disapprove of the principles of the Committee. On this occasion, Carroll and Casey apparently agreed they did not have a strong enough case to bear the light of day. The hearing was adjourned without the taking of evidence. It was adjourned three more times. The couple were finally bound over to appear before Casey on the moming of Wednesday, February 4.

It was apparent to both the constable and the magistrate that they did not have a chance of making out a reasonable case against the Donnellys. An assize court grand jury would have thrown it out at first glance if, indeed, it had ever got that far.

The St. Thomas police chief had expressed an interest in the disposition of the charge against Mrs. Donnelly. From the letter Carroll wrote to him on January 30, it is seen that Carroll had lost his interest in the Ryder case and was looking for other fish to fry:

Sir: As regards the arson case against Mr and Mrs Donnelly it will, I fear, fall to the ground. There has been four adjournments already and Wednesday next has been set as the final day. I have made no arrest yet of any of the sons but will I think pretty soon. I will wait no longer for Robert to be caught. I am getting a case against him for arson with some proof which will I hope return Robert to Kingston for a long term of years. I expect in about two weeks to have a case with evidence strong enough to prove that Robert is the man who two years ago burnt out a farmer of this township against whom the Donnellys had a dreadful spite. You will excuse me for not writing sooner but I wanted the fire case over as I fear it will amount to nothing.

Bob Donnelly, having served his two years, had returned home from Kingston at four o'clock on the morning of January 10. A friendly reference in William Porte's diary records that he "looked well." He remained with his parents only a few days, then travelled to St. Thomas to visit his sister, after which he seems to have gone back to the village of Glencoe where he had connections and the promise of employment. Bob was a man who worked with his hands; of all the sons of James and Johannah Donnelly he was the only illiterate. Pat, the Thorold blacksmith, wrote with some difficulty and dropped the "h" out of words like "thought" and "through" but his syntax was reasonably good. Will wrote with ease in a fine, fluid although often hasty hand. The writing of the others rather obviously betrays great effort, with tongue firmly clenched between the teeth.

What "burning" it was Carroll hoped to pin on Bob Donnelly is not clear; there was a wide variety of incidents to choose from. Aside from this letter there is no other reference to Bob being a fugitive at this time. His whereabouts were no particular secret.

It must have seemed to some of the more respectable residents of the township that the new constable's time might have been more profitably spent assisting William Hodgins and some of the other county constables in seeking out and apprehending the persons who had robbed and beaten R. B. Orme, the Lucan merchant, in October, or in discovering who had burned out a Mr. Jackson in Lucan in the same month.

Carroll was monumentally uninterested in these cases. No shred of suspicion in either instance pointed to the "right" farm on the Roman Line. In his term of less than five months in office there is no record of him participating in any case that did not concern the Donnelly family.

He did not even attempt to injure the friends of the Donnellys; he merely gave them kindly words of advice. In the witness-box a few months later Jim Feeheley recounted some words that had passed between him and Carroll: "James Carroll told me that the Society was going to put down the Donnellys one way or another. . . . He told me to shun the Donnellys. Carroll said the Donnellys had a bad name and that I would get a bad name if I went with them."

It was later claimed that more had passed between Jim Feeheley and Jim Carroll on this occasion than is here recorded. Before a year had passed the police of two nations were looking for Feeheley to learn the rest of the story. However, the Feeheleys, although related to John Cain, an active member of the Vigilance Committee, were accounted friends of the Donnellys in January, 1880.

The closest friends of the Donnelly family were still the Keeffes, as they had been for more than thirty years. The death that breathed on the necks of the Donnellys in that winter eighty years ago, also breathed on the Keeffes. Like the Donnellys they discovered that their neighbours on the Roman Line had stopped speaking to them.

There was a perceptible change in the atmosphere of the township. The loud-mouthed arguments between the partisans of the Donnellys and the supporters of the Vigilance Committee abruptly stopped as though all mouths had been sealed by a single giant hand. Even the Protestant friends of the Donnellys fell silent. There was no more brawling, no more horseplay.

Over the embattled township the roaring flames of hatred were giving place to the cold silence of death, cunningly and deliberately premeditated. The thirteen men who met in the back room of the Cedar Swamp schoolhouse to draw up the agenda for the day of reckoning alone as yet knew the date of that day.

Pat Breen, acknowledged by all to be the president of the Vigilance Committee, may not have been in the chair at the most fatal of all their meetings. According to John Cain, next neighbour to the south of the elder Donnellys, Martin McLoughlin had assumed the chair at the time of the meeting about Ryan's threshing. From that time on, his would seem to have been the dominant personality. This man was no idle brawler. He was a respectable, well-to-do farmer of quiet disposition and retiring habits. He had much more to lose than most of the other members of the Committee. It is difficult to understand what real or fancied insult or injury at the hands of the Donnellys could have driven him into such an association. Whatever the cause, he was now well and thoroughly embroiled.

With the passing of the leadership into the hands of the hot-blooded Jim Carroll and the cool-headed Martin McLoughlin a murderous issue could momentarily be expected. Most of the rest of the Committee were blowhards and bully-boys. Without a firm hand to guide them with a calculated purpose they were men of straw, as Will Donnelly had proved with insulting ease. Carroll and McLoughlin provided the stiffening for their backbones.

Will Donnelly seems to have been honestly puzzled at the change in Martin McLoughlin. In a later statement he said of him:

> I was the best of friends with Martin McLoughlin until he joined the Society. I have nothing to say against the man. I always thought he was a deacent man and I think the public did also. . . . I spoke to him at Morley's funeral and he would not answer me. . . . I met him at the gate when I was at Morley's; he was in his waggon, some ladies were in it with him. I was out of my buggy passing him by. I said "Good day, Mr McLoughlin." He did not answer. I didn't attribute his not answering me to his being engaged; he was looking straight at me.

From the time of the Ryan threshing case in the early fall of 1879, McLoughlin was in the forefront of the Committee's activities. He was at the elder Donnellys in the abortive search for the Thompson cow; he was at Will's place on the same errand; he was the man who threatened Sutherby and he was a signatory of the petition for Carroll's appointment. He later survived two trials for murder and was probably the last of the Vigilance Committee to die, a sage, respected elder of the township. The ways of an Irish vendetta are strange, but no stranger or more devious than the mind of a man, especially a man like Martin McLoughlin.

The first day of February was a Sunday and the faithful streamed down the Roman Line in their wagons and buggies to attend mass at St. Patrick's Church. In the pulpit Father John

Connolly again spoke out sternly against the depredations and the wrong-doings being committed in his parish, and expressed the hope that the malefactors might be brought to justice and so reformed. In the congregation at least forty guilty hearts echoed "Amen" and at least forty grim-set lips silently translated the priest's word "malefactor" into the words they truly thought he meant:

"The Donnellys."

Again neither priest nor congregation would admit the family's name was actually used, but several of the parishioners afterwards were sure that the priest's meaning was clear to them.

A Toronto *Globe* newspaper reporter was later to make a monstrous claim: that Father Connolly was a member of the inner circle of the Vigilance Committee and, further, that he absolved them of guilt before they went out on their work of murder on the night of February 3. This is almost certainly false in all particulars. It is, however, more than possible that some of the Committee attended the confessional that week-end, cleansing their souls of minor offences before committing a greater. Rumour and especially Protestant-inspired rumour could easily have transmuted this simple fact into monstrous fancy. It is worth repeating that *The Globe* at this time was an acknowledged organ of the Orange Order.

Afterwards the parishioners dispersed to their homes in unusual silence and decorum. The rest of the day was spent quietly. If there was talk of the Donnellys, it was hushed and secret. Neither the old folks nor the three boys, Tom, John and Will, had been there since Father Connolly refused to receive John's confession.

When the clocks struck twelve that night behind the tightly-closed windows of the homes on the Roman Line, four of the surviving eight members of the Donnelly family and the niece, Bridget, had forty-eight hours to live.

The Last Night

But ne'er a word would ane o' them speak,
For barring of the door.

Ballad: GET UP AND BAR THE DOOR

IT was the morning of February 3, 1880. The weather was clear and cold with a hint of snow in the air although there was very little on the ground.

The lamps were lit early as the farmers of Biddulph Township bustled about their morning chores. Although Jim Carroll had no stock to feed he, too, was up early; he had a big day ahead of him. He was living at the home of his uncle, Jim Maher, Senior, one and one-quarter miles north of the Donnelly homestead. He and his younger brother, William, usually stayed there, paying for their keep by performing odd jobs about the farm. Neither brother owned any property.

Before leaving his bedroom Jim tucked into his hip pocket a shiny pair of handcuffs he had borrowed from Constable William Hodgins. It was necessary for him to take them with him. He did not intend to return to the Maher place that night. This would not have surprised Mr. and Mrs. Maher, for Jim Carroll frequently spent the night elsewhere.

The elder Maher and his son, James, Junior, were members of the Vigilance Committee, and Mrs. Maher seems to have known more about the Committee's activities than most of the wives of the Vigilantes.

A mile and a quarter to the south Johannah Donnelly fixed breakfast for a diminishing family circle with the help of Bridget, the Tipperary niece. We do not know much about Bridget. We do not know what she looked like, nor what she thought of her new home. The land and its customs must indeed have been strange to her, but she would have been quite familiar with the transplanted Tipperary feuds and family hatreds.

Not that the talk round the breakfast table would have been about such things. The Donnellys, in the sanctity of their own home, seem to have been cheerful people, much given to horseplay and rough-and-ready chaffing. Tom's sense of humour was somewhat primitive and at this time more than a little strained, thanks to the interminable Ryan robbery case. John was his usual ebullient self, his jaunty grin coming and going like the sun on an April day. John loved life; not even the feud could dull his joy in each day's coming.

Elsewhere on the Roman Line children were being fed and prepared for school. Depending on the location of their parents' homes, some went to the Donnelly schoolhouse, others to the Cedar Swamp schoolhouse where the three R's were taught in the front room by daylight, and murder in the back room by night.

Some said there was to be a meeting at the schoolhouse that night; others said it had already been held and the plans laid. Probably at least one member of every household on the Roman Line between St. Patrick's church and the "town line" dividing Usborne and Biddulph Townships, knew what those plans were, except the Donnellys and the Keeffes. Even the intended sacrificial victims seem to have had a premonition of evil which they hesitated to voice.

Pat Ryder, whose barns had been burned, knew about the plans and so did his two sons, as well as their relatives, John Ryder and Dan Ryder. Three Heenans knew—Dennis, Mike and John. Three Ryans had knowledge—Ed, John and "Little Johnny." There were a couple of Quigleys—John and Pat; there was a brace of Tooheys—James, Senior, and Ted. Pat Breen, the Vigilance Committee president, knew and so did James

Kelly, who claimed the Donnelly boys often rode his horses to exhaustion by night.

Sam Everett, the former constable who stayed on in Lucan despite Postmaster Porte's efforts to drive him out, was later to claim that William Casey knew—Casey, the new J.P. who lived midway between the Donnellys and the Mahers on the Roman Line. Everett's deadly little page of notes named others who had foreknowledge: John Dorsey, John Bruin and John Lamphier, Mike Madigan, Mike Blake and Mike Carroll, James Harrigan, John Thompson and Pat Dewan.

No one knows what most of these worthy scions of Munster were doing that frosty morning. We do, however, have a pretty clear idea of what one of their intended victims was about. After Johannah and Bridget cleared the breakfast dishes away old Jim Donnelly settled down at the table for a difficult piece of work—the composition of a letter to Edmund Meredith, a London barrister. The family's former legal counsellor, David Glass, had departed for the Canadian West to add fresh honours and glory to an already distinguished career. The old man, unaware that Carroll and Casey had virtually given up hope of pinning the Ryder arson charge on him, wanted Meredith to undertake the defence of himself and Johannah. It was the last time Jim ever set his name to a document. The letter as later published in *The St. Marys Argus* is reproduced below:

February 3rd 1880

Mr Meredith:

SIR,—On the 15th of last month Pat Ryder's barns were burned. All the vigilance committee at once pointed to my family as the ones that done it. Ryder found out that all my boys were at a wedding that night. He at once arrested me on suspicion and also sent a constable after my wife to St Thomas. The trial has been postponed four different times and although we are ready for our trial at any time, they examined a lot of witnesses but can't find anything against us. Ryder swore that we lived neighbours to each other for thirty years and never had any difference, and had no reason for arresting us only that we are blamed for everything. The presiding magistrates are old Grant and a newly-made one William Casey, who is married to Ryder's cousin. They are using us worse than mad dogs. Mr McDermid is attending on our behalf, and says there is a good chance against Ryder for damages. They had the first trial in Lucan, and then adjourned to Granton simply to advertise us. We have agreed to appear tomorrow again, and I am informed they are going to send us for trial without a tittle of evidence. If so, I will telegraph you when we start for London, to meet us at the City Hotel and get us bailed to take our trial before the judge and I want you to handle the case on our behalf, and if there is any chance for damages I want you to attack them at once, as they will never let us alone until some of them are made an example of. There is not the slightest cause for our arrest, and it seems hard to see a man and woman over sixty years of age dragged around as laughing stocks.

Yours truly
JAMES DONNELLY, SENIOR

It probably took Jim the better part of the morning to compose this letter. He was in his sixty-fifth year, an age which in the nineteenth century was considered old, and he had long been afflicted by rheumatism in his joints. The picture the couple's enemies present for our consideration, that of the aged Jim and his Johannah hirpling across the winter-locked fields at four in the morning to set fire to the barns and stables of a neighbour with whom they had no differences, is ludicrous in the extreme and not for an instant to be believed.

After the letter-writing exercise Jim had his noon meal, which both town and country folk called "dinner" in those days, and then had a rest. Later in the afternoon he got Tom to get out the horse and wagon and they went into Lucan to mail the letter, do some shopping and arrange for little Johnny O'Connor to look after the cattle while they went the next day to their trial at Granton.

A Protestant wayfarer was abroad that day on the Roman Line, blissfully unaware that he was exemplifying in a particularly macabre manner one-half of a popular adage. He was John Robinson Armitage, the township tax collector. As he slowly worked his way north on the Line, receiving a reluctant tribute here, a fervent promise there, he might have reflected that on the Roman Line that day nothing was certain but death and taxes—if he had known what those houses concealed.

However, he did not. He had planned his day carefully. Nightfall would find him at the Donnelly homestead, where he had often stayed before and where he anticipated the usual pleasant hospitality to which he had become gratefully accustomed.

It is worth pausing here to reflect. In a township where robbery, rapine, arson and murder were common aspects of the community's life, an official in the habit of carrying with him temptingly large sums of money elected to bed with a family whom neighbours accused of every crime on the calendar. Either the neighbours were wrong or John Robinson Armitage was wrong.

Of course, it must be borne in mind that John Robinson Armitage was a Protestant.

Three miles away at Whalen's Corners, Will Donnelly may have been discussing with his wife, Nora, the big dance that was to be held that night. In spite of his crippled foot Will loved dancing almost as much as he enjoyed playing the fiddle. Nora does not seem to have shared his enthusiasms.

Like many persons who are hard of hearing she was inclined to withdraw within herself, to shut people out as she fancied they shut her out.

Will and Nora were in many ways an oddly matched couple. While there seems to have been a good degree of rather off-hand affection between them, their marriage could not have been termed a love-match. Nora was as phlegmatic as Will was effervescent. To some extent at least her marriage had alienated her from her family. Although her parents and some members of her family continued on almost aggressively good terms with the Donnellys, her brother, John, cherished a corrosive hatred for the whole tribe and for Will in particular. In consequence, Will had taken to avoiding the home of the elder Kennedys to "try and keep peace in the family," as he put it. Because of John Kennedy's enmity as well as the fact that many of Nora's friends and relatives were members of the anti-Donnelly faction, her husband's friends never entirely accepted or trusted her. In the witness-box later she implied the same thing of her husband: "I have been married to my husband for over five years and know his peculiarities and I know that if he didn't want to tell me anything there would be no use asking him."

In the result, Will decided to go to the dance. It is not clear whether Nora attended or not. The chances are she did not. Will put out a revolver to take with him. Being a Donnelly and being abroad after nightfall was risky.

The various residents of the village and the township passed the afternoon of February 3 in ways best known to themselves. Jim Donnelly mailed his letter, made a few small purchases in the village and then called for Johnny O'Connor.

Few people spoke to old Jim or his son Tom, but many a sharp eye noted their movements carefully. From behind the window curtains William Thompson saw them drive past his farm, eighty rods from the Donnelly homestead. He observed that Tom was driving and that he was driving rather rapidly considering the rutted condition of the road. He remarked sourly to someone in the house that the Donnellys "must have liquor in them."

The "someone" may have been Jim Carroll, who had decided to spend the night with the Thompsons for unstated reasons.

John Robinson Armitage reached the home of John Cain, the next farm south of the Donnelly homestead, near sundown. He collected Cain's taxes and announced that he planned to spend the night with the Donnellys. Cain protested and invited Armitage to stay with him instead. Armitage reaffirmed his intention and then Cain said an odd thing, which is recalled in an Armitage family tradition in these words:

> When he started to take his departure . . . the old man refused to allow him to depart. Cain refused any explanation other than "Your grandfather John Armitage, helped my father out of a tight hole in Ireland, and his grandson must accept my hospitality tonight!"

There is magnificent irony in this incident. Through the intervention of a Tipperary Roman Catholic, a Tipperary Protestant was saved from sharing the fate of a Tipperary Roman Catholic family whose greatest sin was numbering too many Protestants among its friends.

The dance broke up early. Tempers were raw and nerves tense. Miss Murphy, the red-headed school teacher, had a dance with Will Donnelly, to everyone's surprise and consternation. When dancing with him she noticed a bulge in his jacket pocket. She asked him what it was and he told her it was a revolver. She drew him to one side and asked him to promise her there would be no incident to spoil the dance. Gently he assured the teacher there would be no trouble that night, and they finished the dance.

Afterwards some of the young men lingered at front gates and cross-roads in the frosty starlight. Jim Feeheley went to call at the Donnelly homestead. He stayed for a while in the kitchen talking to Tom. He heard the old man talking to someone in the downstairs bedroom but apparently assumed it was John or one of the other members of the family. He did not know about Johnny O'Connor. Feeheley was wearing an overcoat when he arrived. After a while he got up to go. He said he was going to pay a call on one of the Ryders up the road a piece. He asked permission to leave the overcoat and call back for it later. It was so agreed. In case he should be late, the door was to be left on the latch so there would be no need to wake the family. Then he went away.

Nobody knows where Bill Feeheley was at this time but Sam Everett listed him among the forty who were abroad later.

Tom and Jim Keeffe took their time going home too. They stood in front of a Roman Line farm gate for some time chatting. It was after nine o'clock when they saw a man riding towards them with something wrapped in white, half-concealed, by his side. They spoke but he did not answer.

"The faction is abroad tonight," Tom Keeffe said to Jim Keeffe.

There was little conversation after that. The young men went home to bed.

That night Tom Keeffe slept with an axe beside him.

A Night's Work

Fire and fleet and candlelight,
And Christ receive your soul.

OLD BALLAD

THE work of murder began shortly after midnight.

Entry to the Donnelly home presented no problem. The door had been left on the latch for Jim Feeheley.

It appears that the man identified by Johnny O'Connor as Constable James Carroll entered first, alone. The rest of the Vigilantes waited outside.

Carroll found a lamp and lit it. He may first have gone to Tom Donnelly's room, wakened him and placed a pair of handcuffs on his wrists. This is conjecture, but in view of the timing of events it seems probable. His next move was witnessed.

Carrying the lamp, he entered the bedroom off the kitchen to wake the old man. There was an exchange of words between them which wakened the O'Connor lad. He heard only the tail-end of the conversation, but what he heard makes it easy to reconstruct the unrecorded part. It must have begun with the usual Biddulph gambit about having a warrant for arrest.

At this stage Jim Donnelly seems to have had no inkling of what was to come. He was irritated at being awakened, but apparently assumed the visit to be a legitimate legal call. As he struggled into his trousers under the eyes of the intruder he growled:

"What charge have you got against me now?"

"I've got another charge against you," the visitor said; then, apparently convinced that the old man suspected nothing, he went into the kitchen while Donnelly finished putting on his boots. Johnny heard him walking back and forth there, whistling. He seemed still to be alone.

A moment or two later Jim Donnelly went into the kitchen and Johnny O'Connor heard him exclaim:

"Tom! Are you handcuffed?"

Tom Donnelly's voice answered:

"Yes. He thinks he's smart."

The old man immediately returned to the bedroom to get his coat. Carroll may have suspected he was after a weapon; in any case he followed him with the lamp.

The O'Connor boy was using Donnelly's coat as a pillow. He dragged it from under his head and offered it to his host.

"It's here," he said.

If we are to believe Johnny's evidence, this by-play took place in full view of the Vigilante leader. It makes Johnny's later escape from that house of death very remarkable indeed.

By now Mrs. Donnelly was awake, dressed and in the kitchen. Her first concern was a housewifely one. Going to the door of her bedroom she called out:

"Bridget! Get up and light the fire!"

Jim's niece had apparently been wakened by the voices. She came from the bedroom immediately. Johnny heard her lifting off the stove lids.

There was a murmur of voices in the kitchen. Then Tom spoke:

"All right. Now read your warrant."

"There's lots of time for that," the constable said.

At that point, someone shouted. It was the signal. The outside door burst open and the Vigilantes entered.

The rest is utter confusion.

Johnny O'Connor said that when the men poured into the house, Bridget Donnelly raced up the stairs, and he after her.

When she reached the top, she closed the door in his face. He ran back down the stairs, dived under the bed in the old man's room and hid behind a laundry basket.

While this was going on, the Donnellys were being assaulted. Johnny says the Vigilantes were "hammering them with sticks." It is impossible to say for certain who died first, or who last. However, the two old people were probably dead when the Vigilantes dragged Bridget down the stairs and killed her.

Tom Donnelly gave them the most trouble. Beaten, battered and bleeding, he broke away from his captors and ran outside. The blood draining from many wounds created a pool that was still visible in the snow near the house the following morning. With his hands manacled, he was no match for his attackers. They dragged him back into the kitchen and threw him on the floor.

A voice said:

"Hit him with a spade and break his skull open."

Johnny did not see the blow fall. Local legend says the spade decapitated its victim, and that until the end of his days one of the Vigilantes was known by the nickname "Spadey."

Nothing was now to be heard except the heavy breathing of the murderers. Some of them came to Jim Donnelly's bedroom, poured kerosene on the bed and set it afire. Then they all left.

Some moments later Johnny crawled out of his hiding-place. As he fled from the burning bedstead he inadvertently stepped on the body of Mrs. Donnelly. Another of the victims was still breathing. He saw also the body of Tom Donnelly and near it, something that "looked like a dog's head." He did not see the body of Bridget.

A few moments later he was seeking refuge at the home of Pat Whelan.

The Donnelly homestead was a substantial structure. The flames of its burning must have been visible for a considerable distance in all directions. When Pat Ryder's barns burned on January 10, people came from all points of the compass to see the fire. Nobody visited the pyre of James, Johannah, Tom and Bridget Donnelly in the early morning hours of February 4, 1880, except Pat Whelan and his sons.

They would not have gone either had it not been for the unexpected presence and unplanned escape of little Johnny O'Connor.

II

When the murderers had finished at the Donnelly homestead they made their way to Will Donnelly's house at Whalen's Corners, three and a half miles distant.

Some of the Vigilantes may have defected before they got there. There were not as many engaged in the work at Will's home.

They could not have known of Will Donnelly's two guests— his brother John, and Martin Hogan. Hogan, John and Will had talked late. They had been asleep only a little over an hour when the Vigilantes arrived, at a quarter past two.

The murderers went first to the stable where Will's prize stallion was bedded. In one of the most savage acts of a night of unmitigated horror, they beat the poor animal with clubs, apparently in the hope that its screams would bring Will from the house. When this failed of its object, some of them began pounding on Will's door and shouting "Fire!" while others prepared their weapons for the ambush.

Inside the house it was John Donnelly who wakened first. He roused Will and then went to the door to investigate the racket. When he opened it there were two shots—one from a shotgun, the other from a rifle—at point-blank range. He fell back into the house and died within five minutes.

Satisfied that they had killed Will Donnelly, the Vigilantes left after firing a triumphant volley of shots into the air. According to some witnesses they intended one more call that night—at the home of Jim Keeffe. They left clear evidence in the snow that they had started in that direction, had hesitated and then dispersed to their homes.

After five murders, their blood lust had been sated.

Unfortunately for them, they had left two living witnesses to the night's work. Johnny O'Connor had by now already told his story to the Whelan family. Will Donnelly was keeping his own counsel.

Ashes to Ashes

. . . and after the fire, a still, small voice.

I KINGS xix. 12

THE commission of the crimes had been accompanied by a considerable amount of noise and violent commotion. At the home of the elder Donnellys there had been screams, shouts, and cries. Furthermore, the flames of the burning house were visible for at least three miles. At Whalen's Corners a stallion had been clubbed half to death; there had been shouts of fire and much talking. At least eight shots were fired.

Both houses were located in well-populated areas. The distances to the nearest buildings from the Donnelly homestead were measured in rods; at Whalen's Corners houses adjacent to that occupied by Will Donnelly were only a matter of feet away.

Nevertheless, only the Whelans on the Roman Line and William Blackwell, Will Donnelly's next neighbour at Whalen's Corners, ever admitted to having heard or observed anything out of the ordinary. Their admissions were made with the utmost reluctance and only in the face of circumstances that made denial impossible.

The Whelans claimed to have had no knowledge of the events of the night until awakened by Johnny O'Connor. Blackwell admitted to having been aroused by the sound of the shots at Will Donnelly's house, no more than twenty-five feet distant. He reckoned the number at eight, some of them revolver shots. He got up and went to the window and saw in the sky the reflection of the burning Donnelly homestead. William Blackwell was thus the first person aside from the murderers themselves to have knowledge of both incidents.

His reaction was typical of the good citizens of Biddulph Township. He partially dressed himself and then sat down in a chair to have a smoke and presumably to cogitate on what he had seen and heard. The "smoke" was a long one; he was still sitting in his chair more than four hours later when Will Donnelly, lantern in hand, came to rap on his door.

He was later questioned on the witness stand about his inactivity; he gave a typical Biddulph answer: "I did not know but some of the shots might come into my house. I thought the Constables and Donnelly were shooting at each other; that they might be making an arrest, and whoever it was, I did not want to have anything to do with it."

When he admitted Will Donnelly into his house the conversation was laconic and cryptic, in the Blackwell account at least: "In the morning before daylight William Donnelly came to my place and said they shot his brother Jack. I said who done it and he said they done it."

Donnelly wanted Blackwell to go back to his place with him at once. Blackwell insisted on waiting until full daylight. They then went first to the stable where they found a number of footprints in the snow, the door unbarred and the stallion beaten. Around the kitchen door there were a great many more footprints and by the gate still another group.

In the house Nora Donnelly was going through the motions of making breakfast. Martin Hogan was making himself as small as possible on a chair in a corner of the kitchen. John's body lay on the floor, the dirty piece of holy candle still clutched in the dead hands.

Will had not been idle. He showed Blackwell some carefully-prepared exhibits. There was a splinter of wood torn from the door frame by the shotgun blast which John had received full in the throat and upper chest; a rifle bullet which had entered John's groin, passed through his body and lodged itself in the wall opposite the door; and a piece of bloodied paper which had apparently been used as a wad in the shotgun. All three exhibits were placed in envelopes and the bullet marked for later identification in the presence of this witness, whom Will Donnelly had probably brought to the house for that purpose.

Will then saddled John's pony and rode to James Keeffe's place. On the way he traced the trail of footprints to and from Whalen's Corners. He noted that one set went half-way to Keeffe's and then turned back on itself. From this circumstance he assumed that the murderers had intended a call on Keeffe as well, but for some reason had not gone through with it.

After giving Keeffe certain instructions, Will returned to Whalen's Corners. Either from Keeffe or a near neighbour he heard for the first time of the murders at the homestead. No one has recorded his reaction. He probably expected the news.

By sunrise nothing was left of the Donnelly homestead above ground level. The cruelly-beaten, charred and dismembered bodies of Jim, Johannah, Tom and Bridget Donnelly lay sprawled among the potato bags in the cellar. A few feet from the threshold of the kitchen door a pool of coagulated blood stained the freshly fallen snow. Now and then a vagrant breeze stirred little pockets of embers into fitful flames.

The Whelans returned to the scene at nine o'clock and there met Jim Keeffe and a man named Walker from Whalen's Corners. About half an hour later Keeffe rode into Lucan and at the office of the local coroner, Dr. Thomas Hossack, swore out the necessary information for the holding of two inquests.

The news spread quickly through Lucan. Dr. Hossack wired the authorities in London, and someone else, probably William Porte, notified the newspapers. Towards noon Lambert Payne, a young reporter from *The London Free Press,* arrived and went directly to the Donnelly homestead. He was the first of the army of newsmen who descended on the village in the next few days. Between February 5 and March 4, 1880, William Porte filed 90,937 words of telegraph copy for them.

Authentic information was hard to come by that day. The people of Lucan and Biddulph Township were stunned by the enormity of the tragedy. The friends of the murdered family were afraid to talk—the Vigilance Committee's list might still be open. The murderers, of course, dared not talk. Their friends were another matter. They were ready and willing to talk, and did.

By evening enough copy had been wrung out of the anti-Donnelly faction to provide material for three full columns on the front page of the Toronto *Mail* for the following day. The story was heavily biased in favour of the Vigilance Committee. There was no mention of a feud. The emphasis was on the lawless Donnellys, the killing of Farrell, the "volunteers" who had to be called out to check the family's depredations, and the strong-minded mother "taunting her boys with their inferiority to their father who had killed his man."

In these first stories the pattern was set for all subsequent popular accounts. There was reason for it then. The Committee was still in existence, and it had proved its power. The only safe stand was to repeat the "party line." Those who knew better kept silence through fear, and their silence was accepted as corroboration of the "official" story.

In the afternoon, while Payne and other reporters were questioning the villagers, Dr. Hossack empanelled a jury and took them to the scene of the tragedy. Towards evening the body of John Donnelly was brought in from Whalen's Corners by two constables and taken to the home of Michael O'Connor, father of little Johnny. As yet, only Mr. and Mrs. Pat Whelan and two London city constables knew that Johnny O'Connor had been an eyewitness to the murders at the homestead.

The inquest opened in the town hall at 7 p.m. The county authorities had assigned the London police chief, W.T.T. Williams, and two detectives to assist the coroner. The first witness was John Whelan, elder son of Patrick and also a resident of the Roman Line. He was awakened about 2 a.m. by his child, looked out of his window and saw "a light" at the Donnellys. Later his father came to tell him there was a fire. According to his testimony it was half an hour later before he joined his father at the Donnelly homestead. The heat was too intense for them to attempt entry. The front door was locked, the kitchen door unlocked. Around the latter were many footprints and a pool of blood.

Pat Whelan was the next witness. His opening words created a sensation:

> At about half past one o'clock this morning young O'Connor came to my door crying and bawling, saying he was froze. He was barefooted, no hat, and had his coat under his arm. I got up and let him in. I asked him his name and he said he was O'Connor. I asked him what was the matter and he said the Donnellys was killed. James Donnelly was called up. He said he saw them tying James Donnelly.

This was the first public intimation that there had been an eyewitness to the killings. The rest of his evidence merely corroborated that given by his son. The third witness was Joseph, the Whelan boy who lived at home. He had nothing new to add. Neither Mrs. Whelan nor Johnny O'Connor was asked to testify at this time.

After Joe Whelan had given his evidence the coroner, his police attendants, the jury and the spectators moved to the O'Connor home to view the body of John Donnelly. The Toronto *Mail* reporter described the scene in these words:

> On entering the place, a low ceilinged log house in the village, situated near the G.T.R. track, the body was found to be laid out in the principal room of the house. The same clothing in which he appeared at the door when he was shot down still covered the body, which was placed in a coffin. It presented a sickening appearance. The face was covered with blood, while the wounds which caused death were still clotted with gore. After the jury had made their inspection they retired, passing through the main room of the house, which was crowded with friends and relatives, who had come to wake the body. One of the jurymen observed the brother of the murdered man, Wm. Donnelly, to whom he remarked, "This is a bad job, Bill." To this William replied, "I guess I will live through the circus."

Back at the town hall Coroner Hossack told the jury the inquest was adjourned for one week, to give the detectives "time to work up the case." They were informed that the police had information which would lead to the arrest of "a number of persons." They were further enjoined to keep their own counsel and to assist in bringing the guilty parties to justice.

Meanwhile, at the O'Connor home, Dr. C. W. Flock was performing the autopsy on the body of John Donnelly. Examination showed either wound would have caused death. The more serious of the two, however, was caused by a rifle shot in the right groin. The bullet was thought to come from a Minie rifle. The Toronto *Mail* reporter noted in passing that such a rifle had been stolen from the militia armoury in Lucan not long before. Embedded in this wound was another piece of paper apparently used as a wad for the charge. The paper proved to be from a page of *The Catholic Record,* a religious journal published in London, Ontario.

Will Donnelly was present at the autopsy. He was still in a state of shock. The Victorian reporters, unacquainted with such modern subtleties as emotional trauma, merely remarked on his "stony composure." The needful tears did not come until Dr. Flock opened the breast, removed the heart and commented on its exceptional size. Will choked, turned aside and through his sobs cried out:

"Oh God! This is more than flesh and blood can endure!"

After the post-mortem Will and Chief Williams asked permission of Michael O'Connor to speak to young Johnny. Under pressure the boy was produced but refused to answer any questions. It appeared he had already told his story to two constables who had warned him not to repeat it to anyone else. The precautions were considered necessary for it was the general feeling that the lad's life was in danger.

So was Will Donnelly's for that matter, but he was prepared to talk.

At McLean's Hotel in Lucan he told the chief what had happened at Whalen's Corners. It was a story he was called upon to repeat many times in the months that followed. Like the story told by the other eyewitness, Johnny O'Connor, it never differed except in minor detail.

He said that he had had three visitors the previous night—James Keeffe, Martin Hogan, and his brother, John Donnelly. Keeffe left at eleven o'clock and Will's wife, Nora, retired soon after. Keeffe, John and Will had sat up much later than usual, discussing the Vigilance Committee. Will and John pressed Hogan to stay for the night and Will had eventually conducted them to a cold upstairs bedroom. He threw a buffalo robe over them for greater warmth.

Fate had decreed that Nora Donnelly should sleep on the outside of their double bed that night instead of her usual position next the window. She had refused to move from her warm spot and Will had clambered into bed over her.

Will said that he was awakened from a deep sleep about two-fifteen by his brother John's voice. John was asking who was at the door "hollowing fire!" John passed through the room into the kitchen and opened the outside door. There immediately followed two loud reports. One shot was so close that the acrid-smelling powder blew right into the bedroom.

Over the thunder of the shots John cried out:

"Will! Will! I'm shot and may the Lord have mercy on my soul!"

There was a crash as John fell to the floor and then, from the head of Will's bed, the voice of Martin Hogan spoke out of the darkness:

"It's you they want. Lie quiet or we'll all be killed!"

Now came the critical point in Will's testimony.

He said he then sat up in bed and cautiously pulled back one corner of the blind covering the window. It was a clear, cold starlit night. Near the window he recognized Nora's brother, John Kennedy. Farther off were James Carroll and James Ryder. Near the front gate were three men he thought he recognized as James Carroll's brother, William, Patrick Ryder, Junior, and Michael Heenan.

Will was positive as to his identification of Kennedy, Carroll and Jim Ryder. He could not swear to his identification of the three by the gate.

There was talk among the group outside but Will could swear to only two statements. Kennedy said:

"Brother-in-law is easy at last."

Jim Carroll said:

"What next?"

One thing more he could swear to—the voice that cried "Fire!" several times was that of Martin McLoughlin.

The rest of the story was the tale of a long, terror-filled night; of three human beings huddling by the corpse of a fourth waiting for daylight to give them courage.

Chief Williams took copious notes before returning to London at one o'clock on the morning of Thursday, February 5. After a few hours' sleep he secured a number of warrants and returned to Lucan accompanied by Detectives Henry Phair and Enoch Murphy of the London police force.

It was not until then that the charred human remains were brought to Lucan from the Donnelly homestead. Two Lucan constables were sent to the scene with a rough wooden coffin and a quantity of newspaper. In the meantime hordes of the curious had descended on the farm. Souvenir hunters, spiritual ancestors of those who now chip pieces off the Donnelly tombstone in St. Patrick's churchyard, had carried away all but one of the skulls, together with many of the other bones and even some teeth.

In testimony given later Alfred Brown, one of the constables, stated that on his first visit to the ruins on the morning after the fire "there were some of the skulls there. I think there were a portion of all the skulls there at that time." On the second visit part of one skull only remained and it crumbled to dust when handled.

The remains—the four sets carefully separated by sheets of newspaper—were taken at once to Michael O'Connor's home, where Dr. Flock performed a difficult post-mortem examination. So much damage had been done by the fire and the souvenir hunters that Flock could only report that the remains were those of four human beings. He could not tell male from female.

The pitiful relics of Jim, Johannah, Tom and Bridget Donnelly were then released to the remaining members of the family who made funeral arrangements for the following day (Friday). By this time Bob Donnelly and Jenny Currie had come from St. Thomas and Pat Donnelly had arrived from Thorold.

While the Donnelly family was carrying out its sad duties, Chief Williams, his two detectives and four constables were busily executing their warrants on the Roman Line. The first group of warrants were for the arrest of John Kennedy, James Carroll, Martin McLoughlin and James Ryder.

The chief, his two London detectives and Pat Donnelly elected to call at the home of John Kennedy. Kennedy was not there. The visitors made note of certain circumstances:

> There on a rail close by the back door was a pair of wet pants, dark colour tweed pants, not homespun. They were frozen stiff. They had apparently been recently washed. The water was frozen in them and by the end of the side of the dairy there was a pan with a lot of flannel in and a dark liquid, red looking and frozen. . . . Couldn't say what was in the pan. I tipped the trousers off the rail into the snow as if they had fallen down and left them there. Detective Murphy got them next day.

Kennedy was arrested later in the day at the home of Anthony Heenan.

The task of arresting Jim Carroll was assigned to the county constables, Charles Pope and William Hodge. They also had warrants for James Maher, Carroll's uncle, and his son, James, Junior, with whom Carroll normally lived.

The constables, driving a large sleigh, overtook Carroll on the Roman Line about five miles from Lucan near the Maher home. As Pope later told the story:

I stopped him and told him that the chief wanted him to help work up this murder case. . . . He seemed excited; he changed his color. On the way to Lucan we were talking about the murder. He didn't care to make any replies. I pointed to the ruins. He would not look at them. . . . We took him to McLeans Hotel in Lucan. We took him into the sitting room. Hodge and John Larkin were with me. Hodge told him what he wanted with him and what he was arresting him for. He said all right and dropped his head and held out his hands for the cuffs. He seemed frightened and said nothing like as if a shock had come over him. He gave up quietly.

The Mahers were arrested in Lucan about an hour later. When told why they were being arrested, young Maher said nothing. The father said:

"I expected it."

Detective Enoch Murphy arrested Martin McLoughlin at his home. McLoughlin made no resistance and no comment. A rifle was found on top of a cupboard in a front room. Although McLoughlin said it had not been used since August or September of the year previous, Murphy testified that it smelled of powder and gave it as his opinion that it had been recently cleaned, but imperfectly.

Chief Williams himself arrested Jim Ryder. At Ryder's home he found a loaded revolver on top of a barrel. Six chambers of the seven had been recently discharged, there being a quantity of spent powder round the cylinder. By the chief's reckoning "it undoubtedly had been fired off within a few days."

Four more arrests were made that day. Patrick Ryder, Senior, and his son Patrick, John Maher and John Darcy were held on warrants charging them as "accessories to the fact." The elder Ryder was, of course, the farmer whose charge of arson against the Donnellys was to have been heard at Granton on the fatal fourth of February. At the home of John Darcy, County Constables Alfred Brown and S. G. Moore found a gun loaded with buckshot, of which they took possession.

Six of the prisoners were taken to London that night via the London, Huron & Bruce Railway. A great crowd of people gathered at the station to see them brought in. Among them was a reporter from *The London Advertiser* who described the scene:

> On the arrival of the train Detective Murphy stepped on to the platform and motioned to four persons, who were handcuffed two by two, to follow him. County Constable Pope followed up in the rear with his baton drawn, while the detective in front bore a rifle which was found at the house of one of the prisoners (Martin McLoughlin) and which is supposed to be the identical one with which John Donnelly was shot. Police Constable Larkin followed with two other prisoners manacled together, and in this order the procession marched up Richmond Street to the Police Station. An immense throng of people gathered at the station anxious to get a peep at the prisoners. Once inside, however, the doors were shut and the prisoners examined in the usual manner.

The remaining four prisoners arrived later by various conveyances. If the excitement in London was intense, the state of mind of the people of Lucan can only be imagined. The funeral of the Donnellys took place the following day. St. Patrick's Church was packed. There were two coffins in the centre aisle. One contained the body of John Donnelly, clumsily patched-up for the "viewing." (It had earlier been photographed for *The London Advertiser* in this condition.) The second coffin contained the lumps of human charcoal that represented the other murdered members of the family.

Johnny O'Connor was there with his parents and his sister. When John Purtell, the simple-minded farmhand who worked for James Magrath, walked in and took a seat, Johnny whispered excitedly to his sister:

"That's one of them! I recognize him by the cut on his chin."
Will, Bob and Pat Donnelly and their sister, Jenny Currie, were
there in the mourners' pew. The whole Roman Line was there—
and there were enough guilty secrets in the crowd to provide
material for a book three times the size of this one.

It was a moment for high drama—and Father John
Connolly provided it.

What he had to say to his parishioners was not so much a
requiem for the deceased as it was a complaint against the reflection their sudden deaths had cast upon his curacy of souls.
To the eager Victorian reporters it was good stuff. In the main
it followed the party line already well laid down, and they took
notes avidly. However, at the distance of eighty years the priest's
reported remarks seem a trifle specious, a little too self-centred.

He began bravely but after a few sentences burst into tears
and turned his face from his people. After recovering, he went on
to deliver some sound comments on the laws of God and man.
Then he came to the subject that seemed to prey on his mind:

> It may be thought that I was not in friendship with that
> family. I was in friendship with the old people, but of the
> young people I did not know much. Particularly with the old
> woman I was friendly. For two hours she was in my office
> on Christmas eve giving me the history of her whole life
> in Biddulph. She received the sacrament, and the last words
> she spoke to me as she went away were, "Father Connolly, I
> am going to get not only my boys but all the Biddulph boys
> to reform." Here are the consequences. Oh! God of Heaven,
> how terrible!

Here the priest flung himself upon the coffins, crying out:
"Oh God! who would have thought it would come to this!"

The congregation sat in stunned and embarrassed silence.
After a moment the priest rose and several times tried to speak.
At last he said:

"I can't say any more."

At this point Pat Donnelly rose in his pew and said:

"Father Connolly, I would like you to tell the whole matter."

The priest responded to the invitation.

Any hostile feelings towards him, he said, had always come from the younger members of the family, but any trouble he had had with them was "not worth speaking of." William Donnelly had sent him a sharp letter and threatened to drive him from the country, but he was a talented young man. He had never had any hard feelings against any of the family, but "the boys had a hard character."

Then the priest spoke of the Vigilance Committee. He had had nothing to do with that Committee, he had never been at their meetings, but he had had "unbounded faith" in those who were members of it.

"I cannot understand how this has taken place," he said. "I did not believe that there was a man capable of doing anything like that in Biddulph. I believed that there were men who would give a man a clout when half drunk, or waylay him upon the road, but I never thought that they could commit such a butchery as this."

He ended his peroration with fulsome praise for Pat Donnelly whom he found to be "an honest, respectable young man," and with a word or two for John, "who died with a prayer upon his lips." He did not mention his refusal to shrive John a few weeks before his death.

Following high mass, the remaining members of the family visited the presbytery of the church to thank Father Connolly for his kindness. The man from *The London Advertiser* reported: "After a consultation, during which explanations were made to the priest by all of the members, the family left, thoroughly grateful for the kindness, having been reconciled to the Church and to their priest."

Then they were gone, leaving Father John Connolly to reconcile himself with God.

Suspects and Blackfeet

XXVIII

Here's a corpse in the case with a sad swell'd face
And a medical crowner's a queer sort of thing!

R. H. Barham: LAY OF ST. GENGULPHUS

O N Wednesday, February 11, the inquest into the deaths at the Donnelly homestead was resumed in the Lucan town hall. Three witnesses only were heard: Dr. C. W. Flock, who testified as to his post-mortem findings; Alfred Brown, one of the two constables who had brought the remains to Lucan; and Johnny O'Connor.

This was the first time Johnny had told his story in public. It was the moment everyone had been waiting for. The secret of his evidence had been well kept. Had he recognized anyone?

Johnny began by telling of the events of the evening of February 3. He told how Jim and Tom Donnelly had called at the O'Connor house to get him to look after the farm while the family answered Carroll's charges against them at Granton the next day. There were all the small details of the evening—Tom and John putting the horses in the stable, Bridget bringing them apples, supper, John going off to Will's place to borrow his cutter, Johnny helping the old man with the evening chores, then prayers, and bedtime.

Johnny went to bed with the old man, in the bedroom off the kitchen. Just before the boy dropped off to sleep, there was a visitor; he thought it was Jim Feeheley. Then sleep and the rude awakening.

Between 12 and 2 o'clock a.m. a man came into the house to arrest the old man and Jack. He asked where Jack was and the old man said he wasn't in. Then he asked him again and the old man said didn't I tell you he wasn't in. Then the old man told him to hold the light till he dressed himself, then he dressed himself. James Carroll the constable was the man who came in to arrest old Donnelly. I was in bed when Carroll came to arrest old Donnelly. I slept next the wall. Carroll had a candle lighted in his hand when he came in.

To the crowd gathered in the town hall, this seemed like the kiss of death for Jim Carroll. Everyone knew Will Donnelly claimed to have seen him at Whalen's Comers. Now he was doubly damned.

The boyish treble went on to name two more men:

Then I saw Thomas Ryder and John Purtell standing near the same door, the bedroom door. . . . I saw nobody in the Donnelly house when they were being hammered that I could recognize except James Carroll, Thomas Ryder and John Purtell.

After Johnny O'Connor had given his evidence, Dr. Hossack adjourned the inquest for one week. No witnesses were heard with respect to the murder of John Donnelly and that inquest was adjourned for the same period.

Meanwhile the official investigation continued and additional arrests were made. Purtell was taken into custody on Friday the 6th, following Johnny O'Connor's identification of him at the funeral. He cried bitterly, "sobbing like a child," as he left Lucan in charge of Detective Henry Phair. Soon, however, the crying changed to singing, which he kept up all the way to London.

On the same day Detective Enoch Murphy went back to John Kennedy's farm to pick up the suspicious pair of trousers and to check into the mysterious piece of flannel which Chief Williams had noted the day before. Murphy identified it bluntly as a "blood-stained blanket" and queried Mrs. Kennedy and Michael Heenan, whom he found there, as to its present whereabouts. After a search of the house, he found it in an upstairs room. When he questioned the two about it, Heenan said he had taken the blanket and Mrs. Kennedy to Granton that morning to see a Dr. Laing, who had given it as his opinion that the marks were only dye and not blood.

This was a little too thin for Detective Murphy, so he took the blanket, the trousers and Heenan along with him to London. According to a newspaper report, Heenan took the matter of his arrest and the murders very lightly, "expressing his belief in the Missouri and Texas laws as effectual. He also stated that he thought the Donnellys received what they deserved and that no one would be punished for it."

On Saturday Chief Williams concentrated his attack on the home of William Thompson with whom Carroll stayed on the night of February 3, and that of James Maher, Senior, where he normally lived. There were suspicious circumstances at both places. At Thompson's there were indications that the bed Carroll was alleged to have used had not been slept in, but rather rested upon. There were also some blood-spattered pieces of paper between the bed and the wall.

At Maher's it was observed that the room occupied by Carroll was papered with copies of *The Catholic Record*. The chief made an unsuccessful search for a copy of the issue of December 26, 1879, from which a wad had been made for the gun that killed John Donnelly. There were also in the room a number of warrants made out for the arrest of various members of the Donnelly family.

On February 18 a crowd of the curious assembled at the town hall in Lucan for the adjourned inquest, only to be told that, owing to the illness of Dr. Hossack, there would be a further adjournment to the twenty-fourth. The crowd was indignant at being cheated of its entertainment and the constables experienced some difficulty in breaking up the gathering. Some Lucanites said the coroner's ailment was a common one in the Biddulph area and that its name was blue funk.

The Lucan reporter of *The London Free Press* noted a peculiar circumstance. It appears that on this occasion the reporter from the Toronto *Mail* "harangued the jury." We are left to wonder what it was all about.

Owing to the continued illness of the coroner, the inquest was again postponed, this time to March 2. In the meantime the preliminary examination of the accused persons had already begun in the city police court at London before two magistrates, on February 26. The number of those accused of complicity in the crime rose at one time to thirty-three.

When the double inquest resumed, the hearings at London were still taking place and were being voluminously reported by the local press. On March 2 at Lucan many of the same witnesses repeated, and in some cases elaborated, testimony they had given in London. The positive identification of the six most important prisoners by Will Donnelly and Johnny O'Connor was again emphasized.

Nevertheless, the twelve shopkeepers and farmers making up the inquest panel—most of them Protestants, it should be noted—returned an open verdict in both cases, stating that the five deceased had come to their deaths at the hands of "some parties unknown to this jury."

The jurors were severely criticized for their lack of courage— but who is to blame them? The prisoners in the jail at London represented only a small percentage of the total membership of the Vigilance Committee. All the others were at large. Even with all the evidence now available it is difficult fully to appreciate the fear in which this terrorist society was held by all the people of Biddulph Township and indeed by most of the population of Middlesex County.

It was for this reason that the prosecution began early in the case to press for a change of venue for the impending trial of the accused. In the interests of justice it is unfortunate that the application was denied.

The preliminary hearing concluded at London on March 13. Six of the prisoners were committed for trial at the spring assizes—James Carroll, John Kennedy, Martin McLoughlin, James Ryder, Thomas Ryder and John Purtell. The other prisoners were all released.

All through this period the "Biddulph Horror" continued to provide thousands of lines of copy for the newspaper readers of the continent. Some reporters made the village a home away from home. In his diary for Thursday, March 4, William Porte recorded: "J. C. McLean, Globe reporter, left here for good on Clandeboye bus, being here just one month reporting the Donnelly Tragedy."

It was now known that the tragedy was the outcome of a long and bloody feud, although its true nature was still being carefully obscured. The principal points of reference continued to be the killing of Farrell, the stage-coach rivalry, and the establishment of the Vigilance Committee to "put the Donnellys in their places."

With few exceptions the persons interviewed by the press were Roman Catholics, members of the anti-Donnelly, Roman Line faction, and their stories consistently followed the well-worn rut, studiously avoiding any reference to the religious nature of the feud. One of the most popular accounts was that reported in *The London Advertiser* and frequently repeated since. It took the form of a dialogue between a Lucanite and an *Advertiser* reporter:

LUCANITE: If it were known, it will be found that the murderers are the most respectable people in the township, good farmers and honest men, but they had to do it—there was no other way.

REPORTER: Was there no law?

LUCANITE: Law? Well, I'll be—! Law? Where did anybody ever get the best of the Donnellys in law? Why, we never saw them up and get their deserts. The Donnellys had to be killed. They were a bad family, and the only difference between them and a dog was in the shape.

No interviewee was bold enough to point out that the "respectable murderers" had failed in what was generally acknowledged to be their principal task—the elimination of Will Donnelly.

Will and his brother Bob and their families moved into Lucan a day or two after the murders, taking up residence in a house adjacent to Michael O'Connor's home. Pat Donnelly stayed there with them for a few weeks, neglecting his business in Thorold in order to help Will "work up" the case against the prisoners.

The brothers were marked men. The authorities would have been happier if they had agreed to move to London, where it would have been easier to protect them. Will would have none of it. He had not run before; he had no intention of running now. He and his brothers walked the streets of Lucan boldly but warily, armed and prepared instantly to retaliate if violence were offered them.

The first threat came in mid-February, in a letter dated at Port Huron, Michigan, on the fourteenth. It read:

> WILLIAM DONNELLY:
> You and your relatives have been a disgrace and a curse to our country. Your chances are favourable to leave now. If you delay our friends will assist you. So take warning. If your brother Patrick remains at Lucan he will take his chances with our friends for assistance when we think proper.
> Yours truly
> ONE THAT SAW YOUR FATHER
> AND MOTHER FALL

The writer of the letter was almost certainly William Lewis. Lewis was in Port Huron a few days after the murders and boasted in a barbershop there that he had been an eyewitness of the burning of the Donnelly house. *The London Free Press*, which published the report, commented editorially: "It is known that this man Lewis worked at Mr. Hogan's a short time previous to the massacre and was well acquainted with the workings and intentions of the Vigilance Committee."

It might have been added—but was not—that William Lewis was the man who stabbed Mike Donnelly to death in Waterford, Ontario, on December 9, 1879. No reference to this was made then or later.

Once again it becomes difficult to reconcile with the proper ends of justice and the responsibilities of the press, the conspiracy of silence that cloaks all accounts of violence done to the Donnelly family and their friends with the single exception of the final, overwhelming act of villainy and brutality.

Publication of the threatening letter to Will Donnelly unleashed a flood of letters on the subject of the crime. One published in *The London Free Press* on February 21 attacked the Donnellys for their political activities and condemned *The London Advertiser* for supporting them. It also referred to an unlisted crime which the writer apparently attributed to the Donnelly faction:

> Well, did you hear of the murder of Dan Clark, and of the sham inquest held on his body? Do you know who managed that affair and how it was done? Did you make any appeal to Mowat for security for life when Clark was foully murdered in Aleck Lovat's stable at Lucan? . . . Great indignation prevails in Biddulph on account of a reputed member of the Biddulph thieving gang being on the coroner's jury which is to try the prisoners who are now in London jail.

The reference to Attorney-General Mowat was intended as a comment on the prosecution's request for a change of venue for the trial in view of the difficulty of obtaining an impartial jury. The "reputed member of the Biddulph thieving gang" was Michael Crunnican, a Lucan merchant and Justice of the Peace known to be on good terms with the Donnellys.

Now and then a more reasoned voice spoke up, although the writer was usually thickly cloaked in anonymity for personal protection. One such letter, dated at Biddulph on March 8 and signed "Fair Play," appeared in the *Free Press* of the twelfth:

> SIR,—For some time past a good deal has been said about the Donnelly family. They have been blamed by the Biddulphers as perpetrators of many crimes throughout the township. A Vigilance Committee was formed by a few pretended honest settlers as a means of protection from these outrages. But the question is, who needed protection? Well, I think the Donnellys needed protection more than the Vigilance Committee did. . . . A Vigilance man writes to *The Free Press* saying many of them were driven to the poll to vote for Reform government with fear of their barns being burned down by the Donnellys. I think this a shameful excuse for any man of common sense to make. They were not driven by the Donnellys to commit this murder. . . . The Donnellys have not been accused of all the crimes in Biddulph. They were not accused with the burning alive of a man named O'Donogan, nor with the murder of the Englishman on the famous Roman Line. They were not accused with the burning of Andrew Keef's barn and eight horses. They did not entertain the gang who went to cut Mr Coffinger's apple trees. I am taking the liberty of telling the public the kind of people the Vigilance Committee is made up of. It will be remembered in 1876 the Donnellys had a fight in Lucan with John Bawden, John Reid and John Courcey. The Donnellys escaped arrest and the pretended honest settlers of Biddulph came to the rescue, and the Donnellys were not brought to justice that time, simply because the Constables were Orangemen. William Donnelly gave himself up in London afterwards, and when his trial came off those honest men sent their sons to swear him out. The Vigilance Committee declare the Donnellys a terror

to the neighbourhood, but I am safe in saying it is now the reign of terror begins, as those opposed to the Vigilance Committee receive threatening letters. Mr Dennis Carty and his son, James Carty, on the 11th concession of Biddulph, have received several threatening letters, to the effect that if he allows any person to come to his house who is opposed to the Vigilance Committee, he wouldn't be left a beast, as they would be shot down like dogs. . . . There was a fire in Granton on the 7th of this month and a large amount of grain burned—cause of fire unknown. But if the Donnelly family were living today, the Vigilance Committee would have them all arrested for setting it on fire. Jim Carroll would be on the alert.

Some of the references in this letter go back to 1857 and the murder of Richard Brimmacombe. The writer was obviously an old settler with a long memory. It is more than likely that the "O'Donogan" referred to was John O'Donohue, a one-time friend of the Donnellys.

Long before the spring assizes opened at London on April 12, 1880, the case had been tried and re-tried in the columns of the country's newspapers. Virtually every individual in Biddulph Township old enough to talk had been interviewed by a reporter. Sensation piled on sensation. The Toronto *Globe*, arch-organ of the Reform party and the Orange Order, charged that Father John Connolly had cursed the Donnelly family from the pulpit of St. Patrick's Church and strongly implied that the priest had had guilty foreknowledge of the crimes through the confessional.

Father Connolly, through the columns of *The London Free Press*, denied the charge and seized on the opportunity again to refer to the great enmity which Will Donnelly had shown for him. He added that Will had been responsible for a petition to Bishop John Walsh of the Roman Catholic Diocese of London seeking the priest's removal from St. Patrick's parish.

The following day, in an interview by the same paper, Will denied that he had written any such petition. He admitted that, after the affair of the Thompson cow, he had indeed written to the bishop about the state of affairs in Biddulph Township. He also admitted that there had been some criticism of Father Connolly in the letter.

"I told the bishop that Father Connolly had been present at two or three lawsuits against our family, and that I didn't think the courts a fit place for a priest to be," he told the reporter.

The purpose of the letter, he said, had been an appeal against the apparent sanction by the Church of the Vigilance Committee.

"I didn't think that the church allowed a sworn party to exist," he said. "I asked him in the name of God to break up the organization."

This is the full extent of the criticism William Donnelly ever permitted himself officially to level against the priest. In spite of the many circumstances that might have allowed him to make stronger statements and a multitude of temptations to do so, he kept his silence. The remaining years of Father Connolly's life were exceedingly difficult ones. If it had not been for Will Donnelly's respect for the clergy, they would have been very much more difficult.

Biddulph Township continued to swarm with visitors. If one met a stranger on the Roman Line it was an even bet that he was either a reporter or a detective. By mid-April the reporters were beginning to find the pickings a bit thin; the detectives were just getting warmed up.

First of all, there were the Lucan and Biddulph constables, old and new. This was their bailiwick; they claimed to know more about the feud and the Donnellys and the Vigilance Committee than the usurpers from outside. Probably they did, but their knowledge was tinged by factionalism and their techniques were unsophisticated. Nevertheless, they kept at it.

Even Sam Everett, who no longer had a job, was involved.

Then there were the detectives of the London police force, good run-of-the-mill investigators, some with previous experience in murder cases. There were also detectives appointed by the county authorities and others named by the Attorney-General's department. Added to all these were private detectives of varying degrees of proficiency, hired from time to time by the surviving members of the Donnelly family. Finally, there were the three rank amateurs motivated mainly by an enthusiasm for revenge—Will, Bob and Pat Donnelly.

The trial of the prisoners opened at London on April 12 before Mr. Justice Adam Wilson. The Crown was represented by Aemilius (later Sir Aemilius) Irving, Q.C., and the defence by Hugh (later Sir Hugh) MacMahon.

As expected, the Crown immediately requested a change of venue to some other county. Opposing counsel argued the question vehemently for some time. Mr. Justice Wilson finally ruled against the request—a decision later upheld by the court of Queen's Bench in Toronto. Instead, he ordered a postponement of the trial to the fall assizes.

In a blatant display of their power and contempt for the processes of law, the Vigilance Committee or some of its unincarcerated members staged a demonstration in Lucan on the night of April 13, the day following the hearing in London. They set fire to Michael O'Connor's house and burned it to the ground. Fortunately, all the members of the family including young Johnny were being lodged in London by the prudent authorities, who had no intention of losing the Crown's chief witness.

It will be recalled that Will and Bob Donnelly and their families were living in the house next door. Maybe the arsonists hoped the fire would spread. Or perhaps it was intended as a warning. It seems to have been accepted in this sense by Will Donnelly who told Crown Attorney Charles Hutchinson soon afterwards that he had sent his wife and family to stay at her father's house and that it was his practice never "to sleep any two nights in the same house."

A Lucan inquest jury sat for two days on the case, concluded that the fire was incendiary and that it was set "by some persons unknown to this jury." In September Michael O'Connor charged one of the Ryders with complicity in the burning. The case, as usual, was laid over indefinitely and nothing more was heard of it.

Early in May, William Porte received a letter addressed to "The Postmaster, Lucan, Canada." It came from Mrs. D. L. Wilson, of Ballarat, Victoria, Australia, and sought information about the Donnelly murders. Mrs. Wilson represented herself as a sister of the murdered Mrs. Donnelly. She asked for information on behalf of herself and another sister, a Mrs. Jones, widow of a barrister, and a brother, Patrick Magee. All three were apparently well-off and respected residents of their communities.

The Donnelly relatives in Australia were no more isolated from the affairs of Biddulph Township than their Canadian nephews. Pat Donnelly had gone back to his business in Thorold. Will and Bob walked in a core of silence. Their Protestant friends were dominated by fear of the Vigilance Committee; their Roman Catholic friends mostly sought refuge in silence or flight. Jim and Pat Keeffe left Lucan on March 8 for Nebraska, far out of reach of the Vigilantes. Martin Hogan left for parts unknown a few days later. Jim and Bill Feeheley left for Michigan shortly after with, it is said, the good wishes of the Vigilance Committee. All of them had to be dragged back by process of law to give evidence at the trial.

In the first shock of the tragedy and the subsequent arrests, the iron grip of the Vigilance Committee relaxed slightly. A few mouths wagged indiscreetly; by one means or another they were later shut tight. However, thanks to this brief relaxation of vigilance we are permitted two tantalizingly brief glimpses of evidence that incontrovertibly tie the "Biddulph Horror" to the "Tipperary Terror."

One was a fleeting and unsatisfactory reference to "Sheehy's Day" by a garrulous and indiscreet old resident of Biddulph. The other, which also found its way into a brief news paragraph, was a reference to the half-forgotten Tipperary origins of the feud.

It seems that for a time during that spring of 1880 a number of Roman Line residents were in the habit of drawing water from the well of one of them. Among those habitually using the well were some known friends of the Donnellys. One morning the well sprouted a crudely lettered sign:

> NO WATER FOR BLACKFEET

In these two references, plus one or two verbal accounts, the true cause of the Biddulph feud is nakedly revealed. The paucity of evidence is something deliberately contrived by both sides of the dispute. It is the one matter relating to the murders that neither pro- nor anti-Donnelly informants will speak of to this day. Neither arson, nor torture nor murder could ever induce any of them to speak freely on this subject. "Whiteboys versus Blackfeet" was a private feud; no others need apply.

With these facts in mind the problems of the Crown in developing its case against the murderers may be more easily understood. The detectives were beaten before they began. No group of yeomen ever perfected the techniques of evasion as thoroughly as the Munstermen of the Roman Line. When the worst came to the worst a judicious spot of perjury always did the trick, in or out of the witness-box.

Even Will Donnelly was defeated by the combination. Time and again he reported to Charles Hutchinson or Aemilius Irving that he had such-and-such a witness on the point of testifying to the truth, only to have him wriggle away under pressure from another quarter.

The summer months were marked by feverish activity on the part of the prosecution. There is in existence a voluminous mass of correspondence between Will Donnelly and the various members of the prosecution's team. Much of it is cryptic, referring as it does to unrecorded conversations. There are many references to "mystery witnesses" and the efforts of the Crown to run them to earth. None of these leads seems to have worked out well; certainly none of them was used at the trial.

The most dramatic of these wild-goose chases involved the police forces of at least three Canadian and six American cities. A woman in Berlin, Ontario, saw a vagrant drop a paper near the railroad tracks in that city. It turned out to be a torn letter dated at Lucan on August 14 and addressed to someone called "Mike." The letter was signed "Bill" and revealed intimate knowledge of the events of the night on February 3. She turned it over to the police. The parts of the letter that can be deciphered read:

I had a notion to begin with ye are a darn fool to go to try and get money out of McLathlin wife as if wasent hard enouf for her to get along. You had better be after trying to get it out of bill donnely he seems to have lots but Mike sure if you set your foot in London before it is all over you will be arested and get us all in a nise darn fus. bill donnely thinks like everyone here that you are in the state instead of here that night and if you did tell you could only tell on them that is in gal for i sware by the holy Vergin that I never [paper torn] you could not have either. It was that darn Jim carall and McLoughlin and kennedy and X that we sen going in the old donnalys house and you needent get us in to a scrape or yerself for them for all Father connors or all the money in the hole consarn wont hinder them from swinging those to fast.

Jim done it all and ought to. he was so smart he thought that cul conners will be a big man after a while you bet but you better have the duckbillache [duck-bill ache] as well as the duckague [duck ague] if that is what you have for a while longer than come to London or Lucan tramping among the duck [paper torn] can tell yet but will soon. The old fellow is not so bad as that. Now dont make a fool and an ass of yerself because ye have got it in head yer are going to dee divil [indecipherable] but if you want a call from someone ye will turn spout. i send this from London good by and kep good hart. Sure it will soon be all over and ye will be better of then you will if you spout. rite as soon as ye get this. Rite to London next time.

The hunt for the vagrant who dropped the letter continued all through the autumn. Dozens of suspects were rounded up, only to be later released. The identity of the correspondents continued to engage the attention of the prosecution right up to the time of the trial. In mid-October Will Donnelly wrote to Charles Hutchinson:

I have been studying over them letters and know of no one who I supposed was in the States at the time of the murder but a young man named Mike Sullivan who has worked for William Casey but was as we supposed in Michigan at the time of the trouble. He turned up in Lucan at the time of the inquest and was in company with Bill Whalen and a son of Michael Carrol sen. He left at once and has not been in Biddulph sense to my knowledge.

Mike Sullivan was a relative of Ned Sullivan, one of the Vigilantes, who on one occasion was reported to have told Robert Keeffe that "there were not many guns at the murder" and that Will's father and brother Tom "died very soft."

The chase for the elusive "Bill" seems to have ended early in November with a report from Michigan City, Indiana. The police there were holding a man variously known as John, Ed or Charley Teirney, whose description seemed to tally exactly with that given by the Kitchener woman. He had served two years for highway robbery at one stage in his career. No disposition seems ever to have been made of his case and this trail, too, ended in smoke.

Between chasing about the country on leads, good and bad, conferring with the prosecution and eluding the Vigilantes, Will Donnelly also managed that summer to interview an astonishing number of the listed jurymen of Middlesex County. His notes on their character and personal bias or lack of it with respect to the case against the murderers were of great assistance later to the prosecution. If his notes are to be accepted at face value, they strengthen the stand of the Crown in requesting a change of venue for the trial.

Through August and September the discharged Lucan constable, Sam Everett, was employed by Charles Hutchinson on a per diem basis in a desperate effort to unearth additional, trustworthy evidence. Both Dr. Hossack, the coroner, and Will Donnelly advised against using him.

Dr. Hossack felt that Everett would give temporary allegiance to whatever side was employing him and Will Donnelly considered him a "rotten stick" to depend upon, but admitted that even "rotten sticks make good manure sometimes."

In mid-September, enclosed in a letter complaining about the difficulty of gathering evidence in Biddulph, Everett sent Hutchinson a deadly little list of thirty-four names. Against some of the names were brief notations. The list follows:

Denis Henan
Mike Henan
John Henan
James Toohey, Sen.
*   do Harigan*
John Thompson
John McGlochlin
John Ryder
Mike Carrol—he killed the Old Woman
James McGraw
Wm. Casey, J. P.

James Ryder
Dan Ryder
John Quigley
Pat Quigley
Edwd. Ryan
John Ryan
John Cain
Wm. Thompson
James Maher—killed the Old Man
John Dorcey
John Bruin
John Lamphier
Pat Ryder and his two sons
Wm. Feeheley
John Ryan—little Johny
Mike Madigan
Mike Blake
James Kelley
Pat Breen pres. of the Committee
Pat Dewan
Ted Toohey

Along with the prisoners they were all there.

Counting in the six prisoners held in the London jail, this list-adds up to forty names, generally considered to be the number of active members of the Vigilance Committee. The shadow of suspicion had at one time or another touched most of these men. All of them had signed Father Connolly's oath; most of them had signed the petition requesting Jim Carroll's appointment as a constable.

No one now living can vouch for the accuracy of Sam Everett's little list. He may have erred in one or two cases. Certainly there were additional persons with guilty knowledge before or after the fact. However, this little document is probably as close as anyone will ever get to a true and complete list of the persons abroad with murder in their hearts on the night of February 3–4, 1880.

The Trials

A rape! A rape! . . . Yes, you have ravish'd justice;
Forced her to do your Pleasure.

Webster: THE WHITE DEVIL

IF the object in delaying the trial of the six prisoners had been to allow tempers to cool and inflamed passions to subside, the hope was ill-founded. When the fall assizes opened in the old, castle-like Middlesex County courthouse in London in the last week of September, feelings were running even higher than they were in April.

Long before the sessions opened, the dark courtroom with its faded coat of arms dating back to the reign of King William IV was packed and hordes of the disappointed curious were jammed into every inch of the corridors. County constables had great difficulty in quieting the tumult so that proceedings could be conducted with the decorum demanded by British law.

The first day's events were disappointing. They consisted largely of legal technicalities. The prisoners were indicted on charges of murder and arson, and true bills were returned by the grand jury against all of them. Pleas of not guilty were entered on behalf of all the accused. Then the defence asked for and was granted a severance of trials. This meant the accused were to go on trial one by one, rather than collectively.

The Crown chose to put James Carroll on trial first, for obvious reasons. Its case against him was stronger than those against the other five. The opening day of the trial was set for Thursday, October 4, 1880.

Mr. Justice John Douglas Armour, later to become Chief Justice of Ontario, occupied the bench. Aemilius Irving represented the Crown, with the assistance of Charles Hutchinson, county Crown Attorney. Edmund Meredith represented the private prosecution and James Magee represented the people of Ontario. Hugh MacMahon, William R. (later Sir William) Meredith and J. J. Blake appeared for the defence.

The selection of jurymen occupied a considerable time. Will Donnelly sat by Irving, frequently consulting his notes as each name on the jury list was called. Well aware of the problems confronting it in the choice of an impartial jury, the Crown had summoned more than 100 jurymen.

Challenges were frequent, but at last the tale of jurors had been filled, the "twelve good men and true" took their oaths and their seats and the great trial was under way.

Several formal witnesses gave their testimony first. Samuel Peters, a surveyor, testified to the accuracy of various diagrams he had prepared of the scenes of the murders and the buildings in the vicinity. Robert Thompson, a resident of Biddulph, testified that he had built an extension on the house of the elder Donnellys ten years previously, at the same time "framing" the original log structure. J. R. Peel confirmed details regarding the construction of the building and testified as to the accuracy of a model of the building prepared as an exhibit for the Crown.

With these formalities disposed of, the spectators settled down to hear the evidence of the remaining ninety witnesses summoned by the prosecution and the defence. No crime in Canadian history has ever received more thorough press coverage. Most of the evidence given at the trial was already familiar to all through the very full reports given by the newspapers of the proceedings of the inquests and the preliminary hearing, yet everyone followed the repetitive accounts with unflagging interest. A good story bears repeating.

Ann Whelan, wife of Patrick, was called to the stand.

She told again the story of Johnny O'Connor's unceremonious entry on the morning of February 4, the family's unwillingness at first to believe his story, the gradual realization that he was telling the truth, and finally the reluctant decision to investigate. She told of Johnny naming Jim Carroll, Tom Ryder and John Purtell. She admitted she had told the lad to say nothing for fear of reprisals.

Mrs. Whelan was closely questioned as to her knowledge of the Vigilance Committee and its affairs. She added nothing that was not already known.

Pat Whelan repeated his story and gave the same degree of satisfaction with respect to the Committee. His two sons followed faithfully in their father's footsteps.

The anticipated sensation of the trial came on its second day. The first two witnesses were Thomas Keeffe and Robert Keeffe, Junior. The two young men, who were cousins, testified that they had seen Pat Ryder on the Roman Line between nine-thirty and ten o'clock on the night of February 3 with a gun in his hand.

Then the clerk of the court called the name of John O'Connor.

Johnny repeated his story. His evidence was frequently interrupted for clarification of various points such as the exact geography of the house, the type of bed in which he and the elder Donnelly slept, and the exact language used by the persons present that night. He identified the prisoner, James Carroll, as the leader of the men who came to the Donnelly house.

He told of being awakened by the appearance of the prisoner at the door of the bedroom, candle in hand; the brief conversation between Carroll and Donnelly; the old man dressing himself; Johnny producing his coat; the brief conversation between Donnelly and his son Tom in the next room; the outer door bursting open to admit a crowd of men who immediately began "hammering" their victims.

He told of Bridget running upstairs and how he followed her, only to have her shut the door against him. He told of rushing back downstairs and taking refuge under the bed behind a large basket, from which position he witnessed the remaining events of the tragedy.

John Purtell and Tom Ryder were brought into court. Ryder was stolid; Purtell was as white as a sheet. Irving questioned young Johnny about them.

Mr. Irving: Did you see these two men before you?

Witness: Yes, sir.

Mr. Irving: Who is this man?

Witness: Thomas Ryder.

Mr. Irving: And this one?

Witness: John Purtell.

Mr. Irving: These are the two men you spoke of. A light was being held?

Witness: Yes sir.

Mr. Irving: Well, did you know how they were dressed?

Witness: Thomas Ryder had on a pair of grey pants, and a cap with lugs and a peak on it.

Mr. Irving: Did you ever see that cap before?

Witness: Yes, I had seen it when Ryder came to Lucan.

Mr. Irving: You knew Ryder then, and Purtell too?

Witness: Yes.

Mr. Irving: How was Purtell dressed?

Witness: He had on black clothes.

Mr. Irving: Of the people who were there—you say there were others—can you give a description of them?

Witness: Yes; I saw a pretty tall man there, with a moustache and black whiskers. I didn't know who he was. I also saw one with a brown dress on; I mean a woman's dress; he was not short nor very tall. I also saw a man with a long coat and a man with a blackened face.

Mr. Irving: Have you any idea of how many men were there?

Witness: About twenty.

Mr. Irving: How did you know?

Witness: By their tramping.

Mr. Irving: Anything else?

Witness: I heard them hammering and those who were being hammered hollering.

Mr. Irving: Yes?

Witness: Tom also called out "Oh! Oh! Oh!"

He then told of the marauders pouring coal oil on the bed under which he was sheltering and setting fire to it before leaving. He told of his futile attempts to quench the fire by beating at it with his coat and, finally, his flight to the Whelan house.

In cross-examination Hugh MacMahon did his best to trip Johnny up on details of his testimony. Did he not tell Whelan that there were several men there wearing women's dresses and with blackened faces? Johnny said he may have done so; if so, it was not true. Had he not told the inquest jury that he had tipped the clothes basket to get a better view, whereas he had just now stated that he had not tipped it? Johnny could not recall exactly what he had said at the inquest; what he was saying now was the truth.

There was more of this. It was obvious that MacMahon was seeking out every possible small contradiction between the evidence Johnny had given in the witness box on this occasion and the various earlier statements he had given to the Whelans, to his own family, to the inquest jury, and to the magistrates at the preliminary hearing. There were indeed some contradictions. It must be remembered that this young boy told his story during the first few days after the tragedy while in a state of shock and amid a flood of contradictory commands by some very frightened adults, in an atmosphere heavy with tension and abject fear.

The remarkable thing is that the essential points of his narrative did not vary appreciably from the first telling to the last. Hugh MacMahon was well aware of this fact, which perhaps accounts for the frustration evident in the question with which he concluded his cross-examination:

"Who has been reading over your evidence to you the past few days?"

Johnny said no one had.

The one point in Johnny's story that has always been difficult to understand is the reason for his survival. According to his testimony, James Carroll was looking straight at him when he sat up in bed and handed Jim Donnelly's coat to him. If Carroll knew the boy was there, why was he allowed to live? There were, and are, many theories about this, none of them entirely satisfactory. The defunct made the most of this weak point in its summation.

There followed a long parade of Crown witnesses to attest to the condition of the bodies at the Donnelly homestead and their position with respect to the various rooms of the house; to testify to the results of the Crown's investigations and to the arrests of the prisoners, and finally to prove the existence of the Vigilance Committee and to testify to its activities.

Of all the evidence submitted at the trial, the testimony dealing with these last two points was the least satisfactory. With the exception of Will Donnelly, whose evidence as to this and to the circumstance of his brother's death was dismissed rather summarily as being biased and partial, most of the witnesses seemed to suffer from amnesia. A few witnesses admitted, under pressure, that they had signed Father Connolly's declaration. A smaller number agreed that they had been present at meetings in the Cedar Swamp schoolhouse but could not for the life of them recall anything that had been discussed nor even who else was there. One witness described in minute detail the position of the chair he sat in at one of these meetings but could not remember the name of a single person present.

John Cain was more loquacious than most. It was he who had successfully pressed the township tax collector, John Robinson Armitage, to stay at his house on the night of the murders rather than at the Donnelly home as Armitage had intended.

Cain admitted to membership in the Committee. He named many who had been members at the time of the case of the Thompson cow, and he spoke freely of that incident. It was only when dealing with later meetings of the Committee that the memory of the witness began to fail:

Mr. Irving: When did you next go to the Committee meeting?

Witness: After the Thompson affair, as the Donnellys had an information laid against the committee for trespass; the meeting was after the case had been disposed of.

Mr. Irving: When did you go there again?

Witness: Can't say.

Mr. Irving: Was it on account of a charge made against John Donnelly for robbing Ryan?

Witness: I don't think so.

Mr. Irving: When were you there then?

Witness: After the burning of Ryder's barn, the next day I think; I was not there on any other occasion.

Mr. Irving: What was done at the meeting after Ryder's barn was burned?

Witness: Inquiries were made if anybody knew anything about it; there was no prosecution ordered of anyone in reference to the affair as far as I know; I was there till the meeting broke up and heard nothing about a charge against the Donnellys.

Mr. Irving: Did you hear the names of the Donnellys mentioned that night?

Witness: No.

Mr. Irving: Then the Ryders didn't blame the Donnellys for burning their barn?

Witness: No, not that I know of.

Mr. Irving: Did you go to this meeting whenever you were summoned?

Witness: Well, no. Yes. No, I didn't.

Mr. Irving: Did you go to the meetings whenever you heard of them?

Witness: I don't know. Yes, I did.

Mr. Irving: What meetings were you at?

Witness: The one for Thompson's cow, the trespass case, Ryan's threshing and Ryder's barn.

Mr. Irving: What about Ryan's threshing?

Witness: It was to secure Ryan from damage and to get a machine for him.

Mr. Irving: Why?

Witness: Because the Donnellys had forbidden anyone threshing.

Mr. Irving: Where did you hear that said?

Witness: I heard Ryan say it.

Mr. Irving: Where?

Witness: At the committee meeting and before.

Under continued questioning Cain admitted being present at still other meetings of the Committee—on the occasion when Carroll was appointed a constable (by the Committee) and again when William Casey was named a magistrate (also by the Committee). He had signed the petition for Carroll's appointment.

Here the witness's memory began to fail badly. In its questioning the prosecution was getting dangerously close to the date of the killings:

Mr. Irving: At all these meetings you speak of, was Carroll present?

Witness: I wouldn't like to swear that.

His Lordship: Was he present at the meeting about the burning of Ryder's barn?

Witness: I don't know.

Mr. Irving: How did you get notice of the meetings?

Witness: I can't call to mind who notified me of the meetings.

Mr. Irving: How long would it take you to remember who notified you? We could give you a room to yourself where you might think.

Witness: I really don't know if I could think that way.

Mr. Irving: Who told you to attend the meeting about Ryder's burning?

Witness: I think it was one of the Ryders, but can't say which one.

Mr. Irving: When was this meeting about Ryan's threshing?

Witness: It must have been in August.

Mr. Irving: How were you called on that occasion?

Witness: Oh, it was going through the whole neighbourhood; everyone knew about it.

Mr. Irving: Was there a chairman appointed?

Witness: Yes.

Mr. Irving: Who was he?

Witness: Martin McLoughlin.

Mr. Irving: How were you brought in?

Witness: All came in together.

Mr. Irving: Did you take any pledge?

Witness: Yes. There was a kind of declaration or rules.

Mr. Irving: What did you do?

Witness: Agree to them.

Mr. Irving: Was it read to you?

Witness: Yes. Heenan read it.

Mr. Irving: Now, can you tell us what it was you agreed to?

Witness: I can't hardly tell, more than that the rule was to give information if anything was lost or stolen to the meeting.

Mr. Irving: Were they to keep it secret?

Witness: Yes. I guess they weren't to tell everyone about it.

Mr. Irving: You said a declaration was used?

Witness: Oh, I can't tell what it was.

Mr. Irving: Did you take an oath?

Witness: No.

Mr. Irving: Anything binding on your conscience?

Witness: Yes. I felt it my duty to keep this secret. I had never been there before, and what I did I felt was to be kept secret.

Mr. Irving: Were you to keep secret what took place at the meeting?

Witness: Yes.

Mr. Irving: Then perhaps you are not telling us all that took place; this pledge may prevent you.

Witness: If there was such a thing as a warrant it was to be kept secret, but I am not holding back anything. It was not to interfere with my telling the truth under oath.

Mr. Irving: Are you one of the persons who signed the book in the church?

Witness: Yes.

Mr. Irving: All these people you speak of took the declaration?

Witness: I might have seen others take the declaration.

In cross-examination by Hugh MacMahon, one of the intricate Biddulph Township family relationships was revealed. John Cain was a son-in-law of James Maher, Senior. In further questioning Cain admitted hearing of the fire at the Donnelly homestead early on the morning of February 4 from Pat Whelan:

His Lordship: Did you go over to the house?

Witness: No.

His Lordship: But you had seen that the house was burned before you heard from Whelan or your wife?

Witness: Yes, but the reason was because I did not neighbour with the Donnellys on account of their preventing me selling my farm once. The old woman threatened the man who was to buy it.

His Lordship: How did you know it?

Witness: I saw the old woman and the man talking together on the road.

His Lordship: How long ago was this—three or four years?

Witness: Yes.

As far as the Biddulph witnesses were concerned, there was little to choose between those appearing for the prosecution and those representing the defence. Both groups were evasive and shifty-eyed, garrulous in inconsequential details and sphinx-like when the line of questioning seemed to threaten their personal security. One of the worst of the lot was the Vigilance Committee's untried magistrate, William Casey. If, as Sam Everett declared, Casey was one of those abroad on the work of murder on the night of February 3, his account of his actions the following forenoon is a masterpiece of double talk:

Witness: On the morning of the tragedy I started out from home to go to my cattle and on the concession I met Mr Whelan. He was going southward on the 6th concession, The Roman Line. . . . I asked him where the fire was, having seen it when I got up in the morning. I thought the schoolhouse was on fire, but made no inquiries till Whelan came along. Lots of people went to the Ryders' fire, but I saw no one going to the Donnellys. Whelan did not tell me there was any loss of blood at the Donnellys' fire, but spoke merely of the burning. After breakfast I started for Granton, which is something over four miles away. On the way I met Dick Curtin who asked me if the Donnellys were all burned up, and I said no. He said Whelan had told him so. At the swamp schoolhouse James Carroll overtook me on horseback and I asked him if he had heard about the fire. He said there were four bodies in the fire, and that it was a mysterious-looking affair. He was the nearest constable and I was the nearest magistrate to the fire, but I gave him no instructions on the matter. I did not think it my duty to do so. Faith, I can't say who he said had told him there were four bodies in the fire. If he told me it has escaped my memory and that's the best I can say. I can't say whether he told me where he slept or not. I can't say whether he told me whose bodies were in the fire or not. I told Carroll I was not thoroughly posted in the law.

Mr. Magee: You thought it required a deeper mind?

Witness: Well, yes. I thought it required a little practice anyway.

Mr. Magee: What was done at Granton?

Witness: Well I think Mr Whelan asked me to have a treat.

Mr. Magee: That's the way the court began, eh? Well what did you tell Dr Laing at Granton?

Witness: That I knew nothing of the murder only what Whelan had told me.

His Lordship: What was done at the Court?

Witness: It was adjourned for good. Carroll was there but we had no discussion in the Court about the Donnelly fire. I heard Carroll say nothing, nor did Ryder make any remarks.

The case for the defence was based on two main lines of legal strategy—to prove an alibi for the prisoner Carroll and to discredit the evidence of the two principal Crown witnesses, Johnny O'Connor and Will Donnelly.

Carroll's alibi rested on the evidence of Mr. and Mrs. William Thompson and his own brother, William Carroll. In essence, Thompson testified that Carroll had slept upstairs at his house on the night of the crime and could not have left the house without being heard. Mrs. Thompson corroborated her husband's evidence and William Carroll testified that he had slept with the prisoner and that he "did not get up that night."

Then Mr. MacMahon turned his attention to Johnny O'Connor. To cast doubt on Johnny's evidence he sent John Purtell and several members of the family of James Magrath into the witness stand in succession to prove that Purtell had stayed at the Magrath home that night and could not possibly have left without the family's knowledge, since he would have had to go through four doors to get out.

Finally, a number of defence witnesses swore under oath to the untruthfulness and general dishonesty of Will Donnelly, all of them testifying that they would not believe him even if he swore on "a stack of Bibles."

Will sat patiently throughout the character assassination. He had expected no better treatment.

Then came the summing up by counsel.

W. R. Meredith closed the case for the defence. He argued brilliantly against complete acceptance of Johnny O'Connor's evidence. He seized on a discrepancy in the boy's testimony about the place where Bridget Donnelly was murdered; he stressed the unlikelihood of Johnny's survival had he indeed been seen by the murderers; and finally he made much of the good character previously borne by the prisoners and contrasted it with the bad character almost universally ascribed to the Donnellys.

Aemilius Irving for the Crown laid great stress on the Vigilance Committee and charged it with planning and executing the crime. He pointed out that Johnny O'Connor's evidence had not been successfully challenged in any substantial particular and declared the defence alibis to be weak and worthless.

Mr. Justice Armour's charge to the jury was distinctly unfavourable to the accused. He, too, dwelt on the part played by the Vigilance Committee, declaring such an organization to be totally without the law and "the pregnant mother of all kinds of offences:"

> It is a material part of this inquiry to consider whether the murder at the Donnelly homestead was the outcome of this society. If it was, and the persons who committed that crime were members of that society, you may have little difficulty in coming to a conclusion on other parts of the case. Do not the whole circumstances surrounding the murder show that it was the result of a deliberate plan? Are these men members of this society? If you decide that the society made up their minds to exterminate the Donnellys, everything is plain, so far as these alibis and this evidence is concerned; for do you suppose that men who would join hands to perform such an outrage as this would hesitate to swear alibis for every person engaged in it? . . . As for the alibis, it is very difficult to say whether a man could go out of a house at night without being heard. As for Johnny O'Connor's evidence, do you believe that the boy could invent his story? Is there anyone capable of writing such a history as that, and teaching it to a boy afterwards?

In the face of this charge no one in the crowded courtroom expected the jury to take long to decide on the prisoner's guilt. However, in the result the jury was out most of the afternoon and far into the evening. The crowd had dwindled considerably when the twelve men finally straggled into the jury box late on Saturday night, October 9, 1880.

On being questioned by the clerk of the court as to their verdict, the foreman confessed that they had been unable to agree on one. Setting themselves against the Judge's charge and the weight of the evidence, seven had voted for acquittal, four had stood out for conviction and the twelfth had been unable to arrive at any decision.

Astonishingly enough, an application for bail for the six accused was made by their counsel and seriously debated before being refused. The prisoners were then returned to their cells to await trial at the next ensuing assizes.

The second trial began in the same old courthouse in the last week of January, 1881.

Because of the importance of the case, the obvious difficulties in the way of administering justice in the matter and the inflamed state of public feeling in the neighbourhood, the Ontario government decided on a most unusual step. A special commission of two judges was appointed to preside over the case, instead of the customary circuit court judge. It was hoped that two distinguished jurists could succeed where one had failed.

The two judges were Mr. Justice (afterwards Chief Justice Sir Matthew) Cameron and Mr. Justice Featherston Osler, the elder brother of Sir William Osler, Sir Edmund Osler and the famous criminal lawyer, B. B. Osler.

Although the two justices were supposed to have equal standing through the case, it was actually Cameron who played the more prominent role and read the charge to the jury, while Osler acted mainly in the role of consultant.

There was the usual difficulty about the choice of jurors, with Will Donnelly providing *sotto voce* comments on each in turn to the Crown prosecutor, Aemilius Irving. At last, however, the panel was complete and the prisoner, James Carroll, was brought in to face his accusers.

The second trial, so far as evidence was concerned, was a repetition of the first. The cast of characters was the same, the plot was the same. There were no surprise witnesses, no dramatic denouements. The same ninety-odd witnesses trudged to the witness-stand and told the same stories, most of them for at least the fourth time. Even the most indefatigable spectators and newspaper readers began to lose interest. Newspaper coverage was more perfunctory; there were fewer "side stories."

The real drama in this second re-hashing of the Biddulph Horror was in the duel of wits between the opposing counsel and the brilliance of the two presiding justices.

It was apparent, early in the trial, that the principal element of difference between this trial and the first was the attitude of the two judges towards the evidence of Johnny O'Connor and the testimony with respect to the existence of the Vigilance Committee. This was especially true in the case of Mr. Justice Cameron who, as Crown prosecutor at the Middlesex County fall assizes in 1879, had had a brief contact with the Biddulph feud. It was he who had refused to prosecute Tom Donnelly on the charge of the Ryan robbery.

Cameron's attitude was crystallized on the ninth and last day of the trial when he delivered the charge to the jury. He dealt first with the testimony of Johnny O'Connor:

> You must enquire whether there has been anything presented, either in the evidence for the prosecution or for the defence, which shakes your confidence in Johnny O'Connor's testimony, so as to lead you to the conclusion that it would be unsafe to rely upon it, not because you may believe the boy is wilfully telling an untruth, but because under the circumstances he may have been in such a state of mind that it would be unsafe to rely on what he said.

Hugh MacMahon, for the defence, could hardly have done better.

Then the Justice dealt with the matter of the Vigilance Committee:

> Although you may suspect that these witnesses are not telling you the truth, although you may even suspect that in that witness-box we have had men who were actually concerned in this crime, you are not to come to the conclusion without proof that there was a resolution or determination passed by that organization, or a part of it, to destroy the Donnelly household. You are not to assume that, and this prisoner is not to be held responsible on the ground that he was a member of this organization. You cannot assume that this crime was the work of this organization, and then convict this prisoner because he was a member of this organization. You can only convict him if you believe the direct

evidence of the boy in regard to him, because apart from the boy's statement you have no evidence of the prisoner being at the Donnellys' that night.

Surely few juries have ever been given clearer direction. Nevertheless, it took the twelve men nearly four hours to arrive at their foregone conclusion. It was sharp on the hour of three o'clock on the afternoon of Saturday, January 29, 1881, when they filed back into the courtroom. On the challenge by the clerk of the court, the foreman stood in his place and delivered the verdict in a trembling voice:

"My Lords, we find the prisoner not guilty of murder."

There was sensation in the courtroom, promptly suppressed. The business of the court went on. The prisoner was discharged. Immediately after the verdict was recorded, the prisoners, Thomas Ryder and John Purtell were called to the dock to answer to the same charges. The business of empanelling a new jury began. After nearly forty challenges and directions to "stand aside," eleven jurors had been sworn. Just as the twelfth juror had been accepted and was about to receive the oath, Aemilius Irving arose to address the court. He had been in consultation with his colleagues and a decision had been reached. Receiving permission of the bench to speak, he said:

> My Lords, I ask that this juror be not sworn. The Crown, under the circumstances, is not prepared to proceed with the trial of these prisoners. Carroll has just been acquitted. The evidence against these men is the same as that which was presented against the last prisoner. I do not foresee any different verdict in their case from that which has just been rendered. I therefore ask that their case, and all of the other cases of murder and arson, the killing of the unfortunates, and the burning of the building, go over to the next assizes.

The courtroom was as silent as a tomb while the spectators mulled over the meaning of the Crown prosecutor's words. Then, after a brief pause, Irving continued: "The Crown is ready to consider the question of bail for all of the accused."

It was an astonishing anti-climax. There was no demonstration on the part of the spectators as the court droned on with the technicalities of admitting the accused to bail. If there was surprise at the small amount of the sureties demanded—ranging from $250 to $1,000—it was not expressed.

It was carefully explained to the prisoners that the prime condition of their recognizances was that they should reappear for trial whenever called upon to do so.

No such call was ever made, in this world.

There was a demonstration on the part of friends of the prisoners when they walked out of the courthouse into freedom.

The big celebration, however, was held later—at the Cedar Swamp schoolhouse in Biddulph Township.

Thirty Pieces of Silver

Biddulph April 23rd 1881

James Feeheley told me when sleeping with him in his house that he was now about to leave Biddulph and there was only one thing he ever done that he was sorrey for. I asked him what that was. He said he sold Tom the best friend he ever had. I asked him how that was he said he went to the house that night to see who was there for them vigleants son of biches but he said he did not think they were going to murder them. I then asked him why he did not tell that at the trial he said he often tought of telling it but the way they talked to him about being an informer that he did not like to tell but he said if he could give one oath and then leave the country he would hang everyone of them he also told me about his uncle being sent to him by Pat Ryder to try and get him to sware for Carroll he said he was often offered money to sware for them and Pat Ryder said to him one day we did murder them but can they prove it

PATRICK DONNELLY

AT no time during his year of bitter trial had Will Donnelly entertained any doubts about the loyalty of Jim Feeheley. He must have suspected Jim's brother Bill, for Bill's name had been mentioned frequently in connection with the Vigilance Committee. Jim was different. Jim and his father, old Michael Feeheley, had been lifetime friends and neighbours of the Donnellys, next in friendship only to the Keeffe family.

Will should have kept more carefully in mind the tortured genealogies of the Roman Line families. The Feeheleys were related to the Keeffes, who were Blackfeet, but also to the Cains, who were Whiteboys.

Will accepted without cavil Jim's story of his movements on the night of February 3, 1880. Jim had told the story many times—to Will, to the investigators and in the witness-box.

It had been Jim's night for visiting friends. He had seen the younger Keeffes on the Roman Line after the dance where Will Donnelly had danced with the red-headed schoolteacher. He had visited the Whelans and finally he had called on the elder Donnellys. He was wearing an overcoat which at the Donnelly home he discovered was too cumbrous on so fine a night. He left it there, telling Tom Donnelly he was going up the road to call on the Ryders. He would pick it up on his way back, if Tom would be so kind as to leave the door on the latch; that way he would not need to disturb the family should they be asleep.

Will Donnelly, like all who heard the story, must have realized how Jim Feeheley's action had facilitated the entry into the Donnelly home of their murderers. However, like the others, he accepted it as nothing more than a malign quirk of fate.

In March, 1881, he was disabused of this notion.

II

A new chapter in the Biddulph feud was being written before the ink was dry on the clerk's record of the jury's verdict in the case of the Queen versus James Carroll. Even before taking the stage for Lucan and the big welcome that awaited them there, Jim and his five fellow-defendants instructed their attorney, Hugh MacMahon, to enter an immediate demand for the return of the various rifles, shotguns, and revolvers recently displayed as Crown exhibits.

Aemilius Irving termed the demand "preposterous," especially in view of the fact that five of the six were free only on bail and might be summoned at any time to stand trial for their lives. He thought under the circumstances MacMahon might have had "the sense to recommend silence." Far from doing so, MacMahon submitted three more requests in as many weeks.

His audacity was matched and exceeded by that of his clients. On March 5 the Vigilance Committee held its first open public meeting in the Cedar Swamp schoolhouse. The object of this bold move was to appoint committees to solicit subscriptions to defray the cost of the trials.

Meanwhile a situation was building up which promised the Vigilance Committee greater trouble than anything they had yet faced. Thanks to careful planning and committee solidarity six of their number had come through two trials unscathed. By the anniversary of Sheehy's Day in 1881 the carefully-forged chain had snapped and the Committee had to deal with the defection of two members.

It began with the death of old Mike Feeheley on February 9. Mike had lived a blameless life. He died mourned by his friends and deeply regretted by his sons, James and William, for he died broke. There was a $4,000 mortgage on the farm and $2,000 in other commitments. The farm was unlikely to fetch much more than the amount of the mortgage on the auction block and any excess would of course be applied to the old man's other debts. His sons were to be left homeless and without patrimony.

In this pass the sons turned to Michael Carroll. "Mick," as he was generally known, was a Roman Line connection of Jim Carroll. The arrangement Mick and the two Feeheleys effected between them was never put on paper but its terms soon became a matter of public knowledge. Mick was to buy the farm at the auction and was to permit the family to continue to live there, for a time at least. In addition he was to pay Jim and Bill $500.

No one has ever explained what the $500 was for. One witness considered it sufficient to point out that Mick Carroll had two sons with the Vigilantes.

Mick bought the farm for $5,005 and let the Feeheleys remain there until late in April, but he welched on the second part of the bargain.

The Feeheleys did not nurse their grievance in silence. They began to talk.

Bob Donnelly heard some of the talk. He met Jim Carroll on a Lucan street soon after and punched Carroll on the nose. Carroll laid a charge against him. It was heard in magistrate's court on March 14, the eve of Sheehy's Day, and was thrown out.

For the next few days the Roman Line was in a turmoil. Deadly undercurrents were at work, but so well hidden were they that William Porte could note in his diary that St. Patrick's Day had passed off quietly in Lucan "except for a little fracas at night between Jim Feeheley and John Bawden."

Bawden was one of the county constables who had engaged in a gunfight with the Donnellys at Fitzhenry's Hotel five years earlier. The fracas may have been minor by Biddulph standards but it concealed a nest of vipers.

Will Donnelly was not present at the contretemps nor its aftermath, but he was represented. Immediately following the second trial he had engaged the services of a mysterious agent who masqueraded as a music teacher and made it his business to win the confidence of various members of the Vigilance Committee. It was said afterwards that he was attracted to the job by the $4,000 reward the province had offered for the apprehension and conviction of the killers of the Donnelly family.

Some unkind persons said the Feeheleys were attracted by the reward money too, but could not find any way of collecting it without putting their own necks in the noose.

In due course the agent reported to Will some things he had heard on the night of St. Patrick's Day. The information must have shaken Will to his depths. He did not act on it at once. He was recovering from a severe cold, perhaps occasioned by a trip to Toronto which he had taken "to find something to do." It was not until April 8 that he sat down to write a letter to the Crown Attorney, Charles Hutchinson:

> . . . The man I wanted hired has already in his devil may care way found out something very interesting, especially what he found out on last St. Patrick's night. I will not mention it here but it goes to show that Jim Feeheley set the trap at my Fathers and left William Whalen and William Feeheley to watch the house so that no one should leave or come to it unknown until the fixed hour and then Jim Feeheley went to my place at Whalens Corners and watched proceedings there until the gang got over. William Whalen is in Michigan liveing idle. He was run out of two lumber shanties when the men found out who he was. I understand he is afraid to come home. He is a terable coward and would be a good man to work on. Our man is attending to his music teaching but has got to be a great favorite with all the vigilants. He is the sharpest man I ever met but will not work for a reward as he says there is so much discredit always then upon what a man says when working for a reward. You will please let Mr Irving see this letter and if he wants to hear what this man found out let you telegraph me to send him in. Do it in a way that no one will know who or what you want. . . .

As some members of the Vigilance Committee had reason to know, it was one thing to hoodwink the police and elude the law; it was quite another to escape the implacable enmity of the remaining members of the Donnelly family. From that moment the baleful eye of revenge followed every move of the brothers Feeheley.

April was a month of high drama. By way of a curtain-raiser Sam Everett packed up and left Lucan for good on the 2nd. The ex-constable had been a minor but enigmatic member of the cast of characters of the Biddulph feud. His departure was virtually unnoticed save by the village Pepys who sent joyous maledictions coursing after his enemy's retreating figure:

Mr Samuel Lount Everett of Village Constable renown moved out bag and baggage today. I am led to understand that not one solitary individual called upon him to bid him good bye. He left unwept, unhonoured and unsung, without leaving one friend behind who cared a damn what became of him. At one period of his sojourn here had he took it into his head to leave, he would have been dined, wined and testimonialed and escorted to the station by a sorrowing crowd. But he was the greatest unhung scoundrel in every sense of the word that ever set foot in this Corporation. For my own part I did not blame him to fight me, for I told him upon the occasion of our first quarrel that either him or I must leave this village; and I wouldn't if I could help it. But he played traitor to his very best friends upon the slightest occasion; and this alone stamps him as a scoundrel of the first water. I stuck to his heels more faithful than ever I did to any other project in my life, and after a hard fight succeeded in sending him afloat without money, means or reputation. And may all bad luck leave the village and follow close

*to his heels until it overtakes him at last, as it most
assuredly will. Thus endeth the advent of Mr Everett
in Lucan.*

And I am here yet.

The cause of the dispute between Porte and Everett
is obscure, but seems not to have been connected with the
Biddulph feud. Everett had no stake in the feud and was apparently distrusted by both sides. Porte, from first to last, was
a friend of the Donnelly family.

On April 14 James and William Feeheley were arrested
for an assault on Jim Carroll. The case came up two days later
in magistrate's court at Lucan. To everyone's surprise Carroll
withdrew the charge and paid the court costs.

Carroll had had a sudden attack of discretion. It came too
late. Bill Feeheley was on his feet instantly. He wanted a warrant
sworn out against Carroll for "raising an axe" to him.

The magistrate began filling out the necessary document.
He told Bill he would require a statement and also the names
of any witnesses to the alleged offence. Bill lost his patience
with this legal shilly-shallying and told the magistrate, in the
words of a constable who was present, " . . . not to mind it.
That he would issue a better warrant for him [Carroll] and by
Tuesday he would have him in London jail and he would never
come out. . . ."

The fat was in the fire. The brothers Feeheley, no doubt
seeking spiritual catharsis, were seized of a compulsion to "tell
all." No confidant received the full story; it was told in bits and
pieces, tantalizing fragments of the truth accompanied by indi-
gestible seasoning composed of self-pity and self-justification.

To the alarm of the Vigilance Committee the disease began
to spread. In London, where he had taken refuge, the simple-
minded John Purtell began to brag that he could make $4,000
any time he wanted to.

The situation was becoming desperate. The Feeheleys had
to be got out of the way. Direct action was impossible. Will's

letter to Charles Hutchinson had brought the detectives swarming into the township again. If any ill should happen to the Feeheleys, public opinion would demand its retributive victims this time, legally or illegally. The Feeheleys knew the strength of their position and exerted it remorselessly.

Someone went to Father Connolly with the problem. The priest raised $350 which was given to the Feeheleys on condition that they leave the township at once. The Feeheleys hesitated. The amount was $150 less than what they claimed as their due from Mick Carroll. With remarkable alacrity the full amount of the claim was raised by the Vigilance Committee, paid to the Feeheleys, and the $350 returned to the priest. Belatedly, the Vigilantes seem to have realized the danger of involving Father Connolly so directly in their activities.

The story of this transaction soon came to Will Donnelly's ears and was accordingly reported to the Crown Attorney. For the first time there is a distinctly unfriendly note in Will's reference to the priest who had shown himself willing to pay hush money "sooner than have any trouble about the murder."

The Feeheleys began preparations for a move to Michigan. The Crown as yet had taken no action. Charles Hutchinson needed more evidence. Will Donnelly sent for his brother, Pat. Everyone talked more readily to Pat and in the result that included the Feeheleys.

Pat had a chat first with Jim Feeheley. The results of that conversation were reported in the letter to Charles Hutchinson on April 23 quoted at the beginning of this chapter. Three days later he reported his talk with Bill Feeheley:

Wm. Feeheley told me in presence of James Hogan that James Toohey, Pat Quigley & James Maher were the three men carried tom Donnelly into the house after he was killed, also told me that Pat Breen made all the bye laws and Din Heenan kept the books. that there was an oath in connection with the society and that he knew all about it as he had taken the oath himself. . . . He said it was Pat Quigley's spade tom's head was split with after he was carried into the house. he also stated that Joney Oconner was right about what and who he saw all but one thing that was Purtell was not there. he also said they saw Joney OConner but tought him not old enough to tell any thing onely for that they would have killed him. He said there was a wa[t]ch on our house that day and night. Know one went in or came out but they new all about it. he told me Tade Toohey came to him last summer and offered him more money than would buy our farm if he Feehely would sware there was no oath in the society also to have him sware what they would put up for him and they would follow and give evidence to strengthen his. he said he would go and tell it all if his folks were away out of the country but it was not safe to tell while they were here for fere they would murder his family. He told me that Din Toohey one of the murderes told old Whalen all about it. then the Saturdy previous to this conversation I slept in Feehely's house he told me he saw the whole thing he was inside the Whalen's fence. I asked him why he did not tell all this befor, he said he was afraid but one time in the witnes Box he came nere telling the whole thing. . . . he also asked me for god to forgive him as he was led into it by others. I told him I would if he would tell the whole thing he said he would.

The evidence was piling up but still the Crown was not satisfied. The Feeheleys pulled out at the end of April, bound for the lumber camps of Michigan. Will and Pat redoubled their efforts. More statements were forthcoming from other sources. On May 7 John H. McConnell, a Lucan merchant, wrote to Charles Hutchinson:

In conversation with James Feehelly in April last I attained the following information respecting the late Biddulph Murder and thought it wise to informe you of the contents of the above. James Feehelly told me he was sent to Donnellys house on the night of the murder to see who was their and did so on the advice of some members of the Vigilance Committee who stated to him that the[y] intended taking the Donnelly's out and hanging them until they would tell who burned Riders Barns. he after leaving the house said he saw James Carrol, James Maher and others and reported to them who was in the house I asked him if he told them that Johney OConners was their. he said he did not as he thought it was John Donnelly that was in the bed with his father. He told me that he then went to Whalens Corners to watch Wm. Donnellys house and see who went in or out that night as the Vigilant Committee intended going for Will also after they got through at the old mans family. he said when they came to Whalens Corners he told them that Jim Keeffe left Will's house. he said he did not expect they were intending to shoot Will Donnelly until he heard the report. they then went to kill Jim Keeffe and on the way he said boys you will not do it you have done enough tonight.

The following day Will Donnelly witnessed a statement made by Robert Keeffe, Senior:

James Feehely told me the following in connection with the Donnelly murder on the morning the Feehely family moved away to the States.

I moved them to Lucan with my team. James Feehely and I walked together part of the way. In our conversation the murder was spoken of. Feehely counted thirty one men that he said were at the murder and amongst them were Jim Carroll, Martin McLoughlin, all the Ryders he said but the one that had his foot cut, John Kennedy, John, Denis and Michael Heenan and his (Feehelys) own two uncles James Maher & John Cain etc. etc.

I am Feehely's first cousin and do firmly believe that he and his brother were concerned in the murder, and also believe that if they were now visited by some one with whom they were on intimate terms or placed under arest they would tell all about the affair.

Witness   his
Wm. Donnelly   Robert   X   Keeffe Sen.
                                           mark

This seems to have been Will Donnelly's only direct effort to secure evidence. Throughout the whole Feeheley affair Pat was the moving spirit. Will apparently had great difficulty in accepting the fact of Jim Feeheley's treachery. Pat, according to his own statement, had suspected Jim all along, to the extent of accusing him on at least two occasions of complicity in the murders.

So it was Pat and not Will who helped the Crown put together its case. The prosecution worked cautiously and with great secrecy. Charles Hutchinson, Aemilius Irving, and the Attorney-General's department were only too keenly aware of the problems facing them. Any attempt to convict the Feeheleys would automatically implicate from thirty to forty other persons. As Irving wrote Hutchinson:

> . . . the difficulties of dealing with so many prisoners, the unsatisfactory state of opinion in London and the sympathy of the Jailers with the incriminated surrounds this case with a great deal of trouble as well as responsibility & anxiety to you. . . .

There was another and graver problem for the Crown in the Feeheley matter. Nearly every scrap of evidence so painstakingly gathered made reference to Father John Connolly's part in the Feeheley pay-off. The implication of the priest was considered so serious that no expression of it was permitted to appear in the official correspondence. Two documents only—a telegram and an expense account—give any clue as to the importance attached to this element of the case by the prosecution. These two references establish the fact that on May 14 Charles Hutchinson and the Honourable Adam Crooks, Minister of Education in the Ontario government, met the Most Reverend John Walsh, Bishop of the Roman Catholic Diocese of London, at the Bishop's palace on Blackfriars Street in London. Why the Minister of Education should be involved in the legal aspects of the Donnelly murder is a complete mystery. So is the subject of the conversation on that occasion. It is sufficient to note that the name of Father Connolly is conspicuous by its almost total absence from all subsequent official records of the case.

Four days after this visit Pat Donnelly appeared before John Peters, a Justice of the Peace for the County of Middlesex, to swear out an information and complaint against James and William Feeheley for complicity in the murders of the five members of the Donnelly family. He left almost immediately afterward for Detroit in company with Detective Schram of the London force, with instructions from Charles Hutchinson to assist the Michigan police in arresting the brothers.

The story burst on the newspaper-reading public with the force of a thunderbolt on May 21, 1881. Given the proper "news break" it might have provided a long-term sensation second only to the story of the massacre itself. In the result, it was a three-day wonder. On May 24, the holiday set aside for the celebration of the birthday of Queen Victoria, an excursion steamer named for the "widow of Windsor" capsized in the River Thames near London with the loss of nearly two hundred lives. The Biddulph Judases faded into back-page obscurity. There, and in the now-yellowed stacks of legal correspondence, they lived out the rest of their tawdry little drama.

The Feeheleys were arrested at Saginaw, Michigan, on May 23, and taken to jail at Detroit. They put up a stiff battle against extradition and it was the first week in July before they appeared in magistrate's court in London for their preliminary hearing. The evidence presented was considered sufficient to warrant holding them and they were committed to the county jail to stand trial at the fall sittings of the court of assizes.

The rest was anticlimax.

In October the grand jury found true bills against the prisoners. In another of the surprise legal moves with which the history of the Biddulph murder trials abounds, the prosecution announced it was not yet ready to present its case. James and William Feeheley were admitted to bail on October 7, on condition that they present themselves for trial at the next sessions of the assize court.

The brothers swaggered out of the old courtroom, free as air.

They never entered it again.

As in the two previous trials the Crown had had to admit defeat. The combination against them was too powerful. The body of criminal law is more designed for the punishment of the individual offence than for the execution of judgment against a corporate criminal conspiracy. In witness of this we need only consider the American experience in dealing with organized crime. Even in international law a charge of genocide is difficult to sustain against an individual member of a state conspiracy.

In the case of the Feeheleys the Crown had to contend as well with the enormously delicate religious situation created by Father Connolly's implication in the affair. It must be recalled that the Orange Order had a large and aggressive membership in the Province of Ontario at this time. A public revelation of the priest's role or implied censure by the authorities of his action might well have precipitated large-scale disturbances graver even in nature than the unavenged murders of the Donnelly family.

As for the Feeheleys, there can be little doubt that they were guilty. In preparation for the preliminary examination Charles

Hutchinson prepared several pages of notes from which the following comments are abstracted:

MRS FEEHELEY—On cross exam. I suggest that she should be asked respecting the $500 arrangement with Michl. Carroll, especially who interfered to prevent it being carried out. I think it will appear that it was Jas. Carroll & other vigilants (as they were called). This made the Feheley boys & family generally so angry with the vigilants & caused the threats & talk about the village, which ultimately led to the payment of the money. Did she not also use threats. If so & she will hardly deny it, what were they based upon. What is the secret of the power the Feeheleys possessed to intimidate the vigilants & which they used so effectually. Then her transaction with the Priest should be ventilated. Did the Priest pay her $350. If so, why & was this payment followed almost immediately by the payt. of the $500 & the return of the Priest's money. I think it should not be difficult to show that the Feheleys possessed an intimate knowledge of the facts of the murder, altogether inconsistent with the idea of their complete innocence of complicity in it, & that they used that knowledge to compel the payment of the $500. . . . There can be no evidence to contradict the fact that James Feheley went to the Donnelly's that night. What did he go there for at an hour considered in the country late for a winter night. Is any reason for the visit suggested by the defence. He himself gives the reason. He tells Pat Donnelly & J. H. McConnell, 2 witnesses whose evidence has not been discredited, that he went there at the request *of the vigilants, to find out who was there. Was he to find this out for a lawful purpose—and if not, what then. He knew that a violent & in its nature murderous assault is contemplated, & he assists in a most important matter. Is he not responsible for what follows. What matter if he never went to Will Donnellys, what matter if that part of his statement was mere braggadocio. Does it affect the fact that he did go to the Donnellys & that he said he went there at the request of the murderers of the family—and he himself says they were the murderers—to find out who was there, knowing that they contemplated an unlawful & by its nature murderous assault. Can under the circumstances any such evidence as the defence intend submitting be sufficient to justify the Comm. in deciding that the Feheley boys are innocent & that there is not a sufficient case for the consideration of a jury.*

The last sentence in the above extract was written in an agitated hand. Charles Hutchinson knew the answer to his own question. The Crown had a good case—and not a chance in the world of securing a conviction. Neither he nor the commissioners nor the whole body of judicial experience had found a way, in a practical manner, to try half a township for the murder of five of its residents.

The six members of the Vigilance Committee who sustained two trials for their lives for murder had the sympathy of some sections of the public. However stealthy and secret their plans, they had confronted their victims, face to face, and met their "moment of truth" together.

The Feeheleys received no public sympathy.

Judas Iscariot, the betrayer of Christ, had a conscience. He went out and hanged himself. Jim Feeheley, the betrayer of the Donnellys, had none. He went back to work in the lumber camps of Michigan and Wisconsin. Local legend says even the case-hardened lumberjacks would have nothing to do with him once they had discovered his identity.

Some years ago I discovered certification of the legend in a place remote from the Biddulph scene. An autobiographical record kept by a respected early resident of Medicine Hat, Alberta, tells of a meeting with Jim Feeheley in a Wisconsin lumber camp in the late 1880s. The account states that Feeheley was ostracized by the men and eventually drifted away into obscurity.

There let him remain.

The End of It All

Now I can say no more; to the law-board I must go,
There to take my last farewell of my friends and counterie;
May the angels, shining bright, receive my soul this night
And convey me into heaven with the blessed Trinity.

BALLAD OF HUGH REYNOLDS

THE surviving Donnelly brothers—Will, Pat and Bob—
left Lucan in the summer of 1881. For a time they stayed in
London. After the abortive Feeheley trial they dispersed. Pat
went back to blacksmithing in Thorold; Will settled in Appin
and Bob in Glencoe, neighbouring villages in the western part
of Middlesex County.

There was also a notable dispersal of their friends and enemies. The Feeheleys, the Carroll brothers, the Hogans, the
Keeffes and others drifted away to the lumber camps of the
north-western United States or to the Canadian far west.

If this feud had been as simple a thing as the public has been
led to believe for eighty-odd years, this should have marked the
end of the burnings and killings. We should expect to be shown
a picture of a community exhausted by thirty-five years of fear
and hatred slowly and gratefully relaxing into somnolence.

This was not so.

Because there were no more lurid massacres by bands of
night raiders the world outside Biddulph assumed all was over
and the feud ended. The truth was something quite different. For

nearly two decades, arson, manslaughter and murder continued to be a way of life for the feuding families of the Roman Line.

There were still Whiteboys and Blackfeet on the sixth concession of Biddulph Township. Sheehy's Day still came on March 15. Pat Breen and Martin McLoughlin, the Vigilante leaders, still kept their places. Father John Connolly was still curate of St. Patrick's. Will and Bob Donnelly still lived and the souls of six murdered members of their family still cried out for revenge.

Of all these factors, one is constant. The survival of Will Donnelly is the key. So long as he lived, no matter how remote from the scene, the feud continued.

As a matter of fact Will was charged by his enemies with reviving the feud. On October 8, 1881, an attempt was made to set fire to the Stanley, Dight and Company flour mill at Lucan. It was alleged that Will and Bob Donnelly, Cornelius Carty, Pat and Jack Kent, Simon Howe and a private detective, Francis Morrison West, had been discovered in the very act of arson. The private detective immediately declared in magistrate's court that he had set the trap by prior arrangement with the constables and gave information charging the others with the crime.

Of all the bizarre cases with which the history of the Biddulph feud is liberally studded this is one of the weirdest. In none of the surviving records of the case is any motive assigned for the attempt, which if successful would have occasioned a loss of at least $10,000. However, the means employed to set the fire were totally inadequate. The whole venture, on the evidence of the principal witness, West, was ludicrously amateurish, and the apprehension of the criminals certain from the beginning.

For the identification of Will and Bob Donnelly as two of the arsonists we have only the evidence of F. M. West. They were not arrested at the scene but some time later. The big question that immediately rises is:

Who was Frank Morrison West?

From his sworn statement West was a resident of Prescott, Wisconsin, his father being a cattle dealer in that area. He had left Wisconsin the previous year and had drifted into Lucan about December, 1880, with some $700 in capital. He had gone through this money and was living by doing various odd jobs for the people of Lucan and vicinity.

It is the nature of these jobs that suddenly and unexpectedly reveals one of the best-kept secrets in the Feeheley case. Frank West was the "music teacher" whom Will Donnelly had employed to spy upon the Vigilantes and their families. It was he who had secured the first tip about the implication of Jim and Bill Feeheley.

In the succeeding three weeks the character of the mysterious detective was revealed for all the world to see, and a most unsavoury one it turned out to be. He seems to have been a willowy young man with a retreating forehead and a mincing gait. It was strongly suggested that he had a criminal record in the United States and that he may not have given his correct name to the Canadian authorities.

Nevertheless, the London police magistrate decided at the preliminary hearing that there was enough evidence to commit Will and Bob Donnelly for trial at the November assizes. They were released on bail to appear on November 8 to stand trial. Bob went immediately to Glencoe but Will returned to Lucan, from which place he began to bombard the editor of *The London Free Press* with a series of amusing and sardonic letters about conditions in the village.

In one of these he tells of a battle royal one evening at the Queen's Hotel between Bob Keeffe and Patrick Ryder, Senior, whom Will identifies by his nickname "Grouchie." Bob accused Pat of the murders of the Donnellys and also of the killing of Brimmacombe on the Roman Line in 1857. When Will stepped up with the intention of restoring peace he was seized by another of the Ryder family whom he identifies as "Sideroad Jim." Will told him to take his "blood-stained hands" away and added:

"Your hour for striking is four hours and a half-away yet." On that, according to Will, Sideroad Jim "wilted."

The fight ended with Bob Keeffe thrusting the old man's head through a window, glass and all, and holding him there until he cried for mercy.

The trial came off on the appointed day but, as nearly everyone expected, was extremely short-lived. The evidence of Frank West was offered reluctantly by the Crown and in the result was totally disregarded. A strong implication was left that West himself was guilty of the crime and had attempted to throw the blame on the Donnelly brothers at the instigation of the Vigilance Committee.

Will and Bob were cleared of all blame and permitted to go free. Bob went back to Glencoe and Will to Appin.

After the Dight flour mill affair a year passed without major incident. Then on Sunday, September 3, 1882, a small riot broke out on the Roman Line between factions led by Jack Kent, Tom Keeffe and Pat Sullivan on one side, and Hugh and Jim Toohey and Pat Ryder, Junior, on the other. Stones were thrown and revolvers fired, but according to William Porte "no one much hurt." The patronymics of the combatants makes it quite clear that the battle issue was Blackfeet versus Whiteboys. Some twenty warrants were issued and fifteen persons held over for trial at the fall assizes. The grand jury threw the case out and the whole matter, as Porte says, "ended in smoke."

There was an engagement in front of the Queen's Hotel at Lucan on Thursday, July 31, 1884, between Paddy Reilly, Jim Howe and Jim Ryder. All parties concerned were "under the influence," as was also a constable sent to arrest them. After a great deal of rock-throwing a second constable, John Bawden, was sent to arrest the lot, including the first constable. Peace was restored the next day in magistrate's court at a cost of some twenty dollars in fines.

Following this last Donnybrook a long period of relative quiet settled on the village and township. Aside from an occasional Saturday night row and a few fires, some of them accidental, the feud seemed to have almost died out. Off at Glencoe, Bob Donnelly might have permitted himself a few doubts on this score. Twice within a year he was burned out under suspicious circumstances. The first time it was his house, the second time, his stables.

The feud came to life again in 1893. The first incident was a case of arson. John Whelan's stables were burned down with the loss of two horses and a cow. That was on February 23. On March 6 a man named Dingman and "Buckshot Jim" Ryder went at one another with knives on the old Donnelly property on the Roman Line. According to the Porte diary, the only available record of this event, both parties survived the duel.

On August 22, the Royal Hotel in Lucan, together with three adjoining buildings, was burned to the ground. On September 14 an old building at the rear of P. McIlhargey's house was burned. On December 1, the Stanley and Dight grain warehouse was levelled and the following night the Grand Trunk Railway freight sheds were destroyed. There was another fire on Christmas Day at Lucan and a serious one two days later at Clandeboye, a village to the north. All the fires were considered to be the work of incendiaries.

On January 7, 1894, three buildings in the village were burned in two separate fires. There were two fires on January 12, one on February 7 and another on March 1. There were two fires in April and one in May. There were three bad ones in June. All were assumed to be the work of arsonists.

In the midst of all this excitement death returned to the Donnelly homestead. At ten o'clock on the evening of June 23, 1894, Edward Bowers shot William Cain. The scene of the shooting was the Donnelly property which the surviving members of the family had sold to their old enemy, John Cain. The victim, a son of John Cain, died on July 1. Bowers was tried for murder, found guilty of manslaughter and sentenced to five years in penitentiary.

There were seven more incendiary fires in the remaining months of 1894—one a month except for September, when there were two. The following year was quieter. There were only five cases of arson in 1895. One of them occurred at Stanley and Dight's grain store. It was the fifth time these merchants had been burned out. Not long after, Dight gave up the unequal struggle and moved out of the area. A Negro named Jack Williams was charged with the crime but acquitted.

On October 22 the barns on the farm of the unhappy Edward Bowers' parents were destroyed. In the following year there was a final chain of seven incendiary fires, after which peace returned, this time to stay.

The feud had run low on fuel, although it had by no means burned itself out. Nor has it yet, judging by the open and covert threats I have been subjected to in the last ten years of research leading up to the publication of this book.

The Biddulph Township fire record must be one of the most impressive in Canadian history. William Porte kept a careful accounting of all fires, accidental and incendiary. From his first diary entry in 1864 to his last in 1898 he records some ninety-six fires adjudged to be deliberately caused. Of these, sixty-six, or two-thirds, occurred after the last member of the Donnelly family had left the township. At whose door were these crimes laid? With the Donnellys dead or gone there was no convenient scapegoat and no one was ever convicted of carrying the torch.

Nevertheless, as I stated earlier in this chapter, there is a peculiar and perhaps coincidental connection between the Biddulph arson record and the life span of William Donnelly. As Will fell ill at his home in the village of Appin in the dying months of 1896 the chain of fire-settings sputtered to a halt. There was to be one more, the most peculiar of them all.

Will had never been physically strong. After the murder of his parents and his brothers his health steadily worsened. The excitement of the trials of the Vigilantes carried him on its crest for a while. At one time he seriously considered a proposal made by a theatrical promoter who offered Will the princely salary of $100 a week to narrate a play about the Biddulph tragedy. He finally decided not to take up the offer.

At Appin, Will ran the St. Nicholas Hotel and in the spring travelled the area with a stud stallion. Of his reputation there, Charles M. Macfie, former member of the Ontario Legislature, has written:

> While in Appin William Donnelly conducted himself as well as most citizens and had to meet the general fear that was

engendered by the reputation that preceded him. There was a general effort to make himself one of the community in so far as the average hotel man of that day could do.

Will visited Lucan several times during this period to call on old friends—particularly William Porte to whom on one occasion he brought gifts of a little Scotch terrier and a "fancy cane"—and to exhibit and race the horses for which he was so well known.

Some of the incidents that occurred on these visits were distasteful to him. Once he was told that "Sideroad Jim" Ryder was dying and wanted to see him to confess his fault. Will was weary of death-bed confessions. He despised the cowardice that brought these out only at the point of final and perfect safety from the vengeance of the law. On this occasion he is reported to have said: "Let him die with it in his throat!"

In 1897 Will came home for the last time. He died in his Appin home on March 8—one week before the 131st anniversary of the execution of Father Nicholas Sheehy. He was not quite fifty-two. All Jim Donnelly's sons died at a comparatively early age; only one achieved his father's age. Those who escaped the guns, clubs, spades and knives of assassins were killed by grief and care.

Will was buried beside his parents in St. Patrick's churchyard. Father Connolly's successor, Father Gahan, sang the mass. As the mourners drifted homeward, some rode by the ruins of Andrew Keeffe's old tavern where the Biddulph troubles had begun the year Will was born.

The ruins were new. The old buildings had been abandoned for some years, gaunt skeletons of the past. Then, on the night of March 6, while Will lay dying at Appin, some unknown hand set fire to the buildings and some unknown eyes watched it burn to the ground. Their destruction almost appears symbolic. Is it too fanciful to see in this act a final, triumphant gesture by the Whiteboys?

After the funeral, Pat went back to his smithy in Thorold. Bob elected to remain in Lucan. For a time he ran a hotel there known from its geographical location as the West End.

He was a lonely man and an angry one. It is said that any time a member of the Vigilance Committee was buried, Bob would go to the graveyard and wait until the body was placed in the grave. He would then walk up, spit on the coffin and declare: "There goes another of the bastards to hell!"

A son of Michael Collisson, an old friend of the Donnelly family, tells of an incident that occurred in the City Hotel in London. As he entered the lobby he saw the proprietor talking to Bob Donnelly while around the room were seated a number of Biddulph residents—mostly sons of Vigilantes:

> I went and asked my cousin if my brother was in and he said no and he then turned to Bob Donnelly and said: "Do you know this boy, he comes from Biddulph?" I think I can still see and feel the look of hatred which came into his eyes when he looked at me. My cousin said: "Now hold on, this boy is all right. He is the son of Mike Collisson." Donnelly shouted at the top of his voice and held out his hand to me: "Shake, my boy, we don't have to go out in every rainstorm to wash the blood off our hands!"

The same informant tells of picking up his mail in the Lucan post office on one occasion and being shown a post-card on which was written: "Dear Mr.—: When you go to church on Sunday and bless yourself with your bloody hand, think of the poor Donnellys who you sent to their death without any chance of repentance." The message was written in red ink.

There was more than anger in Bob Donnelly's heart. There was pity and Christian charity. Leonard D. Stanley, a Lucan resident, once told this story to a reporter from *The St. Marys Journal-Argus:*

> One morning when I was working in the grain elevator at Lucan I saw something that has impressed me ever since. It was early and there wasn't very much of a stir on the station platform, the elevator being just down the track a few yards from the station and quite close to the hotel then run there

by Bob Donnelly. As I looked out of the end of the elevator I saw the hotel door open and Bob Donnelly come out onto the platform. He looked up and down and I could see that his gaze had fallen upon something at the other end of the platform, for he stood there with tears in his eyes and slowly put his hand in his pocket and I could see he pulled out a bill. I then looked through a crack in the end of the elevator and beheld the object of his pity. There, coming along the track was a poor, terribly crippled girl, almost in rags, a pitiable sight and as she came along, though she wasn't asking for any help, Bob Donnelly stepped out and pushed the bill into her hand and said: "Here, lady, take this, and if you ever come this way again, come into this house here and stay as long as you like and it won't cost you a cent." Now there wasn't another living soul about the place only me, and Donnelly couldn't see me for I was looking out through a wide I crack in the boards, so he didn't do it for show—but that's the kind of fellows they were.

Bob's time came on June 14, 1911. He was fifty-eight. In death he had to share newspaper space with William Carroll, the brother of Jim, the constable, Vigilante and acquitted murderer. William had been convicted of the murder of a fellow lumberjack at a camp in Northern Ontario. He was sentenced to hang, but the sentence was remitted when it was proved that he was an escaped inmate of the Asylum for the Insane at London.

Father John Connolly died at Ingersoll, Ontario, in December, 1911. As he neared the end of his days almost any mention of the Donnelly murders would start him weeping. About him, also, there are many stories told. One, told in some detail, relates that Mike Collisson once asked the priest if he had any incriminating papers in the house. The priest came back with a big bundle of papers which Collisson put in the stove "without looking at them."

As he neared the end of his days in the raw towns and lumber camps of British Columbia any mention of Father Connolly would start ex-Constable Jim Carroll a-crying. Word of Jim drifted back to Lucan on two or three occasions. A Presbyterian minister saw him at a revivalist meeting at a lumber camp. He reported that Jim was "over-shadowed by a guilty conscience and forebodings of evil." Another reported that Jim lived in a house on a hillside where the lights were kept burning all night. Dr. James Weir, of Exeter, Ontario, saw him in the town of Golden, B.C., in 1912. Jim was then an old, sick man with a long, grey beard. He worked at carpentry in a pool room. The doctor found Carroll "friendly, but not communicative." He asked if Father Connolly was still alive. Told he was dead, Carroll wept.

Pat Donnelly died at Thorold on May 18, 1914. He was sixty-five—the longest-lived of the Donnelly brothers. Perhaps that was because he was so far removed from the stresses and tensions of the feud, although his daughter wrote a few years ago that her father "never fully recovered from the effect of the terrible sorrow over the deaths of his people." Pat was buried at Thorold—the only one of the brothers who does not sleep beside his murdered parents.

The story is almost told. One by one the actors in the drama were claimed by death. Will's Nora long outlived the rest. She died at St. Joseph's Hospital in London on February 26, 1937, at the age of eighty-five.

Some time in the years between the World Wars Will's first love, Maggie Thompson, also quit the scene. That love story with its politely impassioned letters, its frustrations and its drama had long since been forgotten by everyone—except Maggie Thompson.

Death had dissolved the marriage forced on her by her father. Death had claimed her Will and all his brothers. Death had all but claimed Maggie a part of her mind had already died.

For several years the desk sergeants at the old London police station on Carling Street would be troubled by a crank complaint around February 4. A little old lady would appear and demand that "something be done" to bring to justice the murderers of the Donnelly family.

The desk sergeant would yawn with irritation. It was the same old thing every time. However, desk sergeants are, by and large, kindly men, so he would go through the motions of making notes and then inquire:

"What's your name, ma'am?"

"Maggie Thompson."

Then at last Maggie Thompson was gone too. They were all gone—the Blackfeet and the Whiteboys. Many of the Whiteboys died violently—enough of them to create the legend that they all died with their boots on. Of course this is not true. As far as I know Jim and Bill Carroll died in their beds after having survived between them three trials for murder. Martin McLoughlin lived to a respected old age. Others died of nothing more violent than the ravages of age and a violent way of life.

The surviving Blackfeet died for the most part of natural causes in scattered parts of the world. Tom Keeffe, for instance—he who slept with an axe under his pillow that dreadful night in 1880—died in 1902 in Paris, France.

For a number of years the two London newspapers, *The London Free Press* and *The London Advertiser*, revived or reviewed the case on each succeeding February 4. Then that tradition too died out. The story was embalmed, with varying degrees of accuracy, in anthologies and collections of Canadian criminal cases. There it was permitted to slumber until 1954, when it was sensationally revived in a new, even more inaccurate and infinitely more biased account.

I do not claim complete accuracy for all that has been written in this book. I claim merely that here you will find more facts than have hitherto been presented concerning this most bizarre of all North American criminal cases.